The Children's Forest

Hawthorn Press

Published by Hawthorn Press, Hawthorn House,
1 Lansdown Lane, Stroud, Gloucestershire, GL5 1BJ, UK
Tel: (01453) 757040 info@hawthornpress.com

Hawthorn Press

www.hawthornpress.com

Illustrations © Allmut ffrench
Design and layout Lucy Guenot
Printed by Melita Press, Malta, reprinted 2020, 2021
Typeset in Scala

Every effort has been made to trace the ownership of all copyrighted material. If any omission has been made, please bring this to the publisher's attention so that proper acknowledgement may be given in future editions.

The views expressed in this book are not necessarily those of the publisher.

Printed on environmentally friendly chlorine-free paper sourced from renewable forest stock.

British Library Cataloguing in Publication Data applied for

ISBN 978-1-907359-91-0

The Children's Forest

Stories & songs, wild food, crafts & celebrations
ALL YEAR ROUND

Dawn Casey, Anna Richardson
and Helen d'Ascoli

Illustrated by Allmut ffrench

Hawthorn Press

DEDICATION

This book is dedicated to the children, the children of people, animals, trees and plants. As people we have a gift to imagine, vision and create. Our vision informs our actions. Imagine our land in the future: ancient woodlands where trees can grow in peace, filled with birdsong in spring, humming with insect life in summer, abundant with colourful mushrooms in autumn, while badgers curl up with their cubs in the winter roots. This place is a safe haven where our children's children will play. May this vision inspire children to plant and tend forests in connection with the Forest School movement. Imagine children of the future thriving in ancient forests that we planted in our lifetimes. Imagine a healthy, abundant living world for many generations to come.

Contents

Foreword

This book is packed full of delightful creative activities and experiences for children, bringing together some key elements to learning, in particular the connection with the natural world that influences our development.

A while ago I was visiting a Forest School leader, who I had trained four years previously, and one thing she said really encapsulated what I mean by *nature pedagogy*:

'It is all about following the children and nature, rediscovering our own rhythms and individual ways of developing in the natural world. It has taken me until now to really get this and take the time to follow the child and nature.'

This is so true – for a deeply meaningful learning experience, we need to follow the seasons and understand the way they influence our own rhythms, feelings, thoughts, actions and, more importantly, relationships in the world.

As I look out at my garden and see the blue tits flitting from willow bud to bird table and veg patch, listening to the local woodpecker drumming out its tune, I feel connected to the spring. I long to be outdoors, savouring the last of the blackthorn blossom and perhaps carving an amulet – maybe a Willow Ogham (see p 81) to symbolise my dreams for this coming season and year.

This book entices us to go outside, to play and interact with the natural world and to celebrate the different times of year. It is learning in action – combining story, song, cooking and craft, weaving in the trees, plants and animals that are the kith and kin for each season – providing some extra knowledge and observation to accompany the 'play'.

With that in mind I am going out to play and to celebrate the willow and all it brings at this time of year. I suggest you do too and dip into this book over the coming year for inspiration and some real nature pedagogy!

Jon Cree, Forest School Association Director and ecological educator

Preface

We hope that the ideas shared within this book will help readers – families and teachers – and the children in their care, to foster deep, meaningful, enriching and lasting relationships with the natural world.

We offer folklore, games, crafts, activities, recipes, stories, songs and celebrations inspired by our own relationships to nature, and our own sense of the energy of each season. We draw on years of experience leading Forest Schools, and are inspired by the many children in our care who 'come alive' in nature. We have chosen to follow the cycle of the seasons, drawing on the traditional celebrations of ancient Celtic peoples in Britain and beyond.

If you do not have access to woodland, the activities in this book can be adapted to any natural space. We warmly invite you to use these suggestions as a starting point for your own unique explorations, and as inspiration to create your own games and crafts, celebrations, stories and songs.

At this time in the history of our planet, we need to renew our healthy relationship to the earth. The earth needs our reconnection. There is such richness available in the friendships we can develop with the natural world and the other-than-human beings. Over many years we have seen how children are naturally open and able to develop meaningful relationships with plants, animals and the forest as a whole. This inspires and nurtures a natural response to love, care for and protect these beings and this precious world. We offer ways of connecting which are practical and hands-on, which speak not only to the intellect, but also to the imagination and the emotions. We offer nourishment for mind, body and spirit – head, heart and hands.

May the children in our care spend countless happy days in the Enchanted Forest, and may its wisdom, wonder and joy live always within them, to sustain and guide them throughout their lives.

Dawn Casey, Anna Richardson and Helen d'Ascoli

Introduction

The Living Forest

Time is slow in the forest. Trees live for many hundreds of years. When we enter the forest it may seem very still and quiet. Looking at the trees, we cannot see that they are breathing and growing. Imagine slowing down so much that we can see in tree time. Feel the leaves unfurl. Watch berries ripen. Hear the trees talk.

The roots of a tree spread twice as far as the crown. Underneath the forest floor the roots entwine and connect with those of other trees and plants. Here the trees talk to each other, communicating over large distances through the 'wood-wide web' – created underground by special fungi (called mycorrhizal fungi). Their tiny, thin threads spread through the forest, weaving a network that connects the roots of all the trees over huge distances. This network carries messages between the trees and enables them to share food and water through their roots. It is a magical web of forest communication.

Trees are sensory beings. They respond to sounds, especially birdsong, growing more quickly to music that they like – so the dawn chorus truly wakes up the forest. Trees also make slow, crackling sounds through their roots; a very slow tree talk that may continue over many moons and seasons. They can smell, communicating through scent on the breeze, and taste, recognising the saliva of certain insects that eat them. They are aware of light and even their winter buds are able to detect the length of the day as they prepare for the growth of spring.

Trees are able to feel and respond to temperature and the movement of the wind.

Within a healthy forest, the trees are always talking to each other, not with words as we do, but in their own language. The oldest trees are known as the Mother Trees. They are the guardians and protectors, the elders of the forest. They have been alive for so long that their underground networks connect them to many trees throughout the forest, and their vast canopies of leaves allow them to make lots of food from the sunlight. They listen carefully to how the other trees are faring and share food with members of the forest community who are in need, telling their neighbours to help too. These Mother Trees are cared for by the forest in return.

Trees support one another, tending their children and making sure they grow strong and healthy, caring for the elderly and those who are sick, giving them extra food and water through their roots. The forest is a home they create together. Being together gives them protection from being blown over in the winter storms and from drying out in the heat of the summer. Trees live much longer lives when they are part of a forest and are stronger together than on their own. They thrive in a living community, which we call a forest.

The forest created by the trees is a special home for many others, from the tiniest insects, to birds and mammals large and small. In this enchanted place, ferns unfurl in shady groves, mosses nestle in hollows and keep the roots of the trees moist and healthy. Here birds sing, spring flowers shine, deer tread lightly, foxes prowl and mushrooms appear overnight. In this special world we can see all the seasons turn in the great wheel, birth and death following each other so that life can continue and flourish. Each season holds magic and beauty of its own.

The forest is a place of great wonder, where we can explore and play with our friends. Here is a place of belonging, which we can learn to care for and protect. A place of deep stillness, where we can slow down and feel peace. This can be a place of friendships other than human, with the trees, plants and animals who have many gifts to share. There is no end to the treasures that this enchanted world will share with us if we open ourselves up to listen, smell, taste, watch and feel the magic of the living forest.

How to Use This Book

This book is designed to offer inspiration through the seasons for families, Forest School leaders and teachers.

The approach is of reverence to nature, the living forest and the other-than-human beings. We encourage a feeling of playful light-heartedness combined with a respect and love for all life, including ourselves and each other. Appreciation and respect are natural and wonderful ways to feel a sense of friendship and belonging. This book offers ways to develop the sense of this through games, activities, song and story, to bring about an embodied connection to the land and seasons.

Each chapter is created to express and evoke a feeling and essential quality of the time of year, conveyed through the introduction, story and imaginative journey, before offering the practical crafts and games that reflect a connection to that essence.

In carrying out the sessions practically, we have found that children need to explore and play before being invited into focused activity, and that the cooking and eating around the fire often lead well into story time.

We have included several crafts and games in each chapter, though in a session we would usually only do one game and one craft. You may choose to do more, or less, depending on how much time you have.

The celebrations usually work well towards the end of a session, once the story and imaginative journey have given children a sense of the energy of the time of year. Often the crafts the children have made are used in the celebration. The simple celebrations offered here relate to the solar festivals in Northern Europe and are open to interpretation and creative adaption. We offer them as an inspiration. We hope that people will feel moved to co-create celebrations with the children in their care as their relationship to the forest and each other deepens.

Trees are present through the year, though they have their own times of wakefulness and rest. They have been placed in this book at specific times of year, either because they seem to embody some quality we feel fits the season, or, in many cases, because there is a relationship to the Ogham (old tree alphabet) which associates them with specific months. We have found that learning about and relating to the trees is an ongoing part of our time in the forest, though we may make things from them or celebrate them at specific times.

The smaller plants have more particular times of growth and presence. We only see the snowdrop, the primrose and the bluebell during a certain window in the year, as with most of the plants. For the rest of the year, they are beneath the ground, in the form of seed, root or bulb. So it is an important and wonderful part of relating to our place to know when those special windows are, when to visit, celebrate and create with those plants.

When foraging and making edible foods from the wild plants, we usually focus in depth on one plant at a time with children, to ensure there is no confusion.

Our approach to gathering wild food and resources from the forest is to ask permission and give thanks to the trees and plants for their generosity and abundance. We do this by offering a gift of oats or song and quietly taking time to listen in to the feeling we get in response. In this way we harvest respectfully.

It is good to keep revisiting the trees and plants each year, greeting them in turn and mapping your area through the places where specific trees and plants grow. For example, in one forest we work in, we know particular areas as Oak Tree Meadow, Primrose Bank and Pine Tree Place.

Our heartfelt wish is that our book will offer creative inspiration and be used in a myriad of ways.

Imbolc

After the dark and cold of winter, life within the land is starting to stir. Imbolc is a time of mystery – life is awakening deep within, invisible from the outside. This time of year is akin to the time of day just before sunrise, the time of stirring, when we begin to surface from our deep dreaming.

The Celtic festival of Imbolc, on 1 February, halfway between the winter solstice and the spring equinox, has been sacred in Celtic lands since Neolithic times. A prehistoric mound at the Hill of Tara in Ireland is aligned with the rising sun on Imbolc morning; when the sun rises, the entrance to the chamber blazes with light.

Imbolc is also known in Ireland as Brigit's Day; a time sacred to the goddess Brigit, goddess of the holy well and the sacred flame. She is a 'triple goddess' – she kindles the smith's fire of the forge, the hearth fire of the home and the inner fire of the poet. Brigit's healing wells and bright springs can be found throughout the British Isles.

When Christianity arrived in Britain, pagan beliefs fused with the Christian calendar, and the sacred day of the goddess Brigit became the feast day of Saint Brigit.

It is said in Ireland that Saint Brigit was the midwife of Mother Mary and that when Mary walked to the temple, to present her son to God, Brigit walked before her with a lighted candle in each hand. The Christian festival of Candlemas, on 2 February, commemorates this day.

The word *Imbolc* comes from the Gaelic, meaning 'in the belly', for at this time of year ewes are carrying their lambs in their bellies. In the belly of the earth, life is quickening.

The Forest at Imbolc

The earth has been sleeping and now begins to awaken. Under the leafy blanket on the forest floor, the shoots are beginning to burst forth. Very gently, pull back the leaves and see the tiny green spears of bluebell shoots. Safely hidden, they arise.

Sap is beginning to rise in the trees, making ready for swelling buds to open as spring draws near. Catkins shine with yellow pollen, and tiny scarlet flowers, hidden treasures of the woodland, appear on the hazel trees.

Elder leaves are emerging. Honeysuckle leaves, soft and furry, open early to seek the pale sun. Wolf-winds howl and bite but blackthorn challenges the cold, blossoming in delicate clouds of white.

Life is stirring in the forest. Take time to be in nature and find the stillness within yourself. Listen to the dreams stirring inside you.

An Imbolc Story

The Story of Brigit and the Cailleach

A tale woven from Irish and Scottish folklore

Long, long, long ago lived the Cailleach. The old one. The cold one. The Old Woman of Winter. Her face was blue. Her teeth were tusks. Her hair was white as frost.

In those long-ago days the Cailleach tramped the lands with her staff in her hand and her creel (her basket) on her back, full of stones and rocks.

She dropped down the rocks, and they went tumbling to earth, crashing and splashing onto the land and into the sea. That is how she made the hills and the mountains, the highlands and the islands.

The Cailleach had lived for hundreds and hundreds of years, for she knew where to find the Water of Life, in the Well of Youth. Whenever she grew weary, she would tuck up her skirt and wade into the ocean. The sea was nothing to her – it only came up to her knees. She would go to the Island of the West, the Island of the Blest. There stood the Well of Youth. In the morning, at sunrise, the Cailleach lifted off the great stone slab that covered the well. She cupped her hands and drank the cold, clear water and was revived. The lid of the well had to be replaced before nightfall, to preserve the precious waters. So in the evening, at sunset, the Cailleach laid the heavy stone slab back over the well.

After the mountains were made, the Cailleach took her plaid, her great white shawl, to the swirling whirlpool of Corryvreckan. She threw in her shawl and tramped it with her feet until the booming of the waves could be heard for miles around. And when her shawl was washed white, she laid it on the mountains to dry, and the land was covered with snow.

The Old Woman of Winter roamed her white world, with her staff of blackthorn in her hand. Wherever her staff struck the ground, the earth was frozen cold and hard as iron. She went wandering through her mountains, followed by herds of red deer. For she was guardian of the wild beasts. The horned herds of grey goats and red deer, the wolves and the eagles all answered her call.

For a long time, the world was gripped by winter.

But, in the belly of the earth, something tiny was glowing, something tiny was growing. The spirit of spring was quickening. And on the surface of the earth, in sheltered spots, green grew. One day, the sun came out. A flower opened. Well, the Cailleach wasn't having that! She towered over the tiny flower and raised up her staff and crashed it down. She snapped the tender stem and dashed the flimsy petals. There lay the flower, crushed.

But still, a bird sang. A bud swelled. The Cailleach laughed and her laugh was a bitter, stinging wind.

Then she put her fingers to her lips and she whistled. She whistled up the winds, her wild winter wolf-winds. From high on the mountain-tops they came. From far in the northlands they came:

> *The Feadag,*
> *The Gobag,*
> *The Sguabag,*
> *The Gearan.*
>
> *The Shrill Wind,*
> *The Sharp Wind,*
> *The Sweeper,*
> *The Shrieker.*

Yowling and howling they came, over the forest, over the seas, whipping up waves, lashing down trees. Budding branches were torn from the trunks. Ancient trunks cracked and fell crashing. Rivers rose in flood. The Cailleach laughed out loud. She kicked up her skirts and hurled down her hail. She danced in the storm, like a child in the rain.

But when at last the winds died down and the hail melted, the Cailleach sighed. She rubbed her back. Her bones ached. Her knees creaked. She was exhausted. She sat staring out to sea and she sang to herself, a sad, sorrowful song:

> *Oh, I am weary and old,*
> *All alone in the dark and the cold.*
> *When the cold winds blow,*
> *When the cold winds blow.*

Once again, the Cailleach hitched up her skirt and waded through the cold ocean to the Well of Youth. She lifted the great stone slab and drank a little.

Then the Cailleach saw a soft mossy spot, and she sat down there, just to take the weight off her tired feet for a moment. She closed her eyes, just for a little rest ...

But before the Cailleach awoke, before she had a chance to replace the capstone, the sun set. And the moon rose.

As the moon rose, with it rose the waters of the well. Higher and higher. Until the waters touched the lip of the well. And still the Cailleach slept. And still the waters rose, and tipped over the lip of the well, and came slipping and spilling over the edge.

Swelling and swirling, urging and surging, rising and roaring – a great wave of water curled and crashed over the sleeping Cailleach.

As the waters washed over her plaid, her snow-white cloak began to melt and to trickle away into the earth. As the waters washed over her hands, her grip loosened, and her staff of blackthorn rolled out of her fingers and away, down the hill, and lodged beneath a holly bush.

And as the waters of life washed over the great shape of the sleeping Cailleach she herself was turned into a great, grey stone. For that is what happens to old cailleachs at the end of their days.

The full moon shone on that old cold boulder of stone. Well water fell like the first spring rain. The moon set. All was still.

Behind the hill the sun began to rise. There was an opening in the hill. And as the sun rose the opening was lit with light, like a flame blazing.

And out into the world a new goddess emerged. Her dress was white. Her cloak was green. Her hair was red as fire. The goddess Brigit came to power. Brigit the Bright. Brigit the White. Brigit the Bringer of Spring.

Now, some say that the Cailleach still sleeps her stone-cold sleep and that Brigit stays only until summer's end, and then again the Cailleach will wake. But some believe that Brigit is the Cailleach herself, transformed, like a great, grey glacier that changes into a bright bubbling spring.

The goddess Brigit had the power of fire within her. The spark of poetry tingled on her tongue. As she walked, she sang, and her song was soft as a spring breeze and bright as birdsong. The heat of healing and the warmth of crafting were in her hands. She knelt and dipped her finger in the frozen river and, though it was cold, it began to flow.

She reached out and picked up the staff of blackthorn from beneath the holly tree. And as she held it in her hand, it began to swell and sprout and the black wood turned white with blossom.

Brigit looked out over the bare, brown earth and she took off her cloak, her mantle of green. Lovingly, she laid it over the land. And Brigit, Brigit the Bright, Brigit the White, walked out into her green world.

Like a dancing flame, Brigit moved over the land, and snowdrops flowered in her footsteps.

A gentle breeze whispered, '*Spring is coming ...*'

A brook murmured, '*Spring is coming ...*'

A bird sang, '*Spring is coming ...*'

And so it was. And so it is.

Imbolc Imaginary Journey

A simple, imaginary journey offers children an inner experience of the energy of the season; it gives them a feeling for the time of year.

It may be a cold day, so children will be wrapped up warm in the forest. Sit or lie near a glowing fire.

When children are settled comfortably, guide them through an Imbolc imaginary journey of the first stirrings of spring:

- Close your eyes and go within.

- Imagine you are sleeping deep under the earth.

- Above you the ground is covered in snow. You are snug and warm.

- From inside you and within the earth, feel the excitement of life stirring from a long winter sleep. As you lie very still, notice the tingling feeling of aliveness within your body.

- You are beginning to wake up – you are at the crossing place between dreaming and waking. Your dreams are still bright within you: lie still and look inwards to see them.

- Bring to mind a special dream you once had. What do you see in the dream? How do you feel? (Give time for children to savour their dream moments.)

- The tide is turning; the sap is starting to rise up from its sleepy depths, pulling with it nourishment from deep within the Earth. Imagine the sap rising up from your toes to the tips of your fingers and the top of your head. Beneath you, within the Earth, the seeds are awakening, like hundreds of stars bursting with life in the dark. Life is awakening.

- Slowly open your eyes and feel life beginning to stir in the forest all around you.

Imbolc Activities, Crafts and Games

Brigit's Cross (Made with Rushes)

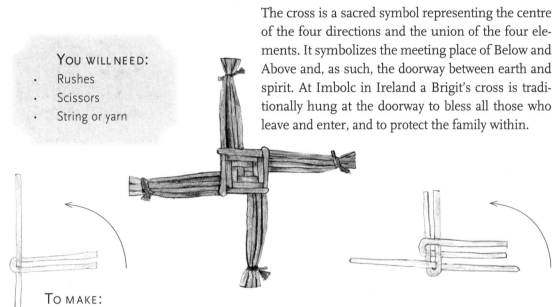

The cross is a sacred symbol representing the centre of the four directions and the union of the four elements. It symbolizes the meeting place of Below and Above and, as such, the doorway between earth and spirit. At Imbolc in Ireland a Brigit's cross is traditionally hung at the doorway to bless all those who leave and enter, and to protect the family within.

YOU WILL NEED:
- Rushes
- Scissors
- String or yarn

TO MAKE:

1. Begin with two straight rushes, A and B. Fold one rush in half (this will be rush B) and place it around the centre of rush A, at right angles.

2. Turn the rushes 90 degrees to the left, then take another rush (C) and fold it around B, at right angles.

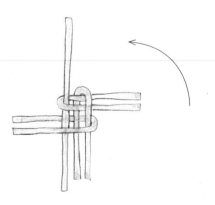

3. Turn the rushes 90 degrees to the left, then fold another rush (D) in half and loop it around C.

4. Keep following this rhythm by turning the rushes 90 degrees left and adding a new rush with the opening to the right each time.

When the cross is the desired size, tie the ends of each 'arm' with yarn and trim the ends of the rushes to finish.

Snowdrop Folk

Snowdrops are a flower of Brigit; they bloom at Imbolc time and their three white petals reflect Brigit's threefold nature. It is said that at this time Brigit walks the land, gently awakening the plants. In her footsteps snowdrops appear and sometimes a flurry of snowflakes swirls in her wake.

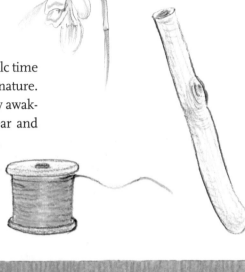

YOU WILL NEED:
- Small hazel stick about 15cm (6ins) long
- Green and white cloth or felt
- Green wool or thread
- Needle for skirt (optional)
- Scissors
- Loppers
- Vegetable peeler

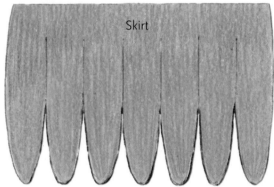

Skirt

TO MAKE:

1. Using the loppers, cut a hazel stick approximately 15cm (6ins) long and 1.5cm (½ in) wide. Alternatively, use a dolly peg. Peel off the bark for the face, using the vegetable peeler.

2. Cut a three-petal flower shape (see right) from the white cloth, for the hat.

   To complete the flower hat, cut a small circle of green cloth. Place the white petals on top of the stick with the green circle on top. Bind them both onto the top of the stick with green thread.

3. To make the skirt, cut a strip of green cloth approximately 10cm (4ins) long and 7cm (2¾ins) wide. Cut the bottom half into long leaf shapes inspired by the leaves of the snowdrop.

You may find it easier to make a card template for the petals. Draw an equilateral triangle of approx. 7cm (2¾ins) and draw the petals as shown within the triangle before cutting.

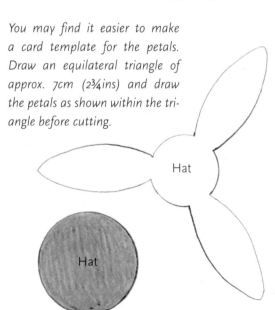

Hat

Hat

4. There are two ways to attach the skirt: either wrap the skirt around the stick and bind the top using green thread, or, using a needle and thread, sew a running stitch along the top of the skirt, pull and gather, then tie on to the hazel body.

(NB: *It may be easier to cut out the shapes before-hand for younger children.*)

Imbolc Plant Song

Song of the Snowdrop

Light and gentle

Snow-drop, Snow-drop, li-ttle drops of snow, what do you do when the cold winds blow? We

ring our li-ttle bells, ding - a - ling - a - ling, ding - a - ling - a - ling, here comes Spring.

Mystery Animal Tracking

Imbolc is the time when we can become aware of that which is invisible. There are many animals who live in the forest, though we rarely see them. When we learn to recognize their footprints and signs, we can become aware of their invisible presence. Maybe they are watching us? Sometimes at this time of year, it snows; tracking animals in the snow is magical – a hidden world is revealed. This game is a fun way to introduce tracking to children.

YOU WILL NEED: (FOR EACH GROUP):
- Sieve or tea strainer
- Teaspoon
- Cup of flour
- A5 card
- Tracking guide
- Craft knife
- (Optional: soft toy animal, e.g. knitted, felted or sewn, of species related to track)

TO MAKE: THE STENCIL:
Using the tracking guide (below), draw one animal's track on the centre of each card and cut with a craft knife to create a stencil. Choose large mammals that live in the forest, such as deer, fox and badger. They are easier stencils to make and are also more likely to be the real tracks that you can find in the forest.

| Badger | Fox | Deer | Wild boar |

NB. Animal foot prints are not to scale

HOW TO PLAY:

1. Choose a minimum of two animals and maximum of four and split the children into that many groups.

2. Split into groups of 5–7. (It works well if there is one adult per group.) Set off in your group, with all your equipment, to find a hiding place; this will be your animal's 'home'. Make the home a suitable distance from the starting point and keep the animal and the location of the home a secret from the other groups.

3. When you have found your hiding place, you will make a trail of animal tracks back to the starting place. The trail should be interesting; use the natural environment, just as an animal would.

4. To make the tracks, clear the ground of leaves and sticks and lay the stencil down flat (toes pointing towards home, so they can be followed from the starting point). Then lightly sprinkle a spoonful of flour through the sieve. Tip the excess flour on the stencil back into the cup.

5. Repeat every 3–5m (10–15ft) to create a trail. Each person in the group can take turns in making a print. Try not to tread on your prints!

6. When all the groups have reached the starting point, one group can hide in their home whilst the other group closes their eyes and counts to 50.

7. Now the tracking begins: as the children discover the trail, encourage them to use their senses and ask questions about what type of animal might have left such a trail. Children can take turns being the leader, so that everyone has a chance to be the first to spot a track.

8. When the animal has been tracked to its home, the hiders remain hidden. The trackers run and hide in their own animal home, ready to be tracked themselves.

9. The hiders count to 100 and then go back to the starting point to begin tracking.

VARIATIONS

- Hide a soft toy relating to the tracks somewhere in your house.
- Use natural face paints of chalk, clay or charcoal to become your animal.
- You can lay any number of trails to suit your group.
- Silent tracking, with hand signals: the first child to find the track stands beside it with their hand in the air and waits there to mark where the track is. The group moves forwards. The child who finds the next track again waits beside the track, with a raised arm. When the third track is found, and the child is waiting with a raised hand, the first child may move on again. This method shows the group where the trail is and gives every child a chance to discover a track.
- Look for real tracks with your tracking guide. This is especially good in the snow.

Clay Love Birds

February is a good time of year to spot native birds, before the summer visitors arrive and while there aren't so many leaves on the branches. In olden days it was believed that by mid-February many birds had begun to seek a mate. It is not by chance that Valentine's Day is celebrated at this time.

Sit quietly in the woods and watch the birds calling and flying in the trees. Many are still in southern lands, awaiting the return of the warm sun. Who is here? Notice that the male and female birds of a species are often different in their markings and colours. Use a bird book or field guide to discover who they are and what the couples look like. What are the songs of each of the birds? Birds are the messengers, telling us so much about the world beyond which we can see. Listen... They are calling about which animals are moving in the forest and where... They are letting all the forest know we are here too... Their movements and song tell about the season, the time of day, the weather and so much more that we may never know.

Making these birds helps the children build a relationship with them. They can then go on to discover the calls of their bird and where it likes to live. Children can look at the field guides and choose a species they would like to make; they can create two birds, one male and one female. Younger children may need help making the basic bird shape but can decorate the birds in their own unique way.

YOU WILL NEED:
- Clay (air-drying is good for this)
- Thin string/thick thread for hanging the birds
- Small black beads for eyes (optional)
- Small sticks for the beak and for hanging
- Paint and small brushes
- Bird field guides – charts that open out are easiest to use

TO MAKE:

1. Take a piece of clay (approximately the size of a golf ball) and mould it into a bird shape. Wings folded in works best. Find or carve a suitable small stick for the beak and insert into position. Push on the black beads for eyes.

2. Cut a length of thread to fold in half as the hanger for the bird. Make it a bit longer than needed and tie the two loose ends together in a bulky knot. Tie the knotted end around a tiny stick (about 1cm long). Once the thread is secure, use a stick to push the tiny stick into the bird, just below its head, so that the thread comes out of the bird's back, as shown above.

3. Smooth the clay over the place where you inserted the stick and thread. Use the pictures of birds to inspire the decoration, using the paint. The clay birds can be left to dry before applying paint, though the air-drying clay can be painted on while still damp.

4. In a classroom a small branch can be brought in for the birds to be hung from. If you wish, you can give them an extra coat of paint and even a coat of matt varnish.

5. Enjoy the beautiful birds, messengers of the forest.

Imbolc Shelter Making

At this cold time of year, being active outdoors helps us to stay warm. Like cutting wood, shelter building warms us twice, not only by providing a shelter but by warming us up through physical activity. Creating a shelter together also builds team-spirit.

YOU WILL NEED:
- Woodland debris and fallen sticks

TO MAKE:

1. When the children have found a space, check that it is safe. Look above to ensure there are no dead branches.

2. One way to make a shelter is to use a whale-bone structure. Stick a sturdy branch firmly into the ground and lean the end in the fork of a tree (or if there are no suitable trees, use a forked branch stuck in the ground). Make sure this 'backbone' is strong (not old, rotten wood) and that it is securely placed, as it will hold the weight of all the other 'rib' sticks.

3. Lay sticks up against this backbone, on both sides, using longer sticks to reach the top and smaller sticks at the bottom. Remind children that when moving long sticks we hold the stick by one end, with a thumb over the stick end, and drag the stick behind us as we walk, so that the back end of the stick is well away from other children. Then cover the 'ribs' with a layer of fine branches.

4. Gather piles of leaves and cover the ribs and branches, starting from the bottom and working upwards. (The leaf layer needs to be at least 30cm (12ins) thick to be waterproof.)

5. To fuel the children's enthusiasm and sense of purpose, you could give them a time-frame: 'Rain is coming!' Children find it exciting to sit inside the shelter, to discover if it is waterproof, while the adult sprinkles over a can of water, the gentle rain.

Magic Wand

A magic wand is a precious tool with a special relationship to its owner that helps give power to magic spells. Explain to the children that it can be used to direct intentions and wishes for goodwill and healing, a tool for good magic. Children can choose the wood of their favourite kind of tree and decorate their wands to add power and strength, either with designs or with feathers, stones or bones they may find.

You will need:

- Branch of wood for your wand
- Loppers (to cut the wood if it is a thumb's thickness in diameter)
- A folding/pruning saw (to cut the wood if it is thicker than a thumb's thickness in diameter)
- Peeler or knife (to shape and personalize your wand)
- Natural dyes to decorate (optional)
- An offering to the tree (such as a sprinkling of oats, flower-petals or a song)

How to choose your wand:

Learn about the qualities of the trees. If there is one you especially like, find a suitable branch of that tree in the woods. Some people believe that a wand chooses you! You could visit different trees that offer a suitable length of wood, and try to sense if you are drawn to a particular one.

You will need a length of wood that is made to measure – the same distance from your inside elbow to your wrist.

How to cut your wand:

When you have chosen, touch the tree and ask if it is OK to take some of its wood. Feel if there is any response inside you to the question. The wood will only be magical if taken with respect. Leave your offering at the base of the tree, with your thanks.

To make:

Personalize your wand in a way that suits you and your competence with the tools. You could peel it and decorate it with crushed charcoal, chalk or other natural paint; you could peel stripes or sections, using a knife to mark the sections; or you could make a spiral pattern by rolling the wood on a log or hard surface. Hold the knife at an angle firmly on the wand and create a spiral as the wand rolls away from you and the knife goes with it. Make another spiral next to it and peel the bark from the middle of the two spirals.

You could whittle your wand, always making sure that you work with the knife pointing away from your body.

A Magic Pouch

A magic pouch can contain a choice of forest treasures. The contents are physical objects that hold personal, symbolic meanings – a touchstone, which when held reminds us of connections and relationships that are important to us. For example, when we feel in need of strength, we might hold our oak Ogham stick (see p 135) to draw on the power of our friendship with the oak. These can be secret treasures. There is no need for children to reveal the contents of their magic pouch if they do not wish to. Other treasures in the pouch might offer practical help, such as a whistle to call your friends or a herbal remedy to heal a friend in need.

Each chapter in this book contains a suggestion for a seasonal treasure to add to your magic pouch.

YOU WILL NEED:
- Cloth – chamois leather, cotton or felt (an old wool blanket can make pouches for a whole class; 30cm x 50cm (12ins x 20ins) makes a bag large enough to hold tinder for two fires)
- Scissors
- Wool or string
- Beads (optional)

Circular Pouch

This is a simple design that does not need to be sewn.

1. Draw a large circle on the cloth. (Using a dinner plate works well for a small pouch.) Cut out and mark equally spaced dots for the holes. A simple way to do this by eye is to mark the centre and the four quarters. Now mark the points in between, so that there are eight marks in total. For a dinner-plate-sized pouch, mark two evenly spaced dots between each of these, until the circle has 16 dots, which can now be carefully cut to make the holes.

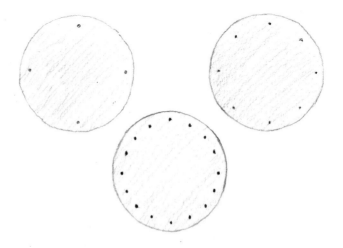

2. To make a cord to close either pouch, you can choose either of the following methods:

Single-cord drawstring

Cut a length of cord which is at least twice the width of the bag, plus a bit extra. Thread from the outside, leaving one length hanging. Thread in and out though all the holes until the cord emerges out of the last hole. Holding the ends of the string together, tie a knot. This can now be pulled to close the bag.

Double-cord drawstring

Cut two lengths of good strong string or wool, approximately twice the diameter of the pouch. Take one piece of string and begin to thread the string through the holes, with the back end of the string dangling on the outside of the bag. After you have reached halfway (e.g. for a bag with 16 holes, after threading eight) add a bead to the threading end and push it along the string, up to the hole. Continue threading and at completion tie the two ends together with a knot.

Now begin to thread the second string in through one of the holes next to the bead, leaving the end dangling outside as before. Thread in and out until the halfway point, and then thread a bead. Continue until you reach the end and tie the two ends with a knot. The two knot ends can now be pulled to close the pouch. To open, pull the beads.

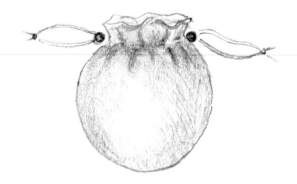

An Imbolc Treasure for Your Magic Pouch – An Animal Disc

Just as there may be certain people in our lives whom we have very close friendships with, there may be certain animals or birds that we particularly relate to. Creating and strengthening these relationships is one way to feel more connected to the natural world. Find out the qualities of different animals, such as the stealth of a fox, or the grace of a swan, and choose a quality that you would love to have. Create or deepen your relationship with that animal, either by direct contact (e.g. by feeding the cheery robin in your garden) or by learning more about the creature from field guides.

Our friend, Cliff, has a friendship with a badger and a fox who come into his garden each night. He sits in the same spot every night at the same time and has done so over a long period of time, since the fox was a cub. The two animals now come (separately mostly and on odd occasions together) and greet him and see if he has some food for them. The fox even climbs in his lap.

YOU WILL NEED:
- A slice of hazel (or other available wood), about 3cm (1¼in) diameter (see p 318 on how to harvest wood whilst honouring the tree)
- Paints
- Field guide for animal tracks/woodland animals

TO MAKE:

1. Saw a slice of wood. If you place your hand through the bow saw – between the blade and the handle – and hold onto the branch you are sawing from, the saw cannot slip and cut you.

2. Paint on a miniature picture of your animal, or the shape of its track.

3. Now charge up your animal disc by holding it with eyes closed and asking the animal to be your friend, thanking them and letting them know how much you admire them.

4. The disc can be added to your magic pouch. When you feel the need to receive the connection or qualities of the animal you have chosen, you can hold the disc and think of your animal friend and ask them to lend you their quality of grace or stealth...

You could drill a hole with a palm drill and thread it with cordage. Wear your animal disc around your neck when you need the qualities of your animal.

Sense Awareness Activity – Special Place

This activity can last between two and 15 minutes, depending on age and experience. It is about learning to become quiet, to tune into your senses, become present and allow yourself time simply to be. Birds and animals come closer when we are quiet and still. Practise this activity all year round to deepen your relationship with the natural world.

🌿 Choose a special place to sit in the forest. Perhaps at the base of a tree or by a stream; somewhere you like the feeling of, that will be a comfortable place to be for a while.

🌿 Be still and listen to the sounds around you. Can you hear the birds, the wind in the leaves? Where is the wind blowing from? Is it gentle?

🌿 Are the clouds racing along? Smell the air. What temperature is it?

🌿 Notice the sky.

🌿 Listen to your heart.

🌿 What is the mood of the forest today?

🌿 Feel the earth beneath you. Touch the leaves gently. Feel the moss. Notice the texture of the bark on the trees.

🌿 Can you see any signs of the animals? Can you feel where they are right now?

🌿 Now close your eyes and relax each part of your body, starting with your toes, moving slowly up to your head, and then your eyes, ears, nose and mouth.

🌿 Slowly open your eyes and smile, look all around you and above you. Has anything changed?

🌿 Use your senses to notice anything new.
Listen ...
Feel ...
Smell ...
Look ...

🌿 Be present to this unique moment. No other moment will be exactly the same again. Slowly get up and shake out your body.

Imbolc Invisibility Game – 'Sink and Fade!'

At this time of year nature is beginning to wake up but the plants are mostly invisible beneath the ground and the rising sap is hidden behind the bark of the trees before the buds burst open. Practising invisibility is fun and instinctive and can be played in many forms of camouflage and hiding games. This game is simple and spontaneous, keeps everyone alert and is best played on a walk whilst moving through the land.

TO PLAY:

1. Set up the game by choosing a seeker and explaining how to play:

2. The seeker is positioned at the front of the group. The seeker calls, 'Sink and Fade!' and then closes their eyes and counts slowly out loud to five. The others find the nearest hiding place behind trees or in the shadows (aiming to become invisible to the seeker).

3. The seeker opens their eyes when counting is completed and, without moving, tries to spot anyone visible and call them out. The seeker then calls, 'Where are you?' and in response the children leap out of their hiding places.

Imbolc Plant Lore

Nettle

GAELIC NAME: *Deanntag* (from the root word 'twist'; nettles have been twisted into cloth since the Bronze Age)

LATIN NAME: *Urtica dioica*

Character

I am Nettle – I'll wake you up with my sting and fiery power.

I grow in big families and have been here since before the last two great ice ages. Your ancestors knew me well for my many gifts: food, medicine, cloth and dye.

I am strong and resilient. I grow upright and bold, my fibres long and strong for twisting into cord or cloth.

My zigzag-shaped leaves bring great strength and energy to those who eat me. So rich and tasty am I that I need my sting to defend myself, or I would not survive.

I am a plant of activation: if you receive my sting, feel the fiery tingle of my touch awakening your senses and know that it is good medicine, and that I command respect.

My companion the dock will cool its touch, though the juice from my leaf can also relieve the sting.

A strong nettle tea, when cooled, will soothe a burn or fever, or a stinging rash.

Gifts

I support many tiny lives; I shelter, protect and nourish insects and butterflies. Be careful when you harvest me: leave those plants with leaves that are folded or have eggs beneath them – I am protecting the tiny creatures in my care.

In every season, nature provides what our bodies need. After the long cold winter, I will help you to wake up and give you the fiery power and strengthening minerals your body needs, ready for the activity of spring.

Nettle Tea

Nettles are one of the first to awaken in the time of stirring, when Brigit walks the land. They are tiny yet potent, so you may need a keen eye and a glove for early harvesting. In February, you can see the nettle's dead stems, long, straight and white. They make good kindling and point the way to the first growth of plants beneath.

Picking nettles with courage and a firm hand crushes the sting. Nettles enjoy this kind of pruning. The sting is destroyed by heat so enjoy nettle's goodness in soup or brew nettle tea.

> *Tender-handed stroke a nettle,*
> *And it stings you, for your pains.*
> *Grasp it like a man of mettle,*
> *And it soft as silk remains.*
> (Aaron Hill, 1750)

To make:
With care and appreciation, harvest 4–5 nettle tips per person. (The tips are the 4–6 leaves at the top of the plant.) Be careful not to pull up the roots and avoid leaves that are curled or folded over, as they could be home to an insect. Steep the nettle tips in boiling water for 10–20 minutes. Bringing out a flask of hot water is an easy way to brew teas whilst in the forest – simply add your tea plants to the flask.

Nettle Soup

Nettle soup is an all-time favourite with children. This is a simple recipe that they enjoy. This soup can be made throughout the next couple of months until the nettle flowers and seeds begin to form. (After this time, the leaves become concentrated with calcium crystals and should be avoided as food or medicine.) Areas where nettles have been cut back will provide fresh plants for longer. Let the children know how strong the nettle soup will make them when they receive the power of nettle.

YOU WILL NEED:
- Nettle tips
- Large bowl
- Scissors
- Cooking oil or butter
- Onions
- Potatoes
- Water
- Organic vegetable stock
- Saucepan

TO MAKE:

1. Harvest the nettle tips in a large bowl using scissors. Wash the nettles if you want to. Cut the nettles into tiny pieces in the bowl using the scissors. Alternatively, children can harvest the nettle tips into cups using small scissors. They can then snip them into tiny pieces in the cup and add them to the large bowl afterwards.

2. Peel, chop and gently fry the onions. While the onions are cooking, chop the potato into small chunks then add them to the onions and add water and stock. Bring to the boil and simmer until the potato is soft. Add the chopped nettles and cook for 5 minutes.

3. Cool for a few minutes and serve by the fire.

Imbolc Tree Lore

Hazel

Gaelic name: *Coill* (meaning 'grove')
Latin name: *Corylus avellana*
Ogham: *Coll* (the letter C)

Essence
Wisdom ~ Divination ~ Creativity

Character

I am Hazel, Tree of Wisdom, of inner knowing.

Throughout the ages I have grown in these forests, a small tree with many gifts.

In February, when life begins to stir again, find my tiny red flowers amongst the golden catkins, hidden treasures of the woods. By autumn, these will have ripened into tasty nuts loved by many creatures of the forest and people alike.

Your ancestors roasted my hazelnuts in shallow pits of sand to make sweet, nutritious food that would last them through the cold times. You can recognise me easily – rather than a single trunk, I grow with many upright stems, useful to you for crafting. I inspire your creativity as you weave your baskets and shelters. I will grow again where I have been cut with care.

Long ago people listened well and discovered a hidden gift within me. My hazel sticks may be used to divine (to find out) where underground streams run and where minerals and metals can be found. This helped them find where to dig wells and where to find precious metals for tools and trade.

With my roots in the wisdom of the earth, I know that which is invisible. The old Irish tale of Finn McCool tells how hazelnuts from the branches of my tree dropped into a deep pool.

Gifts

A silver salmon ate the magical nuts, and a boy, Finn, ate the fish and so gained understanding of all the mysteries of the universe.

Spend time with me in the forest and share my gifts. I offer you my branches to inspire your creativity. Be nourished by my sweet hazelnuts. Find the hidden water with my help. You also have a deep, inner wisdom. Trust the quiet voice within you.

My wood is straight and supple, lending itself to coppicing. My poles are harvested for many uses, including fencing, hurdles, simple dwellings and basketry. My wood is good for making fire by friction; it burns fast and with ease.

My leaves can help heal bruises.

My hazelnuts are oily – a single nut can oil a whole walking stick. Simply rub a hazelnut onto the wood. Enjoy eating my roasted nuts; they are full of goodness, a favourite food of your ancestors.

Imbolc Tree Song

Lyrics by Anna Richardson
Melody by River Jones

The Hazel Tree Song

VERSE

1. 'Make me a fence for my sheep' said he, so I went to the fo - rest to find that tree. There he stood in his cloak of green, sup - ple and lithe, the Ha - zel lean.

CHORUS

Ha - zel Ha - zel, me - rry li - ttle fe - llow, flo - wers red and cat - kins ye - ll - ow. In su - mmer dance in your cap of green, show me the source of the hid - den stream.

2. 'Fetch me some nuts for my Yuletide Store.'
So I went to search on the forest floor.
A feast of nuts lay on the ground,
And there stood Hazel in his autumn gown.
Chorus

3. 'Show me the secrets within the land.'
So he took me dancing by my two hands.
The bright path shone and sang out to me,
'And that is lost shall be found,' said he.
Chorus

Silver Birch

GAELIC NAME: *Beatha*
LATIN NAME: *Betula pendula*
OGHAM: *Beith* (the letter B)

Essence
Birth ~ Cleansing ~ Grace

Character

I am Silver Birch, Tree of Birth.

Graceful and bright in my silver bark, I am the Lady of the Woods. In spring my sweet sap flows strong, followed by the bursting of my luminous leaves.

My catkins grow through summer months and as autumn turns my leaves to gold my tiny seeds flutter free, like flocks of little birds, each seed flying on papery wings.

After my delicate leaves have fallen, see my slim branches glow with a purple hue, supple in the winter winds. I love to dance in all seasons.

I am a pioneer, a tree of new beginnings. After an ice age has cleansed the land, carving new hills and river valleys, I am one of the first to arrive, my seeds flying in on the wind. Here I grow, live and die, my generations short-lived, akin to human lives. I live lightly, embracing change.

Where I grow and fall, the earth is nourished so that other trees, plants and animals may make their homes in these places. So some call me the Mother of the Trees, the homemaker.

Clear the way; brush away the old with brooms of birchen branches. Spend time in my bright presence. I can help you in times of change, to shed the old and embrace the new – to live lightly. In this ever-changing dance of life, I show you how to take each step with grace.

Gifts

My wood is pale gold, perfect for carving. It is used to make cradles for babies and toys and spoons for children; gifts of welcome and protection for new lives. Gather some of my shedding silver bark to catch the spark and birth your fire. My thin flexible twigs, when dead and dry, are perfect kindling. After my leaves fall, my twiggy branches are cut to make brooms. My bark is also used to craft baskets and pots and, in northern lands where it grows thicker, canoes to journey to new places.

My leaves make a cleansing tea that can help heal skin and keep joints supple. When my leaves are young, soak them in oil for a couple of weeks and then strain to make a soothing muscle oil.

My sap can be carefully harvested in early spring, at the time when the hazel leaves begin to open. This is the time I flow the strongest. My sap is a special gift, so enjoy its sweet medicine. It will cleanse and invigorate you, waking your body after the long winter months.

In early autumn, find fly agaric mushrooms beneath me, connected to my roots. Though poisonous, these red and white toadstools glow with otherworldly enchantment.

Later in my life, as I begin to die, mushrooms grow upon my trunks. Birch bracket polypores, smooth, firm and white, offer many healing gifts. Sliced thinly, they make woodland plasters to sooth and mend broken skin.

The Silver Birch Song

Graceful and light

Sil - ver, dan - cing in the mo - on - light,

Sil - ver, shin - ing in th - e sun.

Sil - ver, sway - ing in th - e bl - ue sky - y,

Sil - ver, si - ng Si - l - ver one.

Lyrics by Dawn Casey
Melody by River Jones

Imbolc Animals

Mute Swan

I am the white bird of the waters. See me on lakes and ponds, canals and slow-flowing rivers. I move with grace, my legs invisible under the surface, but strong. Sometimes I lift my wings like sails and catch the wind, gliding through the waters with ease.

I am faithful and true; my mate and I stay together for ever. When we court, we bow our heads to one another and the curve of our necks forms a perfect heart.

My partner and I build and tend our nest together, and we both sit on our eggs to keep them warm. I protect my nest with fierce love. If you come too near, I will hiss at you, and if you do not heed my warning, beware, I can attack. Once our cygnets are born, they stay with us for many moons. You may see us out on the lake, our whole family looking for food together.

I reach underwater with my long neck to find sweet roots and tender greens.

Sometimes I come on land to feed on grain or grass.

Though I am large, I fly. My powerful wings carry me far and fast. Listen for the rhythmic thrum of our wingbeat as we soar.

My ancestors were born in the northlands of the world; I often make my home in the cool countries of the north. Some of my kind, my cousins the Bewick swans and the Whooper swans, fly great distances from the snow-forests and tundra-lands of the far north where they breed each year. Know me from my cousins by my colours. My bill is bright orange ringed with black – like a fire ringed with ash.

The first pens of your people were fashioned from feathers, and the finest quills were from our family. The bards of the Celts wore cloaks of our feathers. May the music in you flow pure and true.

White Hind

I am White Hind.* Unlike the others of my kind, my coat is white. Long have deer lived in these lands. In your Old Stone Age, your people painted caves with images of our herds and valued our antlers for tools.

The ancestors of your people knew me as magical, able to pass between worlds. Legends of King Arthur tell that to follow the White Hind is a spiritual quest. Hunters of old pursued me, not to eat me, but to be led on new journeys, to new wisdom and enchanted realms.

We deer spend the sun's hours resting in the hidden places of the forest, sheltered in long grass or soft ferns. In the cold of winter, resting under a green roof of pine keeps us warm. Even when sleeping, I am always aware; I sleep with my ears open. I hear the smallest branch snap.

In the half-light of dawn, or the twilight of dusk, you may catch a glimpse of one of my kind.

Or perhaps you may see me in your dreams. I will lead you on a journey. Follow...

*'Hind' means female deer. The white hind is a rare white form of the red deer.

The White Hind Song

Lyrics and melody by River Jones

Slow ballad

VERSE

1. Be - yond the dawn, be - fore the day, Fo ——————— llow. Watch well for her and come she may, Fo ————————————— llow.

CHORUS

Foll - ow foll - ow foll - ow foll - ow foll-ow the white hind.
Foll - ow foll - ow foll - ow foll - ow foll - ow.

2. Between the light of gold and green,
Fo - llow.
Twixt all you see and all unseen,
Fo - llow.
Chorus

3. Between the light of green and gold,
Fo - llow.
Many a tale that's yet untold
Fo - llow.
Chorus

4. Is she the Fey in fallow form?
Fo - llow.
The morning mist made quick and warm.
Fo - llow.
Chorus

5. She'll lead you to a crooked door.
Fo - llow.
Will you pass through? Will you see more?
Fo - llow.
Chorus

Imbolc Celebration

Brigit the maiden goddess treads the earth and the shoots begin to appear. The snowdrops, among the first flowers, ring their little bells as she passes by, telling that spring is on the way, though more snow may follow. The light has been growing since the winter solstice, but at Imbolc we sense that the dark part of the year really is behind us, and we light candles to celebrate the stirring of life.

You will need:
- 1 large candle
- Cloak for Brigit
- Cloaks or blankets for children (to hide underneath)
- Small candle or night light for each child (a small candle will need a ball of clay at its base, so that children can carry it safely, and to provide a stand when the candle is put down)
- Bells
- Shrine for lit candles

Create a simple shrine area beneath a tree near the fire circle. A few simple items can be enough to express the spirit of the season: for example, a white cloth, a snowdrop, a bell and a candle.

What to do:

1. Light a fire and tell the story of Brigit and the Cailleach. The children hide beneath their cloaks (or blankets) with their unlit candle. Invite the children to imagine that they are seeds under the earth.

2. Brigit passes by with her bells chiming, singing 'Dreams of Green and Gold' (p 47). The song can be gently sung until all the candles have been placed on the shrine.

3. The children begin to stir. They slowly come out from under their cloaks and light their candle from Brigit's candle.

4. Children take their candles and, one by one, place them at the shrine. As they place their candle, each child can say out loud something in nature that they feel thankful for, and silently they can make a wish for the coming year.

5. Come back into a circle, and celebrate by sharing a pot of nettle tea (p 34) or a bowl of nettle soup (p 35) together.

Dreams of Golden Green Song

Lyrics and melody by River Jones

Slow ballard

Up a - bove the sn - ow i - s fall - ing, warm a - nd dark in earth we dream.

Gent - ly, mo - ther's voice is call - ing, wake ou - r dreams of gold - e - n green.

Stir now th - e hearth fire's warm - ing. Heal - i - ing herbs grow o - n he - r dress.

Hark - en birds, i - t's near - ly morn - ing. Bri - dey bright, Bri - dey blessed.

Spring

Spring is the dawn of the year, the time of awakening and the time of birth. The spring equinox falls on 21 March. The Latin word *equinox* means 'equal night'; at this time, the day and the night are of equal length all over the planet. As with the autumn equinox, spring equinox is a point of perfect balance in the earth's journey around the sun. From now on, each day will bring us more light than dark.

Anglo-Saxons knew this time of year as *eostre*, the root of our words 'east' and 'Easter'. The Old English word means 'dawn'. Eostre may have been Goddess of the Dawn, for in European and Asian languages Eostre is also referred to as the Daughter of Heaven.

After the long night of winter, spring is the sunrise of the year. We feel warmth and colour returning, and we rejoice.

The Forest in Spring

Grey skies are turning to blue. Bare branches are glowing green. The spring flowers are opening. The forest is brightened by yellow – primrose, wild daffodil and celandine. Dandelions bring a flash of sunshine, reflecting the sun. Windflowers dance in their white dresses.

We welcome the return of the birds from the south. All around, they are building their nests and laying their eggs, white and gold as spring flowers, fragile yet strong, full of potential. The eggs are hatching – life begins anew.

In joyful response to the spring sunshine, life is opening: leaves unfurl; flowers blossom. Buds are bursting; shoots are stretching; insects are returning, along with the birds. The land is turning green. We close our eyes and feel the warmth of the soft breeze; it is full of birdsong and the scent of the waking earth.

A Traditional Story for the Spring Equinox

The Golden Egg

A creation myth from the Finnish epic poem, the *Kalevala*

In the beginning, there was only endless ocean and empty air.

Alone, in the emptiness, Ilmatar was floating. Her hair curled like wisps of cloud. Her skin was dew-soft. Her eyes were mist-grey. She was the daughter of the sky, the great goddess of the air.

The all-father, Ukko, spirit of the sky, was somewhere high above, far and distant. All Ilmatar knew was loneliness. Longing tugged in her tummy.

Tears welled in her eyes and rolled down her cheeks, rolled and dropped, down into the water. And Ilmatar herself followed, rolling and dropping, down into the water, which caught her. The water caught Ilmatar. And Ilmatar rolled and played, dived and swam.

Until, from the east, came a breeze, lively and leaping, skipping over the surface of the water, lifting up splashes of spray. The wind turned the water into waves. The waves danced and Ilmatar danced. They danced as one.

These two life-forces, breathing, flowing, wind and wave, air and water, together woke life in the sky king's daughter. In Ilmatar's belly a baby began to grow. She held her hands to her round belly and smiled. Her baby was no ordinary child; a baby made of wind and wave, air and water.

Months passed but the child was not born. Years passed and the child was not born. And still, Ilmatar swam the sea. Ilmatar, the Mother-in-the-Waters, swam and swam.

And again, Ilmatar began to weep. She called up a prayer to Ukko, the all-father, the thunderous spirit of the sky:

> *How my days grow grey and dreary,*
> *Always wandering in the waters!*
> *Ukko, hear me, I implore you!*
> *I am cold and I am lonely!*
> *Ukko, hear me! Ukko, help me!*

And no sooner had she spoken, than down from the sky flew a creature Ilmatar had never seen before, feathered, white: a duck.

It was a mother-bird, with her belly full of eggs. She was circling, looking for somewhere safe to land, somewhere to make her nest and lay her eggs. The duck, the Mother-in-the-Air, flew and flew but all she found was endless water.

Ilmatar knew just how that mama-duck felt, and so she lifted up her knees, out of the water, to make a place for the duck to land. Gliding down, the duck tucked in her wings and landed on Ilmatar's lap. In Ilmatar's lap, snug against her big belly, the mother duck made her nest. She settled there, content. Ilmatar was content too, to have a companion at last, a kindred spirit. Ilmatar stroked the duck's feathers and talked softly to her.

The duck laid seven eggs; six eggs of gold and the seventh egg of iron. Ilmatar had never seen an egg before. She marvelled at their colours – shining yellow and rich red-brown. Very gently, she touched them. They seemed lifeless, hard and cold.

The mother duck snuggled her eggs to warm them. The eggs grew warmer and warmer. The nest grew warmer and warmer. Ilmatar's legs grew warmer and warmer, hotter and hotter, until she felt her knees were on fire, her skin was burning. She shifted her legs, her knees shook, and the nest tipped...

The duck flew up into the air and the eggs fell down, into the water. Down, down, down, into the sea. And the seven shells, bright gold and rich iron, cracked.

But what was broken was not wasted. For in that moment was a wonder. The broken pieces came together, making two great eggshell pieces; one the upper, one the lower. One great egg, bright as gold. One great egg, rich as iron. One great egg, broken open...

With eyes wide, the duck stared. And still the wonder-change continued... The lower part of the egg became the earth beneath our feet. The upper part of the egg became the sky above our heads. The yellow of the yolk became the gold of the sun, the white of the egg the silver of the moon. The speckles of the shell became the sparkles of the stars. And thus the world was born. And how that mama-duck puffed up her feathers with pride!

Ilmatar watched the duck with smiling eyes. But for Ilmatar the world seemed empty still. She put her hands on her big belly and her smile spread to her lips; she knew change was coming.

Ilmatar explored the seashores with her companion the duck always flying alongside her. She lifted her face to the sky and closed her eyes, enjoying the warmth of the new sun.

Wherever Ilmatar cooled her feet in the sand, caves were formed. Where she dived beneath the water, the ocean depths were shaped. Where she rested her head on the shore, curving bays were made. And, when the land was fully formed, Ilmatar's child was born at last. No ordinary child, born of wind and water, to the Great Mother. Her child was Vainamoinen. No sooner was he born than he was grown; a full-grown man, full of power. With her friend the duck beside her, Ilmatar gazed upon her son, her eyes shining.

Rising from the primal waters, Vainamoinen looked around him. Looking over all creation, he felt a mighty inward surging, felt a rising impulse urging... On his tongue was music glowing. From his lips came magic flowing. Vainamoinen opened his mouth and he sang:

> *Grass arise, be green and growing.*
> *Flowers open, yellow, glowing.*
>
> *Willow, Alder, Birch of silver,*
> *Flourish by the rushing river.*
> *Fir trees grow on mountains high.*
> *Pine trees spread towards the sky.*
> *Grow now Linden, Hawthorn, Rowan.*
> *Grow now Oak, Great Tree of Heaven.*
>
> *Be joyful birds. Rise up singing.*
> *Set the very treetops ringing.*
> *Buds, uncurl your tender leaves.*
> *Bugs awake. Buzz bumble bees.*
>
> *From out of slumber, rise, Oh Earth.*
> *Release your seeds, and give them birth.*

Vainamoinen sang the land to life. Now, instead of silence, there was birdsong. Instead of cold wind, there was scented breeze. Instead of bare earth, bright flowers.

And as new life arose in beauty, three figures stood and watched in wonder. A mother, a son and a little white duck.

Spring Imaginary Journey

It is spring, the sunrise of the year. Ask the children to find a comfortable position to lie on the ground. It can be cold at this time of year; if it is, they can sit safely round the fire for warmth. When everyone is settled, begin the imaginary journey.

- Close your eyes. Imagine that you are inside an egg. The white is soft and silky like a sheet. The rich, gold heart feeds you with its glow. You are growing.

- There is a feeling of excitement in the air. Life is awakening around you. A new world is waiting. It is time to hatch! Imagine stretching and bursting out of your shell into the golden light of dawn. Birds are singing and rejoicing. Let your heart rejoice that you are alive!

- As the warmth and energy rise within you, imagine you have wings and fly up, up into the sky. You are flying over the land, watching the sunlight touch the forests, fields and hills. The rivers sparkle in the morning light, winding to the sea.
  Pause to allow the imagination time to be free.

- Now you are returning. You land and fold your wings. Feel the tingling in your toes, your legs and your torso, your arms and hands, up through your neck to your head. Gently open your eyes and slowly sit up, stretching your arms and fingers to the sky.

- Take a deep invigorating breath and feel your body filled with spring energy.

Spring Activities, Crafts and Games

Natural Egg Dyeing with Gorse

The egg, so fragile and so strong, with its promise of new life, has always been a potent symbol. Traditionally in these lands, gorse flowers were gathered to use as a dye to transform hens' eggs into a cheerful Easter yellow.

Gorse (known also as whin or furze) has bright yellow flowers all year round. As the old country saying goes, 'When gorse is in flower, kissing is in season.' In spring, gorse blossom is at its peak and its delicious scent of coconut and vanilla attracts bees and humans alike.

YOU WILL NEED:
- White eggs (which take the dye better than brown eggs)
- Pan
- Gorse blossom
- Slotted spoon
- Gardening gloves (optional)
- Cardboard egg cartons

TO MAKE:

1. Fill a large saucepan with gorse flowers – gorse is a prickly bush, so gather with care! (You may like to wear gardening gloves.) Cover the blossom with water, bring to the boil and simmer until the water turns yellow, about 10 minutes. Add the eggs and boil for another 10 minutes, or more if desired.

2. Remove the eggs from the pan with a slotted spoon, dry them off gently and place them in the egg carton to cool.

Natural Egg Dyeing with Leaf Imprints

When dyeing eggs, you can also use leaves and flowers to create patterns and shapes on your coloured background. This method uses onion skins as a dye material – it is easy to save onion skins when preparing food and they give a good, strong colour.

YOU WILL NEED:
- White eggs
- Pan
- Onion skins* (white onion skins make an orange-brown dye; red onion skins a green dye)
- Vinegar
- Tights cut into pieces to go around each egg
- Small elastic bands
- Slotted spoon
- Cardboard egg cartons
  *You can also use red cabbage to make a blue dye

TO MAKE:

1. Place the onion skins into the pan with enough water to cover the eggs (which are added later). Boil for fifteen minutes with the lid on. Strain the contents into a bowl, pressing the pulp to remove any remaining liquid. Remove the pulp and pour the dye water back into the pan and cover.

2. One at a time, place leaves and flowers onto the egg, arranging them in a pleasing pattern. Simple shapes work best. Some of the plant materials will stick better if dipped in water first. If the eggs are to be eaten, only use edible plants such as calendula. Gently place the egg inside the tights, making sure your plant material is still in place, then pull the tights around the egg and secure with elastic bands.

3. Return the dye to a gentle boil and stir three tablespoons of vinegar into the pan, to act as a natural mordant. Lower the eggs carefully into the pan and simmer for 10 to 20 minutes. Turn off the heat, cover, and let the liquid stand until the desired colour is obtained.

4. Remove the eggs with a slotted spoon and place them back in the egg carton to cool. Carefully untie the elastic bands or cut the tights and unwrap the eggs, and gently pull off the plant materials.

Giant Nest

This group project celebrates the wonder of nest-building and gives the children an idea of how much work is involved in making a nest. The children can look out for birds' nests wherever you go.

It's fun to sit in the nest all together; you can use it as a special place to relax and gather, read stories or play games.

(NB: You could also do the Spring Imaginary Journey (p 53) while the children are inside the nest. The children can then can fly away around the forest.)

You will need:
- 16 x 1m (3ft) hazel poles for a nest 1.5m (5ft) in diameter (see Staff Making, p 282)
- Mallet
- Billhook and/or loppers
- Saw

To make:
1. Angle the bottom of each pole with a billhook or loppers, to help it slide easily into the ground. Hammer the poles into the ground angled slightly away from the middle, in two staggered circles as shown below:

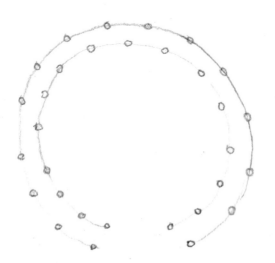

If you don't have space for a permanent feature, you could make a temporary giant nest without the poles to secure it, and then scatter the sticks again after the activity.

2. Fill the space between the circles with piles of sticks, one layer at a time, making it as high as you want, while leaving a space for the entrance.

3. With the saw or loppers cut the tops of the poles flush with the top of your nest. You can fill your nest with hay for a cosy nest-like feel. When the structure is in place, add all the sticks and straw necessary to make it feel like a real nest.

Alder Cone Bees

A mild spell as early as February will bring out the first bumblebees, the fuzzy familiar wild bee of the British Isles. The queen bee has spent all winter hibernating, sheltered underground. When the weather warms up in early spring, the queen bee wakes and looks for a place to nest and lay her eggs. Look out for her low-flying zigzag flight as she searches for a nest-site. Once the queen bee has found one, she builds herself a wax honey-pot and fills it with nectar. She lays her eggs and sits on them to keep them warm, feeding from her honey-pot. Her eggs hatch into larvae, which she feeds with nectar and pollen. Each tiny larva spins itself a cocoon and inside develops into a bumblebee. When the bees emerge, spring flowers provide them with nectar to drink (which they lap up with their long tongues) and pollen to eat (which they gather in 'pollen baskets' – tiny pockets on their back legs).

Alder seed cones, with their tiny size and rounded shape, make lovely fuzzy, buzzy bumblebees.

You will need:
- Alder cones
- Short lengths of yellow yarn
- Thin thread
- Tissue paper

To make:

1. Fold the tissue paper in half and cut out a wing shape.

2. Wind your yellow yarn around your alder cone, tucking it in between the scales to keep it in place. This makes the stripes of your bee.

3. Take a piece of thin cotton thread and place it underneath your alder bee in the middle of its body. Place the paper wings on top of the alder body and lift both ends of the thin thread around the alder cone and over the wings, tying a knot to secure the wings to the body. You can gently twist the wings into place if necessary.

4. Leave the thread attached, so you can fly your bee around or hang it from a branch.

Log Bee House

As well as honeybees and bumblebees, in Britain and Ireland we have over 200 species of wild bees known as solitary bees – because, unlike bumblebees and honeybees, they do not live in large communities. It is especially important to help bees in cities, by providing them with a place to nest. Different bees need different kinds of homes. Many species of bumblebees nest in wood piles – you can create a home for them simply by making an untidy pile of logs, stems and branches. Some solitary bees nest in tunnels in the ground or on grassy banks. To offer a home for these bees, just leave the grass in your garden to grow tall, perhaps planting some pollen-rich plants along the edge. Clover is nectar-rich, and borage flowers re-fill with nectar every two minutes, so both are loved by hungry bees. Other solitary bees make nests in hollows and holes.

YOU WILL NEED:
- Pre-cut log slices, at least 20cm (8ins) deep and without cracks or splits (which might allow fungus to spread)
- Hand drills
- Sandpaper
- Paper straws / brown paper

Wet, mouldy wood can harm developing bee larvae, so bee homes also need a roof to provide shelter from the rain. Prepare the logs in advance for the children by cutting them as shown and screwing on a plank of wood to create a sloping, overhanging 'roof'.

Cut away the top of the log slice at an angle of approx. 45° before attaching the roof.

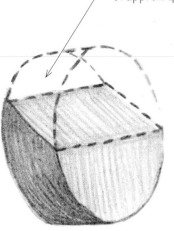
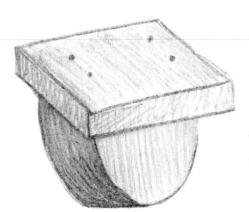

To make:

1. Use a hand drill to make holes in the log slice. The holes need to be 2–10mm (⁵⁄₆₄ – ⅜in) in diameter, and at least 2cm (¾in) apart. (Though solitary bees do not live in great communities, bees of the same species do like to live near each other. So, for example, one child's log could have many small holes, and another child's log could have fewer larger holes.)

2. Stop drilling before you come through the other end of the log – the bees need a closed tunnel so the wind doesn't blow through. Smooth the entrance to each hole with sandpaper. This ensures the bees don't damage their delicate wings on sharp splinters. Blow away all the sawdust.

3. Take a straw or roll brown paper to create a paper tube. Fold down one end of the paper tube to close it. Line the inside of the drilled holes with the tubes (inserting the closed end first) to protect the bees from tiny splinters of wood.

4. Unlike bumblebees, solitary bees have no furry coat to keep themselves warm. They warm up in the sunshine in the morning. So, find a sunny, south-facing spot (at least a metre above the ground and un-obscured by plants) to secure your bee home.

Maintaining the Bee Homes

In mid-September, after all the bees have flown, the paper tubes can be gently withdrawn and stored in a cool, dry place, such as a shed or porch. (This protects the larvae from diseases caused by mould, which can grow on wet wood.)

Before the bees emerge in spring, make new bee homes. In mid-February to March, once the wet winter weather is over, but before the bees emerge, the paper tubes can be hung in a bundle near the new bee homes. Alternatively (again, close to the new bee homes) place the bundle of straws on dry ground beneath a container with a small hole, such as a flower pot. From April onwards, newborn bees will fly out through the hole.

You can leave the straws under the box throughout the summer, as some species of bee emerge months later than others. Check under the box occasionally to remove any predatory insects. After the summer, you can dispose of the old straws.

Sense Awareness Activity – Listening Man

This simple craft creates a focus for opening up awareness of the sounds in nature. It can be used at any time of the year but is especially rewarding in springtime, when there is such an astonishing array of birdsong. Listen to the gurgling brook, to the birdsong, to a tree blowing in the breeze. What can your listening man hear?

It is even possible, with deep listening, to hear the buds opening.

YOU WILL NEED:
- Clay (or mole mud)
- Hazel stick or a strong stick found on the ground
- Leaves, moss, lichen, twigs, etc.

TO MAKE:

1. Make a ball with a small handful of clay or mud and firmly push onto the stick. Mould the face by pulling the nose out and making indents for the eyes. Add leaves for the ears, then for the hair, eyes and mouth use tiny twigs, moss or lichen. There you have your listening man.

2. Ask the children to come on a silent journey of discovery with their listening man, to find all the sounds of the area, from the loudest noise to the tiniest whisper.

Sit awhile in your special place with your listening man, listening...

Egg Hunt – 3D Mapping Game

A map is a picture of a place which can be used as a guide to find our way. We all carry maps within us; for example, when we close our eyes, we can picture the layout of our homes, or the route we walk to school. As we spend time in the forest, we create an inner map of the trees, pathways, streams and special places. This activity is a fun way of creating an outer map of the familiar places in the forest. By making the map, we look more closely at the landmarks and pathways that connect them. Maps always guide us to the treasures we seek, whether it is a mountain view, a friend's home or chocolate gold.

To play:

1. Hide your hidden treasure.

2. Mark out a rectangle with sticks, clearing the ground of debris if you are in the woods. Using twigs stuck in the earth, leaves, stalks, etc. to represent trees and other features of the landscape, create a replica of the area where the eggs are hidden. Make an 'X marks the spot' where the treasure is hidden.

> ### You will need:
> - Locally available hens' eggs, boiled, (one for each person) or use foil-wrapped chocolate eggs

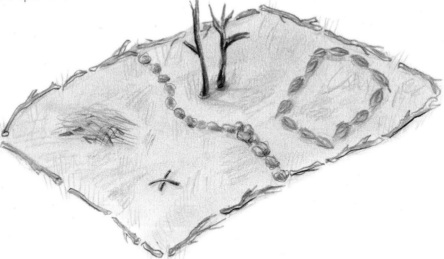

3. The children look at the map and decide what the main features are, so they can discover where the treasure is hidden.

Variations

When the children have successfully found and eaten their treasure, they could set up maps for each other. In autumn you could use nuts or berries that the squirrels have 'hidden' as treasure.

Birds and Beetles Game

In the forest in spring we hear the birds sing in their many voices as they mate, build nests and tend their young. But this time of year is also fraught with danger, as predators also need to feed their babies. This active and energetic game gives us a glimpse of the life and language of birds.

YOU WILL NEED:
- Bag of objects to represent beetles/insects, e.g. pine cones, marbles or hazelnuts (20–50, depending on group size)
- At least eight people

TO PLAY:

1. Two players are predators. The rest of the group are bird families; groups of three with one or two parents and one or two chicks. Create and clear a central area for the game, which will be the feeding ground. Here the beetles are scattered.

2. Each bird family finds a secret nesting area some distance from the feeding area. Create a nest and also invent a bird call that will be specific to your family.

3. When one predator, a sparrowhawk – the silent fierce hunter of the skies and forest – flies through the game, arms outstretched, everyone must fall completely silent and still. Any bird moving or making a sound can be caught and will then be out of the game until the next round. Create a space for those who are out to sit and watch.

4. The other predator is a cat. When the birds see the cat prowling through the forest, they must get off the ground and call, 'Cat, cat, cat!' warning the others of the danger. Any birds caught on the ground will be dinner for the cat and sit out of the game till the next round.

5. The adult calls, 'Sunrise!' Birds sing the dawn chorus – each family singing the song they created earlier – and feeding begins. Parent birds fly to the feeding ground and gather one beetle at a time to bring back to the nest where the chick stores them. Watch out for the predators who are hiding and will occasionally come hunting, one at a time.

6. Any parents who are caught by the predators sit out till the next round. After a few minutes the adult calls, 'Sunset!' and the parent birds can take the last beetles they have gathered back to the nest.

This is the end of round one. Bird families now bring their beetles to the central area to count them and need at least six beetles to survive.

Talk with the group about the birds that did not survive.

Now it's time for another day (round of the game). Change roles so that each player will get a chance to be a predator, parent or baby bird as the game moves on.

Spring Flowers Inspiration Walk

The forests and hedgerows are graced with a succession of flowers, blessing the land. Their beauty is welcome after the dark, bare winter months.

- Take a walk, greeting the return of the plants to the upper world.

- Magnifying glasses and jewellers' loupes are magical eyes for looking into the hearts of flowers and opening leaf buds. See their intricate inner worlds.

- Flowers offer many gifts, including the gift of inspiration.

- Spend time drawing or painting flowers.

- Write poems and create songs to celebrate the plants. These islands have been long acclaimed for their poetry and song. Call upon Brigit for inspiration.

- The songs that follow were created together with children in the forest on a spring morning.

Spring Plant Lore

Celandine

GAELIC NAME: *Grianne* (meaning 'sun')

LATIN NAME: *Ranunculus ficaria*

Character

I am Lesser Celandine, shining gold like my cousin Buttercup.

I am also known as Butterstar.

See me growing in the forest, small but as bright as the sun.

My heart-shaped leaves are not good to eat, but when I sleep underground, my little tubers are good food and have been roasted and eaten by your ancestors.

My name Celandine comes from the Greek for swallow, *chelos*, for when I open my flowers it is a sign that the swallows are on their way home to these shores.

Spring Plant Song

by Anna Richardson,
Helen Thomms and Oak Tree class

Celandine Song

Light and breezy

Ce - lan - dine shin - ing bright, pet - als of pure sun - light,

joy in our hearts as win - ter de - par ————— ts

Ce - lan - dine shin - ing bright, song of the swa - llow's flight,

no long - er roam, we're ca - lling you home.

Wood Anemone

GAELIC NAME: *Lus na gaoithe*
(meaning 'plant of the wind')

LATIN NAME: *Anenome nemorosa*

Character

I am the Windflower, daughter of the wind also known as Wood Anemone.

I am one of the first flowers of spring. I bloom across the forest floor like a galaxy of stars.

I grow in the windy months, bending and swaying in the breeze on my supple stems.

I spread slowly. Indeed, to cover six feet of ground takes over 100 years. See me carpeting the ancient woodland floor.

I am bold yet shy, closing my flowers when the clouds and rain come by.

Song of the Windflower

By Anna Richardson,
Helen Thomms and Oak Tree class

Steady

Wind flow-ers, wind flow-ers, daugh-ters of the wind.

Shine your white pe - tals like stars in the spring.

Dance when the wind blows, hi - de when the sun goes.

Wind flow-ers, wind flow-ers, daugh-ters of the wind.

A Spring Treasure for Your Magic Pouch – Herbal Medicine Tea Bag

This re-usable herbal teabag is useful for making tea in the forest and can also be used as a poultice on wounds. It can be used as a storage pouch for dried medicine. Herbs for making medicinal teas are good used fresh, but for storage through the year it is best to dry them.

Pick herbs on a dry day. They can be tied in bunches and hung upside down to dry, out of direct sunlight, or they can be dried in a warm cupboard, in a basket, cloth or paper bag. Children can make their own pouch and gather herbs to store inside. Some of the medicines of the year include:

- Nettle leaf – for strength and vigour
- Dandelion (young leaves can be dried, flower petals can be used fresh for tea) – for internal sunshine and cleansing
- Daisy – leaves and flowers for bruises
- Honeysuckle – leaves and flowers for sore throats
- Elderflower – for colds and fever
- Meadowsweet – for tummy ache, headache and pains
- Bramble leaf – for diarrhoea
- Elderberry – for coughs, colds and flu
- Sphagnum moss – for wounds

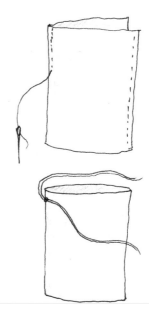

You will need:

- Unbleached cotton
- Needle and thread
- Cotton string
- Scissors

To make:

1. Cut a rectangle approximately 30cm (12ins) long and 10cm (4ins) wide. Fold it in half and sew up the sides.

2. Cut a length of string about 20cm (8ins) long and sew the middle of the string to the bag approx. 2cm (¾in) from the top. Sew a few stitches on top of each other for strength. Use your cotton bag to store dried herbs for tea and for healing.

Deadly and Poisonous Plants in the Forest

It is essential to know the potentially deadly poisonous plants that grow in one's world. This way we can give these plants the respect and space they need. In the forest, the children can learn to identify these plants and then to show them to others. The deadly species are often common. Although they can be fatal for humans, they are not necessarily poisonous to others, and are often essential for animals and insects. They are important in their gifts and roles within the forest, seen and unseen. Many of our most poisonous plants (and mushrooms) also provide the most potent medicines used in modern drugs today. Many mushrooms are deadly, so it is usually best to avoid touching them, just in case. Let us honour these plants with the respect they deserve. Please refer to a good field guide for identification.

Deadly plants in the forest

- Yew
- Foxglove (very common in woodlands and used in modern medicine for heart problems)
- Water hemlock (these can be found growing in wet places in shady forests – it's best to avoid all wild umbellifas generally)
- Monkshood (rare but can be found growing wild in Britain – also known as wolfsbane)
- Lords and ladies (also known as cuckoo pint)
- White and black bryony (these are two different species and prefer hedgerow and woodland edges – they are climbing plants with shiny berries)

Poisonous plants in the forest

- Dog's mercury – eating aerial parts causes sickness
- Bluebells – all parts are toxic if eaten
- Snowdrop – all parts are toxic if eaten
- Wood spurge – all parts are toxic if eaten and leaves can burn the skin though are useful for removing warts
- Honeysuckle – berries not recommended for eating, as they can cause tummy upset, the seeds especially
- Bracken – leaves are toxic if eaten
- Daffodil – all parts toxic if eaten; take care not to confuse the bulbs with shallots
- Holly – leaves can be used as tea but berries cause vomiting
- Privet – leaves and berries are toxic if eaten
- Wood anenome (windflower) – toxic if eaten
- Woody nightshade – all aerial parts (above the ground) are toxic if ingested
- Lesser celandine – all parts are toxic, except the little tubers, which can be eaten when cooked
- Ivy berries – toxic if eaten
- Spindle – leaf and berries toxic if eaten
- Butcher's broom – berries toxic if eaten

Dandelion

GAELIC NAME: *Bearnan Brìde* ('the notched-leaved plant of Brigit')

LATIN NAME: *Taraxacum officinale*

Character

I am Dandelion, bright flower of Brigit.

I always grow in full sun, bringing hope in springtime and cheering up gardens and pathways.

The place where I grow is said to be blessed by the light.

My name comes from the French *dent de lion*, meaning 'tooth of the lion', because my leaves have jagged toothy edges.

I offer both food and medicine. My leaves, roots and flowers are all good to eat and can be taken as a tea.

Brew my yellow petals in hot water and drink a cup of sunshine. My bitter taste is cleansing for your body and is refreshing in today's sweet and salty world.

My roots can be roasted to make dandelion coffee.

My petals have the mildest flavour; you can eat them raw, straight from the flower.

Gift

I help your body to clear away the heavy foods and moods of winter, bringing cheering sunshine into your being.

Dandelion Song

Sunny and bold

From the poem 'O' Dandelion' by
Marlys Swinger

Dand - e - li - o - n yel - low as gold, what do you do all day?   I

just wait here in the tall green grass til the child - ren come to play.   And

Dand - e - li - o - n yel - low as gold, what do you do all night?   I

just wait here til the dew falls down and my hair grows long and white.   And

what do you do when your hair turns white and the child - ren come to play?   They

take me up in their ti - ny hands and they blow my hair a - way.

Dandelion Drop Scones

Collect dandelion flowers in the sunshine, as they close up on rainy days and at night.

YOU WILL NEED: (TO SERVE APPROX. 6–10):
- Dandelion petals from 15–20 flowers (only use the golden petals, as the stem and sepals are bitter)
- 125g (4½oz) self-raising flour
- Approx. 175ml (6floz) milk
- 1 egg
- 2 tablespoons butter or coconut oil
- Honey and butter to serve (optional)

TO MAKE:

1. Mix the flour and dandelion petals in a jug or bowl. Then make a well in the centre and crack in the egg. Pour in a splash of milk and mix to form a smooth paste. Add milk steadily until the mixture reaches the consistency of thick cream.

2. Heat the frying pan and add a spoonful of coconut oil or butter. Carefully pour in 4–6 separate spoonfuls of mixture, depending on the size of your pan. After a few minutes turn the scones with a spatula.

3. Your dandelion scones are ready when both sides are golden brown.

4. Serve with butter and honey.

NB: For a wheat-free, vegan alternative, omit the egg and use buckwheat mixed with water.

Dandelion Wands

Dandelions are like joy-bursts of sunshine. Make these yellow pompom wands with the children and bring sunshine blessings to one and all.

YOU WILL NEED:
- Cardboard
- Scissors
- Yellow wool
- Green wool
- Sharpened sticks, approx. 20–30cm (8–12ins) in length

TO MAKE:

1. It is easier to prepare the cardboard discs in advance of doing the activity with the children. Cut two cardboard ring shapes with a slot, as shown. These are placed precisely together.

2. A length of green wool, approximately 1m (3ft), is then wrapped around a quarter of the cardboard, working from the inner hole out and around the disc. The slot makes it easier to wrap.

3. Cut a length of yellow wool approximately 2–3m (2–3yds) and wrap the rest of the ring.

4. Now cut approximately 1m (3ft) of green wool for tying the pompom together.

5. The next part will need adult help. With one hand, firmly pinch the centre of the circle, holding the wool in place. Insert scissors into the slot between the two layers of cardboard and carefully cut the wool along the circumference of the circle.

6. Keeping a firm grip on the centre of the woollen circle, insert the middle of the length of green wool between the cardboard layers, so that the place where the ends meet is within the green section of the ring. Tie a firm knot that will pull the pompom together and fasten it.

7. Remove the cardboard. There should now be two lengths of green wool hanging from the pompom. Insert the sharpened end of the stick into the green fluffy section and wrap the green threads down and around the stick in a crisscross pattern. Before the wool runs out, wrap tightly in one place a few times and secure with a knot.

8. If need be, trim the dandelion into a pleasing ball shape.

Now the dandelion wand is complete. Lead the children around the woodland, touching the sunshine wand upon the growing buds of trees and young plants with wishes and blessings for their growth and health in the seasons to come.

Ramsons

COMMON NAME: Wild Garlic or Wood Garlic, Broadleaved Garlic, Bears' Garlic, Buckrams ('garlic' comes from the Anglo-Saxon *gar* meaning 'spear' and *lac* meaning 'plant')

GAELIC NAME: *Garleag*

LATIN NAME: *Allium ursine (ursinum* means 'bear' or 'belonging to bears', for this plant is a favourite food of brown bears)

Character

I am Ramsons, Wild Garlic of the Woods, living in the damp forest hollows by the streams.

My flowers are white six-pointed stars that shine from April to June.

Growing from bulbs, my young blade-shaped leaves greet the light in mid-February.

Brown bears, who lived in these lands, loved to dig up my bulbs and shoots for food and I am still eaten by the wild boar in some forests.

People have gathered me for many thousands of years for the healing food I give. By spring equinox I am strong and succulent, offering my broad leaves for harvest.

I love to grow in great communities in ancient woodlands and here I am good for harvesting, where I am healthy and plentiful, but please only take what you need.

Gifts

I am held in high esteem for my flavour and health-giving powers; for example, I lower blood pressure, help to protect against infection and aid digestion. The bears know the healing plants.

Ramsons Paté

This simple recipe is easy to make in the woods and is adaptable as pesto to add to pasta or pizza. The children can help with the chopping, roasting, blending and spreading. The ratios of ingredients are totally flexible and the results will be delicious.

YOU WILL NEED::
- A good handful of ramsons
- Nuts or seeds (hazelnuts or sunflower seeds work well)
- Olive oil
- Salt
- Lemon (optional)
- Oat cakes or crackers
- Bowl
- Chopping board
- Knife
- Mechanical grinder or large pestle and mortar (another simple option is for children to each use a cup and clean-cut stick to pound and mix the ingredients together)
- Plate to serve

TO MAKE:

1. Gather the ramsons and chop finely with a knife.

2. Dry roast the seeds or nuts in a pan, stirring until they start to turn brown and smell 'nutty'.

3. Grind or pound the seeds until they become tiny pieces. Add the ramsons and pound together with the seeds Add salt, plenty of olive oil and lemon juice to taste.

4. Spread on crackers and enjoy.

Be careful as you gather, for there is another plant that likes to grow in the shady forest in the same places as me. This plant is called lords and ladies and it is poisonous. It is also known as cuckoo pint (*Arum maculatum*). Though different in shape when fully grown, it too emerges with a coiled, blade-like leaf among my sea of green and you will need a keen eye to see the difference. Be aware and try to find them. Learn the poisonous plants (see p 70)and greet them but do not touch, for they have other roles to play in the forest.

Ramsons can also be confused with lily of the valley, *Convallaria majalis*. This plant is deadly poisonous if ingested, though is not indigenous to British forests. It is grown in gardens and can escape into the wild. Great care must be taken to correctly identify plants properly, especially when working with children.

Spring Tree Lore

Alder

GAELIC NAME: *Feàrna*
LATIN NAME: *Alnus glutinosa*
OGHAM: *Fearn* (the letter F)

Essence
Protector of the Waters
~ Hidden Realms ~ Strength

Character

I am Alder, protector of the waters. I stand firm and strong.

I grow by rivers, streams and lakes. Here I nourish the earth and strengthen the banks. My roots weave through the rock and earth into the stream bed. In the water, my roots do not rot, but grow hard as stone.

My catkins are long and purple-red, sending pollen on the wind to my seeds, which are safely held in their cone homes.

When they are ripe, my cones fall into the flowing waters and begin their journey, floating down the river currents to be lodged in the banks. The waters choose where my children grow.

In winter, see my iridescent violet buds waiting to unfold. In spring, tiny flowers spiral around each of my catkins, echoing the spiralling journey of the earth as the world moves once more into birth and new life. My spring buds too grow in a spiral around my twigs.

I clean the air, feed the earth and protect the waters. In the hot summer, enjoy my cool

shade and bathe your feet in the flowing streams. When the waters of strong feelings flood you, spend time beside me and let me hold you firm, bringing to light that which is below the surface.

My spirit is strong; I am the Alder King, the Elf King, protector and warrior of the hidden realms. I have the strength of sun-fire within me, balanced with the flowing power of water. My presence can help bring balance between the masculine and feminine within us all – fiery and direct whilst connected to inner knowing, flow and feelings. We all have gifts to share. To share your gifts, go within and listen deeply. Use your inner knowing to guide your actions.

Gifts

My wood is solid when immersed in water. Because I am strong in water, my wood has been used for making the feet of bridges and the soles of clogs, a traditional shoe for people working in damp places.

My shoots can easily be hollowed to make flutes and whistles – one of my old names is 'whistle wood'.

My charcoal was traditionally used for the forging of swords and, as befits a tree of protection, I was also carved into shields.

My wood can be used to make fire by friction.

I yield three dyes, brown from my twigs, blood-red from my bark and green from my flowers. In days of old, my green dye was used to colour and camouflage the clothes of forest dwellers such as Robin Hood and, according to folk belief, dyed the green clothes of the little folk.

I am a healer of damp conditions, a transformer and nourisher for your body's vital fluids. An oil infused from my leaves and green cones soothes rheumatism, inflammations and sore skin. A gargle from my leaves and bark soothes sore throats and can help diarrhoea. Place my fresh green leaves in your shoes on summer days to soothe hot tired feet. Feel your feet cooled, just as my feet are cooled in the waters.

Alder Song

By Anna Richardson and River Jones

Steady and firm

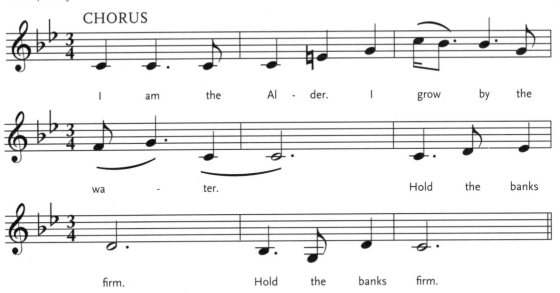

CHORUS

I am the Al - der. I grow by the wa - ter. Hold the banks firm. Hold the banks firm.

VERSE repeat chorus after verse

Where the clear wa - ters flow, here I will al - ways grow.

Down in the va - lleys, I grow by the wa - ter ways.

Dance on the banks in the clogs I will give you. To-geth - er pro - tect our lands, hold the banks firm.

Willow

GAELIC NAME: *Sùileag* (the Old Irish name –
sùil – refers to 'the look' of a thing)
LATIN NAME: *Salix alba* ('white willow' – the
word *salix* comes from the Latin word *salire*
meaning 'to leap' – a sudden burst of expression or action)
OGHAM: *Saille* (the letter S)

Essence
Dreams and Intuition ~ Growth ~ Expression

Character

I am Willow, Tree of Dreams.

I love to grow by the water, reaching my roots
into the damp earth as my leaves reflect in the
shimmering currents.

In spring see my catkins, pussy willows, silver
and soft, shining in the sun, soon to turn gold
with pollen before my white downy seed-chil-
dren are carried away by the wind.

See the willow warblers in my trees; listen to
their sweet song, like a flowing stream.

My branches are elegant and supple, with
dancing leaves of green and silver swaying
in the wind. Spend time with me; see how I
move, feel all resistance fall away as you bend
gently in the wind, soft and free.

Weave a basket from my flexible branches
as your ancestors have done for many ages.
Hold a strong vision of the shape you wish
to make. Follow the patterns, the rhythm, the
dance between your hands and my branches.
I shall become a basket to hold all that you
wish to gather.

Where I fall, I may sprout anew, for I am filled with the power of vigorous life and grow with ease.

If you take some of my shoots to craft, cut a small piece or two and push them into the damp earth. They will easily root and begin to grow.

Grow into the dream you carry within you. My roots are in the river, connected to the flow of life. The River of Life is guiding your way; your heart knows where it is calling.

Come and sit beneath my tree by a woodland stream and look up into the green boughs. Listen to the waters and the whisper of the wind, and follow your dreams.

Gifts

My wood has many uses. My flexible branches are used for weaving baskets, domes and tunnels.

My wood is strong and can absorb strong impacts – it is used to make cricket bats. It is also used to make harps, creating a vibrant sound.

When dry and seasoned, my wood can be used to make fire by friction.

My roots offer a purple dye, my leaves a dye the colour of cinnamon.

My bark contains the main ingredient of aspirin.

Tea made from my bark offers a remedy for many ailments caused by damp, such as stiff muscles and rheumatism.

My leaves, after being chewed to make a simple poultice, can be applied to a cut to help stop bleeding.

Tea from my leaves soothes sore throats, colds and fevers. If you feel stiff and sore, I will ease your pain and help you to flow free.

Willow Tree Song

By Anna Richardson

Gentle and steady, can be sung as a round

VERSE 1

Down by the brook with her feet in the wa - ter

Stands the green wil - low, green wil - low, and she

dan - ces and sways in the heart of the wind so.

Grow the green wil - low, green wil - low.

CHORUS

Wil - low, dream with your roots in the wa - ter.

Wil - low, dance with your head in the sk - y.

Grace - ful and green, you're the for - est man's daugh - ter.

Grow the green wil - low, green wil - low.

2. We'll dance round the willow who grows by the water,
Dance in the wind and the sky oh.
We'll dance in the water with never a care oh,
Round the green willow, green willow.

3. Through the whispering leaves in the silver moonlight,
The song of the river is calling.
'The song of your heart knows the dream you must follow,'
Whispers the willow, green willow.

Spring Animals

Swallow

I am Swallow, the swift sky-sweeper.

I live on the wing, flying fast and far – when cold freezes the land, I fly over the sea and far away. It takes me just three days to fly the length of your whole land. I fly over the cold sea and the baking desert to spend the winter in the south.

Watch for my return. The celandines, yellow flowers of the spring, bloom to welcome me. See me flying over the meadows with my flock of friends and family, catching insects in mid-air, or see me skim the surface of the pond to quench my thirst.

In the autumn, see me before I leave to follow the sun – gathered in great numbers with my flock, perched on telegraph wires.

If you are lucky, in the springtime, you may hear us feeding our babies in our nest; look in barns or outbuildings, on ledges or beams, to find our cup-shaped nests of mud and straw.

We often use the same nest each year, so if you spot a swallow's nest you know where to look for us again.

You will know me by my glossy blue back, my pale tummy, my throat of red and by my long forked tail, which streams behind me as I swoop and soar.

Hare

I am Hare, the light-foot, the jumper, the wild one. The race-the-wind, spring-the-hedge, shake-the-heart Hare!

I am larger and lither than my rabbit cousins; my legs, my snout, my ears are longer and tipped with black. Some call me Long-Lugs.

If I sense danger, I hug the ground, ears flat, but when I spring into action I am swift as the wind; the swiftest land animal in Britain. Even the champion runners of your people cannot outrun me!

I like open land where I can run – I am the stag of the stubble, creature of the corn. By day I rest in hedgerows and woodlands; it is rare to catch a glimpse of me. I venture out at dawn and dusk when the moon is bright.

Look up at the moon when it is full. My shape shines there.

At only one time of year do I change my timid ways. Springtime! Look out for us leaping and chasing as we court. We jills, the female hares, accept no nonsense – if we are not interested in the advances of a jack, a male hare, we box his ears!

I scrape away plants to nest in a shallow hollow on the earth, sheltered by tall grass. I line my nest with fur from my own coat. Unlike the young of our rabbit cousins, my babies are born with a full coat of fur and with their eyes open. How adorable they are; little bouncing balls of fluff – my babies!

Spring Equinox Celebration

At this special time of new beginnings and renewal, we celebrate the return of life. Eggs have become an integral part of this celebration because they embody the potential and mystery of new life. Egg rolling is a tradition that dates back hundreds of years in Britain and Europe. Rolling eggs is a playful way to rejoice in the rebirth of nature and to celebrate the spirit of springtime.

YOU WILL NEED:
- A simple crown woven from ivy or sticky weed (cleavers)
- Spring flowers (one for each person)
- Green cloak or cloth
- Hard-boiled, decorated eggs (see natural egg dyeing, p 55) – one per person
- Basket (you could weave coloured ribbons around the handle of the basket – use the colours of springtime flowers: pink and blue and yellow)

WHAT TO DO:

1. Together, make a crown for Lady Spring by binding ivy or cleavers into a circle. Each person weaves a spring flower into the crown. Lady Spring (who can be an adult or a child) puts on her green cloak and is crowned.

2. Each child holds their egg, closes their eyes and makes two wishes, one for a talent they would like to cultivate and the other a wish for the earth. Everyone then places their egg into a basket in the middle and stands in a large circle around it.

3. Lady Spring picks up the basket and carefully weaves in and out of the people, while they all sing 'My Lady Spring' (p 87; or a spring song of choice).

4. When the circle is completed, Lady Spring stands in the centre and declares that the eggs have been blessed and the egg rolling can now begin. Children come one at a time and take their egg from the basket. Everyone goes together to roll the eggs, preferably downhill. This releases the wishes and is a lot of fun!

5. Afterwards, everyone can come together to crack, peel and eat the eggs. Looking around the forest, we can see life bursting all around and feel it bursting within us.

It is time to celebrate. Sing songs and cook dandelion drop scones on the fire. Spring is here at last!

Spring Seasonal Song

By Nancy Foster

My Lady Spring

Slow

My La - dy Spring is dressed in green, she wears a prim - rose crown, and

all the lit - tle leaves and buds are cling - ing to her gown, and

when she smiles, the sun does shine, and when she cries, the rain - drops fall, my

La - dy Spring, my La - dy Spring.

Beltane

Beltane takes place on 1 May, exactly halfway between spring equinox and summer solstice. The word comes from the Old Irish, meaning 'bright fire', and the day is now often known as May Day. Beltane marks the transition between spring and summer and celebrates the start of the light half of the year. It is the time of fertility. In the cycle of day and night, this time of year is akin to mid-morning – when we are active and moving.

At Beltane, spring has flung open her doors and the sun's warmth and energy has called forth new life. Lady Spring has reached her full potential and the Green Man takes her by the hand and the great marriage is celebrated as together they dance the land green once more. Beltane was traditionally the time for hand-fasting, when couples can express their commitment to each other. Like the hawthorn flowers in May, our hearts open with love. It is a time of enthusiasm, joy, vigorous growth, love, harmony, fertility and the fire of creation.

The bluebells ring their faery bells in celebration, perfuming the green forest glades, May blossom flowers in all its glory in the hedgerows, while birds and animals everywhere are busy feeding their young.

The Forest at Beltane

The forest is bathed in the fresh green light of the trees' new leaves. Beech trees glow with new life, their luminous leaves haloed by fine downy hair. The great oaks wear their crowns of golden-green and their tiny catkins of flowers can be found amidst their leaves. The green trees rejoice in the sunshine, drinking in the light and breathing out fresh clean air for us all. The forest is alive, growing fast and strong. Bramble tendrils forge their vigorous way towards the light, growing visibly everyday as ferns silently unfurl. Birdsong fills the air with music and stories of the woodland. Fox cubs tumble and play.

A great enchantment has come once again to our ancient forests as the bluebells transform the woodland floor into a shimmering haze of purple-blue. The air is scented with their soft perfume and perhaps, if we listen carefully, we can hear the faeries' bells tinkle. Walk gently through these forest bells of blue.

In forest, hedgerow, moor and meadow, the hawthorn, tree of May, shines bright with white blossom, scenting the wind. Beltane has arrived and we dance in celebration of the life and fertility of this green, green land.

A Story for Beltane

Tamlin

A folktale from the Lowlands of Scotland, retold from a Scottish ballad

Jennet sat at the window of her father's castle, sewing. But she could not concentrate on small, neat stitches. For outside the sun was shining and the birds were singing. And beyond the meadow, in the forbidden forest, everything was glowing green.

Jennet hitched up her skirts and ran down the stairs and out into the meadow. She ran barefoot through the cool grass, but at the edge of Carterhaugh Forest she stopped. She knew it was forbidden. Her father had told her, 'It isn't safe. It is enchanted. On All Hallows' Eve, bogarts and boggles, hobgoblins and tricksy little pixies all fly out of the Faery-land and troop through the forest, making mischief. You must not go there.'

But it was not All Hallows' Eve. It was the first of May.

Jennet saw the tangles of brambles and sharp-spiked briars. No one had dared to go into the forest for many years. But she looked deeper. She saw pools of bluebells, and they were all nodding their heads. The birds were singing to her, the trees were waving to her and all the plants were calling to her...

Jennet stepped out of the meadow, and into the forest. She went wandering along, trailing her fingers over tender leaf-tips and singing a lilting song... Until she came to the heart of the forest. There grew a hawthorn tree, alight with white blossom. Beneath the tree was a well, overgrown with wild roses. Jennet plucked a rose, just flushed with pink, and tucked it into her hair. She put her hands on the soft moss and cool stone of the well, and looked down at the rippling reflections.

The bright water darkened – over the well fell a cold shadow... Jennet looked up, and there, where before there was nothing, stood a milk-white horse. On the back of the horse was a young man, no older than Jennet herself.

But his eyes! Storm-grey, so he didn't seem a human man at all, but a dark Elfin knight.

'How dare you come into this forest,' the boy demanded, 'without asking leave of me? How dare you pick that rose? No one picks these roses. They belong to the Queen.'

Jennet felt her stomach clench with fear, but she wasn't a girl who liked to be told what to do, and she also felt a tickle of laughter, and the laughter won, and bubbled out.

The boy stared at Jennet. He was not used to laughter.

Jennet stared back. 'I belong in the forest as much as you do,' she said. 'I'll go where I like and do what I feel.'

And seeing the way Jennet's eyes were twinkling and the way her nose was wrinkling, the boy found that he was smiling too.

Jennet picked another rose. She inhaled its honey scent and held it out to the boy. He had to get down from his high horse to take it.

From outside the forest, in the meadow, Jennet heard the brilliant trill of a lark. 'What's your name, boy?'

'Tamlin.'

'Well, come, Tamlin,' said Jennet. 'The lark is singing! Let's go and listen...' and she ran, laughing, into the sunlit meadow.

Tamlin tilted his head, as if he had not noticed the sound of a lark for a long time. Light flickered in his grey eyes and he followed her. But at the edge of the forest he stopped.

'Come on!'

The colour was ebbing from his skin, the new-born light in his eyes dimming. 'I... cannot. The Queen's magic is too strong.'

'What?'

'The Queen of the Faeries...' And he suddenly looked very young, like a lost child. 'I fell asleep beneath the May tree. I didn't know it was a Faery tree. When I woke up, she was there. And I was in her power. I am bound to this place, bound to do her bidding. I cannot leave the forest.'

So Jennet turned and walked back to Tamlin. They spent all that day together in the green wood, amongst the flowers and the birds and the bees. And the next day. And the next.

What they did there, I cannot tell, for the green leaves were about them.

What they did there, I cannot say, for the roses grew around them. But when Jennet came out of the green wood, she came with child.

The white of May turned through all the colours of summer, to autumn's gold. And as the year turned towards the dark, Tamlin grew troubled.

'What ails you, Tamlin?' Jennet asked.

'All Hallows' Eve is near. On All Hallows' Eve, the Queen of the Faeries makes a sacrifice of one of her knights, a sacrifice to the Netherworld. This year, I am the chosen one.'

Jennet's eyes flashed. 'But there must be a way to save you.'

'There is one way,' said Tamlin. He lowered his head. 'But it is too dangerous for a mortal. I would never ask it of you.'

Jennet just grinned. 'Ask.'

It was All Hallows' Eve – the night the Fair Folk ride out. In the dead of night, Jennet flitted through the meadow, through the skirling wind and the scowling rain, to the forest. The forest, which in summer had looked so light and inviting, but now was grim and dark. Jennet pulled her cloak closer. It was dyed green, the colour of the first hawthorn leaves. Jennet felt heartened. She stepped into the forest.

She waited, exactly as Tamlin had told her, at the place by the well, where four paths meet and cross. She crouched beneath the thorn tree. She hid herself. She watched the crossroads. She waited.

The church bell tolled twelve. And at the stroke of midnight, there came the answering sound. Jangling, thundering; hooves.

Out of the night and the mist-light there came a great black horse, the first of the Faery troop. It was bridled in silver and shod in gold. Stamping and steaming.

Jennet's heart hammered but she remembered what Tamlin had told her. She waited; she let the horse pass.

Then again, jangling, thundering, and into the clearing came a great brown horse, brown as a polished chestnut. Again, Jennet waited; she let the horse pass.

Then came a sound so high and so clear that Jennet could hardly hear it with her human ears. But she felt it, and it made her skin tingle.

Out into the moonlight, leading the Faery troop, came a milk-white horse, its mane twined with silver bells. On the back of the horse was the Faery Queen. And behind her on the saddle, death-pale in the moonlight, was Tamlin.

Jennet's heart beat with hope and fear, and she ran and caught the cloth of Tamlin's shirt in her hands. She gripped him and, though he was heavy, she hauled him down to earth, into her arms.

The shrieks of the Faery Folk rent the air. Slowly, the Queen turned her head. She fixed Jennet in a silver stare. 'Tamlin belongs to ME! Let him go.' But Jennet held her true love in her arms and she did not let go.

The Queen narrowed her eyes. 'Foolish child. You will let him go.' She raised her hand. Tamlin began to shrink and shift. Jennet's hands held not a man, but a snake; a viper, writhing and winding up her arm, hissing and spitting.

The laughter of the Faery Queen rang in her ears, but Jennet did not let go.

The Queen's laugh died. She raised her other hand. 'Now, you will let go.'

Again, shifting, changing. Bulging, bristling. Hot breath, huge jaws. A bear. But Jennet looked into his wild grey eyes, and she did not let go.

Darker grew the face of the Elfin Queen. She sat tall in her saddle and drew in her breath. She raised both her arms. 'Let him go!'

Lightning flashed. Fur burst into flame. And the bear was a bar – a burning bar of red-hot iron.

But Jennet held Tamlin in her heart, and she did not let go. One step, another step. Jennet carried the blind-hot bar to the well and slid her hands into the water. Fizzing. Hissing. Swirling steam.

And out of the well, stepped Tamlin. Mother-naked, dripping wet and grinning. Jennet wrapped her green cloak around him.

The Faery Queen knew then that she had met her match in a mortal woman. And the Faery Queen let go. Her spell was broken. Tamlin was free.

The Queen glared. 'Love!' She spat the word. 'I should have turned his heart to stone!' She tossed her hair, and with a clatter of hooves, she was gone. Her troop followed and the thunder of a thousand hoof-beats faded.

The sky began to glow with the first light of dawn. Jennet and Tamlin took each other by the hand, and together they walked out of the forest, and home.

Beltane Imaginary Journey

The light of the sun is warm at last and the earth delights in it. The land is clothed once again in green. Find a dappled place beneath trees and lie down in the forest. Look up at the play of light through the green leaves and take a few deep breaths and relax.

- You are held by the earth and are being bathed in the green light of the trees. Let your eyes be soft as you look at the plants growing all around you.

- Feel the vitality of all the growing green. Imagine there is a cocoon of green light surrounding you. Close your eyes and, as you breathe, imagine the fresh green light filling your body with new life. Feel the tingle of aliveness from the tips of your toes to the crown of your head. The earth is supporting you as if you are rooted like a growing plant.

- Feel how free the air is, how spacious the sky. Breathe the fresh, clear air. Imagine your body filling with the light of the sun, the breath of the wind, the movement of the clouds.

- Feel the spaciousness of the sky inside you, from the crown of your head to the tips of your toes. The warmth and light of the sun are bringing life to all the growing plants around you.

- Close your eyes and relax into the green earth, breathing with the sky.

- Now wriggle your toes and gently open your eyes. Stretch.

- Take in the beauty of the green earth, and the smell of the new growth of the forest.

Beltane Activities, Crafts and Games

Elder Fire Blowing Sticks

Beltane is traditionally a fire festival. Long ago, people lit fires upon the hills – beacons across the land. The fertility of life is connected to fire, to passion. The elder tree has branches with a pithy core that is soft and easy to remove. Its Latin name *sambucus* means 'pipe' and alludes to its ancient use as wood to make instruments. The root of the word *elder* is thought to come from *aeld*, which is the Anglo-Saxon word for 'fire'. One of the traditional uses for the hollowed sticks of elder is as a blowing stick or bellows for a fire. It is very effective and the sticks can be decorated beautifully. Remember to ask the elder mother respectfully and take only what you need. Dead elder sticks can be used but need to be solid, not rotten.

YOU WILL NEED:
- Campfire
- Elder sticks, approx. 30cm (12ins) in length
- Loppers
- Peelers or knives
- Wire cutters
- Pliers
- Pith-removing tool made from coat hanger as described (right)
- Colours for decoration (e.g. natural paints like clay, chalk or charcoal) or tools for pyrography

TO MAKE A TOOL TO REMOVE THE PITH:
1. Take a wire coat hanger and unwind and straighten it. Using wire cutters, cut to approximately 50cm (20ins).

2. Using pliers, twist one end two or three times into a circle for the handle. On a flat surface, hammer the other end so that it is flat, like a tiny spade. Using the pliers, carefully bend the spade end to a slight angle. This enables the sharp spade end to scrape the sides of the elder wood, thus removing the pith, rather than trying to push the pith all the way through, which is difficult. It may be helpful to make several for a larger group.

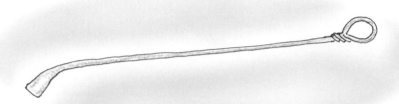

To make:

1. Find an elder with plenty of sun-shoots, which are the branches that grow straight up, usually from a larger, more horizontal branch.

2. Ask respectfully and, when you have a good feeling, harvest the stems using the loppers. Cut just above the collar (where the smaller limb meets the bigger one). This enables the tree to heal easily. Cut one 30cm (12ins) length per child.

3. Peel the stick using peelers or knives. See further notes on tool use (p 317). Use the special wire tool to twist and pull the pith out.

4. Decorate the stick with unique fire-inspired designs.

5. Some children can peel and decorate while others are de-pithing.

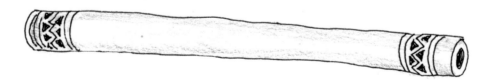

The sticks are ready. Trial them one at a time. When blowing on any fire to get it going, it is important to tie hair back and to lean down close to the ground, blowing into the heart of the fire from a side-on position. This is both safer and much more effective.

The blowing sticks are used in this way: bend near the ground and put one end of the blowing stick in your mouth, then point the other end towards the heart of the fire, at least a hand's distance from the fire. Be sensible and don't breathe in through the stick. Now blow and watch the flames roar and grow!

Green Man

The Green Man is the spirit of the green plants, a symbol of man's reliance on and union with nature. He embodies the underlying life-force of nature, and the renewed growth of spring, which is especially revered at Beltane. Look carefully at tree trunks and you can sometimes see naturally occurring Green Man faces.

YOU WILL NEED:
- A fist-sized lump of clay or mole mud: collect mole mud from mole hills in a bucket, add water and mix with a stick until you have a workable consistency
- Green leaves (you can often find fresh green leaves dropped by the trees at this time)

TO MAKE:

1. Find a tree to make your Green Man face on.

2. Take your clay/mole mud and smooth the outside edge firmly onto the tree trunk. Mould the shape of the face by pulling out the nose and pushing in the eyes and shaping a mouth.

3. Add green leaves to make a beard, moustache, eyebrows and hair.

Twig and Yarn Hearts

The heart is a sweet symbol of the love of life which blazes bright in animals, birds and people alike in the fertile month of May.

YOU WILL NEED:
- Lengths of flexible plant stalks, all approx. 30cm (12ins) – dogwood, which bends easily and has bright-coloured stalks, is ideal. Willow is also ideal if it is cut fresh so it will bend with ease. Otherwise, soak withies prior to using
- Elastic bands
- String
- Yarn (wool is best, as it is biodegradable)

TO MAKE:

1. Take two twigs and fasten the twigs together at the bottom (the thickest end) using an elastic band.

2. Bend one of the twigs around and down, so the loose end of the twig is brought together with the two thick ends in the elastic band. This curve creates one half of the heart and determines the size of the heart you will make. Fasten the thin end into the elastic band.

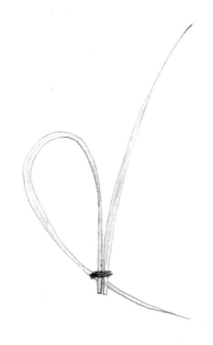

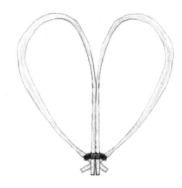

3. Take the other twig and bend it around and down in the same way, fastening the thin end into the elastic band. This creates the whole heart shape.

4. Adjust the shape of the heart until you are satisfied with its form. At the place where the elastic band is holding all the twigs together, tie a tight knot with string to secure the shape. Trim the ends of the twigs to complete your heart.

5. Now you can begin to weave. Tie your length of yarn onto the heart (e.g. onto the inner point at the top of the heart) and bring it across the heart. At the edge of the heart, wrap the yarn around the twig to secure it, and pull it back across to the other side of the heart.

6. Continue wrapping the yarn around the heart, filling the shape with coloured yarn. Children can weave until their heart feels complete. (There is no need to completely fill the space with yarn; the hearts are just as lovely with plenty of gaps amidst the yarn.)

7. Finish by tying the yarn at the top of the heart, leaving enough thread to make a loop, and hang your twig and yarn hearts in the branches of the trees.

A Beltane Treasure for Your Magic Pouch – A Tinder Bag

Making fire is an ancient art and every forest provides, hidden within its depths, the potential to create fire from scratch. Knowing which woods to use to make fire by friction and how to carve and shape all the tools needed are skills known well to our ancestors and may take a lifetime to learn. Tinder is a dry material, fine enough to catch a small spark or ember. Learning about which plants and trees offer good tinder is a wonderful learning journey, and children can make a simple pouch of their own to gather and store tinder. Our ancestors knew that tinder must be dry to make fire, so we gather on dry days and bring our tinder bag with us to the forest, prepared and ready for whenever we want to make a fire.

To make a tinder bag, please see the instructions for the Magic Pouch on p 28. You can adapt the size for your needs. A small tinder bag is good for gathering nest-lining materials – the finest and easiest to light. The adult may also take a larger bag (a cotton shopping bag works well). A simple sewn pouch, which is less bulky than a circular pouch, can also be used as a tinder nest bag – simply sew two identical pieces of cup-shaped cloth together, use running stitch along the curved edge and make holes for a drawstring along the top edge. (The rounded shape is recommended, as rectangular bags tend to trap tinder in the corners.)

Good Forest Tinder to Collect for Your Tinder Pouch

- Birch bark – the thin, loose bark the tree sheds naturally
- King Alfred's cake – round charcoal-coloured mushrooms growing mainly on dying or dead ash trees. They must be dried to hold the fire's spark
- Dried bracken – must be dead and dry. It makes good tinder nest
- Dried cleavers/sticky weed – makes an excellent tinder nest
- Honeysuckle bark – use bark that is peeling naturally from the stem
- Dried inner bark – lime or chestnut inner bark on dead wood is often good

Experiment with natural tinders and go on the principle that any material that is dry and fibrous could work well.

Sense Awareness Activity – Smelling Game

Animals sense prey and predator alike with their extraordinary sense of smell. A deer's ability to smell is a thousand times greater than our own, and their wet noses enhance their sense of smell still further. A deer can smell a human from a mile away. Explore your own sense of smell with this simple game.

YOU WILL NEED:
- Blindfold

TO PLAY:

1. One child will practise their sense of smell. Ask their permission to put a blindfold on them. Gently turn the child around.

2. Another child volunteers (silently!) to come forward to be smelled. This child lifts up their hair to reveal the nape of their neck. The blindfolded child sniffs the neck of the volunteer – can they sense who it is? Children often do recognize their friends by their scent.

Animal Partners Game

Beltane is the time of togetherness. Animals have found their partners; they have very good senses and instincts compared with humans and use them to help find each other. Let's imagine we are able to hear as well as a fox, a deer or a mouse. Can we use our hearing to find our partner?

YOU WILL NEED:
- Blindfolds

TO PLAY:

1. Gather the children together and ask them to get into pairs and choose an animal they both like. Ask them to practise their animal sounds and movement. One of them can be the male, the other the female. Remind them of any differences between the male and female of their species, such as antlers, colouring...

2. One in each pair of children is blindfolded. Those with blindfolds hold hands in a small circle, facing outwards, while their partners go a short distance into the forest, forming an approximate circle (i.e. each standing about the same distance away from their partners, though not opposite their own partner).

3. When everyone is in position, the animals without blindfolds remain stationary, and begin to make their animal noise. The blindfolded partners follow the sound until they are reunited.

4. Swap roles and play again. The distance between partners can be extended as the children's hearing becomes more fine-tuned.

Beltane Seasonal Song

Summer Is a Comin' in

The English folksong 'Sumer Is Icumen In' is one of the world's most famous medieval songs. It is a rota – a kind of round – from the 13th century.

It also works well as a call and response song, especially whilst walking through the forest. The song has an easy, joyful chorus.

Steady beat

Su - mmer is a com - ing i - n, loud - ly sing cuck - oo,

Grow - eth seed and blow - eth mead and spring the woods a - new,

Sing 'Cuck - oo' Sing 'Cuck - oo'.

Beltane Plant Lore

Bluebell

GAELIC NAME: *Brog na cubhaig* (meaning 'the cuckoo's shoe', since the bluebell appears at the same time as the cuckoo)

LATIN NAME: *Hyacintoides nonscripta*

Character

I am Bluebell, flower of enchantment.

I grow where forests have grown since ancient times.

To grow from seed to flower takes me four to five years.

Your people used to say that my bells were rung to herald gatherings of the Faery Folk; we are sometimes known as faeries' doorbells or faeries' thimbles.

Gifts

My bulbs, poisonous to people, are a favourite food of badgers and wild boar.

My scent fills the May woodlands and sends some into otherworldly dreams.

The gummy sap from my bulbs was used to attach arrow fletchings and also to bind books.

My magical plants are protected by law as well as by the Fair Folk, so leave them to perfume the forest and dance in their honour.

Beltane Dance

In and Out the Dusky Bluebells

In and out the dus - ky blue - bells, in and out the

dus - ky blue - bells, in and out the dus - ky blue - bells,

who will be my lead - er? Ti - ppy tap - py tip tap

on my shoul - der, ti - ppy tap - py tip tap on my shoul - der,

ti - ppy tap - py tip tap on my shoul - der, you will be my lead - er.

To play:

1. Stand in a circle and all hold hands, with arms raised like arches. One child goes in and out of the arches.

2. All sing:
In and out the dusky bluebells,
In and out the dusky bluebells,
In and out the dusky bluebells,
Who will be my leader?

Tippy-tappy, tip-tap on my shoulder ...
Tippy-tappy, tip-tap on my shoulder ...
Tippy-tappy, tip-tap on my shoulder ...
You will be my leader.

3. When singing, 'Tippy-tappy, tip-tap on my shoulder', the child going in and out of the arches stops behind another child and taps their shoulders. That child then becomes the leader.

4. The first child puts his or her hands on the new leader's shoulders, and follows in and out of the arches.

The song is complete when you have no more people to add onto the line of dancers or when only the adults are left holding their arches.

Daisy

GAELIC NAME: *Neòinan* (meaning, 'the noon-flower')

LATIN NAME: *Bellis perennis*

Character

I am Daisy, small and bright.

My name comes from 'day's eye', for when the dew dries on my petals my flowers open and follow the sun through the sky till sunset, when I close and sleep until morning.

I grow in the open places where grass is short.

I am delicate and small yet strong and resilient; when I get mown or grazed, I bounce back quickly: 'as fresh as a daisy'.

Gifts

I am good for those who need to deal with life's knocks and blows.

In Scotland my old name was Bruisewort, or Poor Man's Arnica.

I am sacred to Angus Og, the old Celtic god of love, consort of Brigit. See how my flowers grow amongst her sacred dandelions; these are special places.

Daisy Ointment for Bruises

A simple recipe for an ointment to heal bumps and bruises.

YOU WILL NEED:
- A generous handful of daisy flowers and leaves per pot
- One small jar with lid and label per person (miniature jam jars are ideal)
- Olive oil / other vegetable oil
- Beeswax, chopped or flaked
- Water
- Bowl for bain marie
- Sieve
- Jug
- Wooden spoon
- Fire or heat source
- Labels and coloured pencils

TO MAKE:

1. Collect the daisies when the dew has dried and tear them into the bowl. Bring to the boil 5–10cm (2–4ins) water in the pan. Add one small jar of oil to the bowl of daisies.

2. Place the bowl on top of the pan, which is half filled with hot water. Warm the mixture in this bain marie for 15 – 30 minutes over the small fire, stirring occasionally, checking water levels.

3. Add the beeswax to the oil (approx. 1:4 wax to oil). Once it has melted, test the setting consistency by pouring a small amount into the bottom of a jar. If it is too hard, add a little more oil, if it is too soft, add more wax, to create a mixture with a consistency similar to lip balm.

4. Sieve the mixture into a jug and pour into the pots. Wait for the ointment to set, put on the lids and label with the plant name, use, date and place.

The ointment will last up to one year. Use freely on bruises and bumps.

Beltane Tree Lore

Hawthorn

GAELIC NAME: *Drioghionn geal*
('whitethorn' – *geal* means white)
LATIN NAME: *Crataegus monogyna*
OGHAM: *Huathe* (the letter H)

Essence
Heart ~ Protection ~ Fertility

Character

I am Hawthorn, the Tree of the Heart.

I grow throughout these isles, wild and gnarled on mountain, moor and windswept coast or protecting the boundaries in hedgerow and field.

I am the ancient whitethorn, sacred to your ancestors and tree of the faeries. Be careful about cutting me down for they can be fierce guardians.

I am the May tree, blessed of Beltane in my beautiful dress of white blossom. Come close and see my tiny rose flowers. In their hearts my stamens are dusky-pink.

The May wind carries my scent across the land and in time my spent petals scatter like confetti, celebrating the great wedding of life.

At many Beltane fires I have been honoured, sharing in the dances as blossom in your crowns. For many generations my flowers have crowned the maypole as the men and women dance with the ribbons, weaving in and out in joyful celebration of fertility and love.

In the autumn, my blood-red berries are abundant and ripe upon my branches; hedgerows turn to a rosy glow. I give generously to the birds and animals, providing food through cold times as they carry my young to new homes in their droppings.

You too may eat my berries. Some have called me 'bread and cheese', as my berries are creamy and golden inside.

My thorny branches give me protection and offer safe haven for small birds and animals.

As a tree of heart, I am generous and inspire love, but hearts must be protected to be strong. Spend time with me when you feel soft and tender. Joy and dancing strengthen you and protect your heart. Feel the warm sun and celebrate life.

Gifts

My wood is strong and hard, often gnarled. It burns bright and slow and is good for charcoal. Carve and shape me for walking sticks, rakes and mallets, spoons and bowls.

My thorns are sharp and strong and can be used as fishing hooks.

My larger boughs are used as 'brush-barrows', tied in bundles and dragged across the fields over newly sown crops.

My leaves, blossom and berries (known as 'fairy apples') are good to eat. Apple and I are related – look closely at the base of our fruit and you will see we both bear the five-pointed stars. We are safe to eat, unlike other less friendly red berries. Eat my berries from the tree and spit out the hard pips. For pies, jams and fruit leathers, use a sieve and a spoon to push my fruit through.

My squashed berries can be used to draw out splinters and my medicine is used to strengthen the heart and move the blood, so I can help you keep warm in winter. My blossoms and berries will make fine woodland tea.

The Hawthorn Song

By Anna Richardson

Bright and lively

SPRING: Haw - thorn green, Haw - thorn green, Ten - der in Spring - time

Haw - thorn green,

Ten - der in Spring - time, Leaves so sweet, Lea - ves so sw - e - et.

Ten - der in Spring - time, Leaves so sweet.

SUMMER
Hawthorn white (Hawthorn white)
Flower of May light (Flower of May light)
Dance of love (Dance of love)

AUTUMN
Hawthorn red (Hawthorn red)
Generous berries (Generous berries)
Tree of heart (Tree of heart)

WINTER
Hawthorn bare (Hawthorn bare)
Sleeping in winter (Sleeping in winter)
Fearies dream (Fearies dream)

The Hawthorn Dance

This simple dance can be danced either to the song itself or to instruments improvising to the melody.

To dance:

1. Form two lines facing each other, with a spacious corridor between through which people can dance. The people opposite each other will be partners.

2. The bottom couple link hands and hold them high to form an archway. The top couple link arms and gallop down the middle and through the archway, while the others clap in time to the music.

3. The lines shuffle up and repeat until all pairs have danced the line.

4. To finish, the lines form a circle and skip one way and then the other.

Hawthorn Syrup

You will need:
- 5 cups hawthorn blossom (removed from the stalky stems)
- 2 cups sweetener (e.g. honey)
- 2 cups water

To make:

1. Dissolve the sweetener in the water over the fire and boil for three minutes.

2. Pour the sweetened water over the flowers, stir, and return the mixture to the pan. Bring back to the boi, and then remove from the fire.

3. Keep the lid on the pan while you leave it to cool, to strengthen the delicate hawthorn flower flavour. Strain the mixture.

4. Dilute the syrup with sparkling water and raise your glasses in celebration of Beltane.

Beech

GAELIC NAME: *Fhaibhile* (from *fai* – 'to eat')
LATIN NAME: *Fagus sylvatica*
(connected to the Greek word *phagein* –
also 'to eat')

Essence
Wisdom ~ Mother ~ Beauty

Character

I am Beech, Tree of Beauty and Wisdom,
mother of the woods.

Visit me in the sunny spring and see the green
luminescence of my leaves, each surrounded by
a halo of fine downy white hairs. My spring light
shines with otherworldly beauty.

In early summer, my delicate flowers, soft and
subtle, await the touch of wind-borne pollen
among my strong waxy leaves. I hold my presence with stately grace in the forest. My wide,
embracing arms create a canopy of spacious
shade in the summer months.

Autumn arrives and green follows gold to
orange-brown. I am radiant in my glory.
I scatter to earth my tiny triangular nuts in
their elf-hat husks lined with silky down.

As I dream through the winter, I stand in
smooth-skinned majesty. A mother's work is
done for a season.

Beneath my sheltered arms I give a feast for
the people of the woods, large and small. Soon
it is time to let go of my leaves and shake them
down for blankets and beds for animals and
seeds. Strong and leathery, they will last the
winter long, to warm and shelter the children
of the forest.

Now my fallen leaves will nourish the earth
with rich minerals and goodness.

My roots will create caves for small ones.
Spend time in my presence through all the
seasons. I will nourish you with my beauty
and hold a sanctuary for you.

I also hold knowledge and wisdom. When people began to use writing to pass on knowledge, the first books were written on thin tablets of my wood. Later vellum leaves were bound between beech boards. I am guardian of knowledge of the written word and even today people are drawn to carving words on my smooth bark.

My name comes from the Anglo-Saxon *boc* and the German word *buche*: both mean 'book'. Perhaps I can help you find the words you need.

Gifts

My wood has a yellowish-pink hue and is heavy and strong. It has many uses as a carver's wood and makes good furniture.

I burn hot and bright in the fire.

I make good hedges and my leaves make excellent bedding for hibernating animals. People used to use them in their mattresses, as I stay sweet for seven years or more.

My name, *Fagus*, means 'to eat' and my spring leaves are delicious in salad. My beechnuts are edible and full of goodness. They need to be peeled and are most tasty and digestible when lightly toasted.

In the past beech oil was used for lamps and cooking. I will look after many of your needs.

Beech Song

Lyrics by Dawn Casey
Melody by River Jones

Slow and steady

1. Beech heart, Shin-ing go - ld, Strong and wise, Mo-ther old.

2. Beech roots,
Deep deep down,
Anchoring
Sunshine crown.

3. Beech arms,
Reaching wide,
Shelter little
Ones inside.

4. Beech leaves,
Dappled green,
Shade and light,
In harmony.

5. Beech skin,
Smooth and scarred,
Perfect beauty,
Never marred.

6. Beech Queen,
Matriarch,
Power and grace,
In our hearts.

Beltane Animals

Turtle Dove

On summer days, listen for my gentle purring song, from which my name derives. The French call me *tourterelle*, after my call, 'Turrrr turrrr...'

I live in open woodlands, meadows and farmlands. At dawn, I wake and hunt for titbits, nibbling on seeds, fruits and nuts. Each day at mid-morning, I retire to my nest to rest. In the afternoon I forage again, enjoying leaves, cocoons of earthworms and teeny tree snails.

During the winter, we stay in small flocks over the seas in Africa, then in May each year we return to our breeding places. I will find a place for a nest, in a tree or shrub, and together we build our nest. Early in the morning and in the evening, we shape our nest.

I court my mate by flying to her with whistling wings. I puff out my chest and bow to her, stretching tall and bowing low. I bow to my mate again and again, and sing to her a tender love song. I am a devoted partner. We turtle doves mate for life and you often see us sitting side by side.

Our eggs hatch within two weeks. Unlike most other birds, we pigeons can make 'milk' for our babies, in our crops – a place between our throats and our bellies, where we store our food. We both make this milk for our babies and we both feed our nestlings. Our milk helps our babies grow strong and healthy. When our babies are a little older, we mix the milk with grains to make porridge for them.

You can tell me apart from my cousins, the other pigeons and doves, by my dainty size and by my colours – my neck and head are pale lilac-grey – and I have a patch of striped black and white upon the side of my neck. Each of my wing feathers has a diamond of dark brown in the center, with chestnut brown around the edge.

NB: In recent years the number of turtle doves in the UK has declined rapidly. We can all help them in many simple ways. Allow or grow plants that turtle doves eat: fumitory, black medick, red and white clover, common vetch, bird's foot trefoil. Even in a pot, these plants will provide the summer seeds turtle doves rely on.

Otter

I am Otter, sinuous as a stream. I am of the weasel family, but I am the only one in our family who lives with the water. My river-bank den has entrances above and below the waterline.

I am sleek and supple – I swim through the waters swaying my body side to side, or I mosey slowly along, paddling with my webbed feet.

My long whiskers sense the vibrations and movements of fish, so I can hunt even in murky water. Eels are my favourite meal. Those of us who live by the coast teach our young the art of opening a shellfish with a stone. Small stones are good to play with too.

We otters love to play! We use muddy banks to make water-slides! We love to frolic together – you call a group of otters a 'romp'. We are chatty creatures – listen for our loud chirping noises as we chase around.

Those of us who live in the sea often float in groups (which you call rafts) whilst we eat, rest and sleep. We sleep floating on our backs, holding each other's hands.

Beltane Celebration

The Beltane Fire

Along with Samhain, Beltane is the most important of the Celtic fire festivals. For both festivals, bonfires were lit on the evening before. Livestock were driven between Beltane fires to burn off parasites, thus preventing disease.

You could light a Beltane fire on Beltane Eve. Dance and sing and jump over the fire to cleanse, purify and bring good luck for the growing season.

Traditionally, each family would receive some of the embers from the fire the next morning, to light their own hearth fires and bring luck and prosperity. The ashes could be spread on the fields to fertilize them.

In the following Beltane celebration we make simple offerings to the fire followed by the time-honoured tradition of dancing the maypole around a nearby tree. This is a joyful expression of the dance of union that brings forth life. After the dance we return to the Beltane fire and leap over the flames, igniting our love for life.

Fire Offering Stick

This simple stick offering helps children to connect with the tradition of the Beltane fire, while learning the practical skill of how to safely place wood on the fire. The two coloured threads represent the masculine and the feminine woven together within us.

YOU WILL NEED:
- A dry stick for each person
- 2 lengths of natural fibres in different colours (such as red and green) – raffia, string or wool

TO MAKE:

1. Tie the coloured threads together with a knot, lay the length of thread out and place the top end of the stick over the knot.

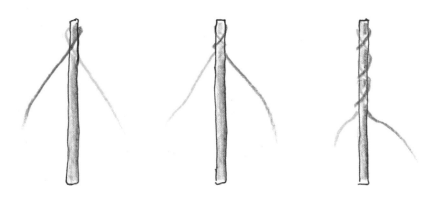

2. Now crisscross the coloured thread around the stick and tie the two threads at the bottom.

3. Create a simple ceremony by giving the children the opportunity to take turns to offer their sticks to the fire as a thanksgiving for life.

4. Place the offering stick on the fire by holding the bottom end of the stick and placing the top end in the fire first, then gently letting it go.

Forest Maypole

YOU WILL NEED:
- A tree with a clear space beneath
- An even number of coloured ribbons approx. 3m (3yds) each
- Long strip of fabric or tape to wrap around a tree

TO MAKE:
Tie long ribbons onto a strip of fabric, using two colours or more in an alternating pattern. Tie the fabric strip around a tree with a wide girth, with clear space underneath for everyone to dance. You will need an even number of ribbons and dancers.

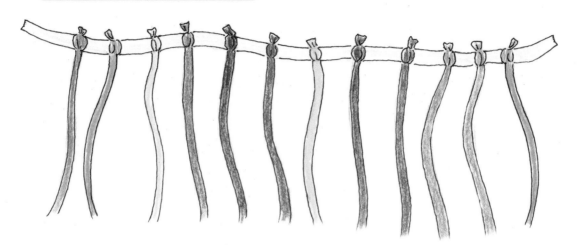

TO PLAY:

1. Each person holds a ribbon. The first person will be A and the next B, so everyone is A or B. All A's turn right to face the person standing on their right, and all B's turn to face the person on their left. The pair facing each other are partners. Each person will move in the direction in which they are facing.

2. The A's start by going under their partner's ribbon, then over the next person's ribbon. B's start by going over their partner's ribbon, then under the next person's ribbon. Keep following the rhythm 'under, over, under, over...' until the length of ribbon is used up, or until everyone has returned to their original partner. The ribbons should entwine around the tree in a pattern.

3. When the ribbons run out, you can dance back to the start in the same way, or simply leave the ribbon in the pattern around the tree to decorate it. If you can, ask musicians to play for you as you dance. Even without music, you can sing!

4. We sing the following simple rhyme, to the tune of 'Here We Go Round the Mulberry Bush':

Here we go round the old oak tree,
The old oak tree,
The old oak tree.
Here we go round the old oak tree
On a sunny May Day morning.

5. After the maypole has been danced and woven, return to the fire. It is time to jump the flames in celebration of the renewal of life. Make sure there is a clear area to do this and younger children can be helped by two adults holding their arms and lifting them over as they jump. Overcoming this challenge gives children a great feeling of achievement and pride. Jumping the flames renews our inner fire and our passion for life.

Summer

Midsummer is around 21 June and is akin to the time of midday, when the sun is at its peak. The sun shines in the sky at its highest point of the year, when we have the shortest night and the longest day.

Throughout the year, the point on the horizon where the sun rises and the point where the sun sets change each day, little by little. In the winter, the sunrise and sunset are close together on the horizon – the sun has a shorter journey across the sky and we have a shorter day. In the summer, the sunrise and sunset are wider apart on the horizon – the sun has a longer journey across the sky and we have a longer day. On the solstice, the sun appears to rise and set in the same position on the horizon for three days in a row. The word *solstice* means 'sun stand still' in Latin. After the summer solstice, the sun's journey through the sky will once again begin to shorten, though the days still feel warm.

The Forest in Summer

At midsummer everything is growing and glorious – nature is shining! The forests, hedgerows, meadows and gardens are alive and wide awake, plants stretched high, flowers of every colour open to the sun. Bees and butterflies are busy in these long days of light, foraging sweet nectar from flower-filled gardens and wild flowers. Birds feast on the insects. See the swallows dive and swoop, sweeping low to catch bugs and flies. Elderflowers bloom like creamy clouds in the hedgerows. Delicate roses and sweet honeysuckle scent the air. The evenings are lovely – look for glow-worms, shining luminous green. We celebrate summer with fêtes and fairs, opening our gardens for cream teas and summer treats.

The woodlands offer cool, green shade on a hot day. The trees are basking in the sun. Although they seem silent and peaceful, they too are at their busiest, turning the summer sunshine into food. Life is at its fullest, bright and beautiful.

A Summer Story

The Children and the Sun

A folktale from the San people of the Kalahari

L et's sit in the sunshine and listen for stories that drift from afar...

Here is a story from the Kalahari, land of red earth and dry sand. For countless years, the life of the Kalahari people was unchanging... Children rose early to fill their flasks with water and gather wild cucumbers and melons. Little ones went out with their mothers to pick nuts and nin berries. Men sunned their shoulder blades, hunting gemsbok, spring-bok and ostrich.

But it was not always so. In the time of the First People, there was no sun up in the sky. It was always cold and grey and gloomy. At that time there lived three boys: Kabbo, Karu and Kau. Kabbo was the eldest, Karu was his brother, and their friend Kau was the littlest one. They loved to play together. One day, they were playing ball with a wild melon, small and round and yellow. Kabbo threw it high in the air. Karu squinted his eyes and reached out his hands. Boof! The melon landed in the sand.

Karu frowned. 'I can't play in the dark!' And he kicked the ball away. The melon went bouncing and rolling through the gloom, towards an old man lying slumped and alone at the edge of the village, snoring.

BUMP! The ball rolled right into the old man.

'Eh?' He sat up and stretched. As he raised his arms, a bright light shone from out of his body! Hot, bright, radiant light! The children stared.

'Old man,' said Kabbo, 'Grandfather, you have light within you!' The old man snapped his arms shut, and the world shrank back to darkness. 'Grandfather,' said Kabbo, 'open your arms again!'

The old man glared. 'It would burn you like fire! Get away!'

'Grandfather,' said Karu, 'please share your light.'

'Away, I said!' the old man growled.

'Grandfather,' said Kau. 'Please.'

The old man scowled at the children. He turned his back and curled up tight.

There was a white-haired woman who lived then, who had lived and lived, and now she was very old and knew many things. The children went to the old woman's hut.

'Grandmother, help us,' said Kabbo. 'That old man there has light within him! But he is all closed up. What can we do?'

The old woman sat quite still, sensing the wisdom within her body. She looked at the children's ball. She grinned. Then the old woman called the mothers of the village together. The young ones crowded round.

The old woman announced, 'These children are going to help that old man. They are going to help us all. The children will throw that old man up into the sky, to make the sun!'

The women's faces crinkled with laughter. 'Heh, heh!'

'Yes, yes!'

But the children stood with mouths agape. 'Eh, mother!'

'Eh, hey! We cannot do that!'

'He is too big!'

'He is too heavy!'

'He is too hot!'

'You can,' said the old woman, 'altogether.' Then she said no more.

The old man sat hunched outside his grass hut, all alone.

The children hid, watching, waiting. After a while, the man let out a giant yawn, like a lion's roar, and he closed his eyes. Slowly, stealthily, the children stalked up to the old man...

WINK! One eye flicked open! The children froze. The old man scratched himself and turned over.

The children crept closer...

BLINK! Two eyes flashed open! The children held their breath. He stretched, settled back down.

The children crept closer, closer...

NOD! His head nodded and he began to snore. His arms slumped to his sides. Burning light blazed out of him. The children stared in awe.

'Can we?' asked Kabbo.

'I don't know,' said Karu.

'I'm scared,' said Kau.

But the children remembered the old woman's words. And her words made their hearts brave, like the leopard's heart.

Kabbo took hold of the old man's shoulders. Karu took hold of the old man's legs. Kau took a pinch of buchu herb. He rubbed the leaves, so the soothing scent rose to the old man's nose. The old man breathed deep and smiled in his sleep.

'Hold him tight!' whispered Kabbo.

'Lift him up!' whispered Karu.

'Throw him up!' they all called together, and with a great heave the children threw that old man – the sun – high up into the sky.

The sun-man went spinning through the skies, his eyes open wide with surprise.

The children called up to him, saying:

Oh Grandfather, become the sun!
Be hot! Make the whole earth warm!
Be bright! Make the whole earth light!
Shine! Chase away the darkness!

As the sun-man flew higher and higher, the sky brightened; it was clear and blue. Yellow sunshine lit up the land.

From way up high, that old man, the sun, could see the whole world below him, all glorying in his light, all the people basking in his warmth. He saw the old people warming their backs and easing their bones. He saw the women smiling up their thanks as they set out their clay pots to dry. He saw the men hunting, taking perfect aim. He saw the children smiling and waving. And the sun-man began to smile.

His light shone brighter and brighter within him, until his whole being was smiling and shining.

That evening, for the first time ever, the sun set. The people sang. The women clapped their hands. One beat the drum. The men danced and danced in celebration of the sun. The children beamed with delight.

As time passed, the sun's light shone in every direction, and he grew round.

Now, that story is finished; it drifts away with the wind. But up in the sky the sun is still shining. And our many hearts are glad.

NB: The language of the San uses 'click' sounds with some of its letters, such as the one shown as ||, as in: '||Kabbo'. Pronounce the click || by placing your tongue against your side teeth and flicking it down as if encouraging a horse to move.

Summer Imaginary Journey

Summer is here. Find a sunlit glade or meadow. Using a compass to find north, ask the children to stretch out comfortably on the earth with their heads in the north and feet in the south. The earth is constantly spinning around the sun, towards the east. (To help the children gain a sense of this, they can point towards the east for a moment.)

🐝 Close your eyes. Imagine yourself lying on the giant ball that is our Mother Earth. Feel your body held without any effort at all by you. The earth is spinning around the sun. Feel this movement. Feel the sun shining on you as it shines on the earth. Feel the warmth of the sun on your skin.

🐝 Now imagine a golden ray of light radiating from your heart upwards into the sky.

🐝 Imagine the golden stream connecting with the sun. Imagine light shining out of the sun, through the golden ray, filling you up with light. Allow it to warm you with its glow, from the top of your head to the tips of your toes.

🐝 Enjoy the feeling of warmth, light and energy. (Pause to allow children time to savour feeling the sun's energy.)

🐝 Silently thank the sun. Imagine the thread of golden light drawing back inside you. Look within at the sun in your heart. Feel its warmth, shining your love on everything around you, just as the sun shines on us and gives us life.

🐝 Wriggle your toes and fingertips. Feel the earth beneath you, gently circling the sun. Softly open your eyes and slowly sit up. See the light shining in your friends' eyes.

Summer Activities, Crafts and Games

Summer Sunshine Balls

Making a felted ball is an easy first felting project for children and on a warm summer's day you can wet felt outside, splashing in the sunshine.

TO MAKE:

1. Ask the children to roll up their sleeves and keep the towels to hand! Set a bowl (or bowls) of warm soapy water on the ground.

2. Start with a strip of wool roving about the length of your hand. Roll it up into a tight spiral. Give each child a spiral of wool to roll in their hands, to form a ball. Roll with slightly cupped palms, rather than squashing with flat hands.

3. Add another strip of roving, covering the first little ball. Again, children roll their balls in their hands. Children love the warm feeling of the wool. Carry on covering your ball with wool roving, making it bigger and bigger with each new layer of wool. The final layers of wool will be the yellow colour(s) to create a ball of sunshine.

YOU WILL NEED:
- Woollen roving for the inside of the ball ('roving' is sheep's wool that has been washed and carded into lengths, but not spun into yarn. Use undyed or pale colours that won't show through the yellow)
- Woollen roving for the outside of the ball (a sunny yellow colour)
- A big bowl of warm water
- Washing-up liquid
- Old towels

4. When you have covered your ball with yellow, the wet felting can begin. Put a generous squirt of washing-up liquid in the palm of each child's hand and get them to roll their ball in it so it is completely covered. The children can now dip their hands in the warm, soapy water and roll their ball in their hands again, nice and gently at first, with not too much water. Roll the balls round and round until they feel the fibres of the wool begin to tighten up as they felt together.

5. Now the children can roll the ball more firmly, squishing it between their hands, getting it wonderfully soapy, round and round and round. They can even take off their shoes and socks and stand on their soapy ball, squishing it between their feet...

6. When the ball is nice and firm, rinse it thoroughly in fresh water to remove the soap.

The children can take their balls of sunshine home to dry, but they'll also enjoy playing with them straight away – throwing them as high as the sun!

Summer Sunshine Weaving

Weave yellow sunshine in celebration of the sun.

YOU WILL NEED:
- Yellow yarn (wool is best, as it is biodegradable)
- Lengths of flexible plant stalks, 60cm (2ft) or longer (e.g. dogwood, which bends easily, or willow. If willow is cut fresh, it will bend with ease. Otherwise, soak withies prior to using)
- Scissors

TO MAKE:

1. Begin by creating a circular frame. Bend the plant stalk around into a circle, overlapping the ends and weaving them under and over the circle to strengthen the weaving frame. If your stalk is long enough, your circular frame can be made of two rounds of stalk.

2. Secure the ends of the stalk together by tying with yellow yarn. Wind the yarn all around the circumference of the circle – this secures the stalk pieces and creates a decorative frame for your weaving. When you get back to the place you started from, tie the end of the yarn to the frame and cut off any spare.

3. Cut three (or more, if desired) lengths of yellow yarn – long enough to span the diameter of your circle. Tie each length from one edge of the circle to the opposite edge, overlapping in the centre – like the radial spokes of a bicycle. These will be the rays of sunshine.

4. Now take a little ball of yarn and, with one end, tie a knot in the centre of the frame, around one of the radial yarns. Weave the yarn in a sun wise (clockwise) direction, under and over the rays of sunshine, to create a circular yellow sun, growing outwards from the centre.

5. When the sun reaches the desired size, tie the yarn end to one of the radial yarns, and cut off any spare.

6. Tie a loop of yarn onto the top of the frame to hang your sunshine in the branches. Children can take their weaving home to hang in the window or bring a ray of sunshine to the nature table.

Flying Butterflies

Butterflies warm their wings in the light of the summer sun. Their patterns and colours are intricate and unique. Their beauty blesses our day.

Choose a sunny day to make these, in glades or meadows where butterflies flutter by to feed on nectar from the summer flowers. It brings great joy to the children to recognize the butterfly that they have just made.

YOU WILL NEED:
- Thin card or thick paper
- Butterfly templates for younger children
- Indentification chart or butterfly book
- Pencil
- Oil pastels
- Scissors
- Sticks

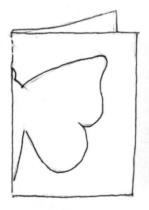

TO MAKE:

1. Choose the butterfly you want to make from the chart. Fold your card in half and draw on the wing shape, with the body of the butterfly at the fold. Younger children can draw around the butterfly template.

2. Cut the card to the shape of your butterfly. Copy the markings on both sides using the oil pastels.

For younger children, show them how the patterns are symmetrical and see if they can create a symmetrical pattern on the wings.

3. Make two additional folds either side of the central fold as shown. Fold the wings back and forth several times; this gives the stiff cardboard more movement so that the wings can flap.

4. Make two small slits between the folds to thread the stick through the middle, so that you can fly your butterfly and flap its wings.

Centre card fold

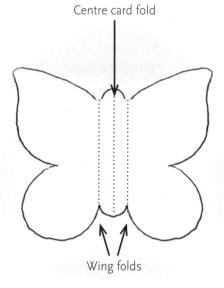

Wing folds

5. As an extra activity, you can research, find and draw the plants that your butterfly feeds on and lays its eggs on in a meadow or woodland glade.

Sundial

The sun and its dance with the earth are the original clock. Our ancestors knew how to read this clock accurately and, with the help of the moon, knew exact times throughout the year, without a calendar, and understood the profound effects of these changes upon the land and their lives.

This simple sundial makes visible the movement of the earth around the sun, to help clarify our understanding of time. Choose a sunny day to make your sundial and find out the time by the sun.

To make:

1. Set up your sundial somewhere in the open on a sunny day.

2. Plant a straight stick in the ground and place the compass flat on the earth next to it. Find and mark north, east, south and west in relation to the central stick by laying smaller sticks flat on the ground as shown.

You will need:

- A sunny spot
- Compass
- 13 straight sticks: one approx. 30cm (12ins) long (for the shadow stick); 4 sticks approx. 15cm (6ins) long (to mark the cardinal directions); 8 sticks approx. 10cm (4ins) long (to mark the remaining hours on the clock)

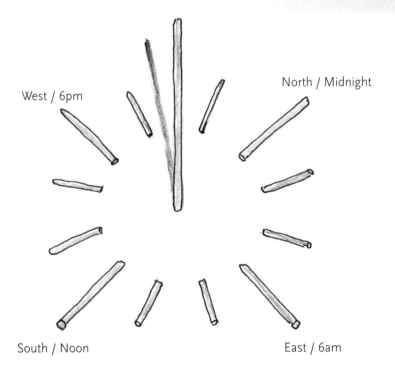

West / 6pm

North / Midnight

South / Noon

East / 6am

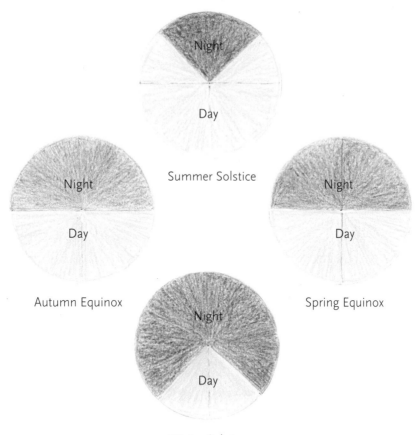

Summer Solstice

Autumn Equinox

Spring Equinox

Winter Solstice

3. Explain that in Britain the sun is precisely in the east at 6am, the south at midday (12pm), the west at 6pm and the north at midnight (12am). Of course we cannot see the sun at midnight because it is shining on the other side of the earth. Remember that during British Summer Tme, which is from March till October (dates vary), you will need to add an hour.

At midday the shadow from the stick will point directly north, so when the sun is in the south we know that it is nearly lunchtime.

The time of actual sunrise and sunset changes through the year, which is why the length of day and seasons vary in this land, but the sun will still be in the east at 6am and in the west at 6pm, even in summer when the sun rises much earlier in the northeast, for example.

4. It will depend on the age of the children whether they can understand these principles, but they will be able to look at the sticks in the sundial and mark where the shadow is falling.

5. Ask them to turn around and notice where the sun is in the sky. Remember its position in relation to a landmark. Go and enjoy time in the forest and when you return see how the shadow has moved round like the hands on a clock.

6. Mark again with a small stick. Turn around and see how the sun has moved through the sky from left to right like writing on a page, except it also moves uphill through the sky until midday and downhill until sunset.

A Summer Forest Fayre

It's time for fun and games! All across the land, people are having fairs, picnics and fêtes, harking back to the outdoor gatherings of people throughout time in the warm months of summer, when travel was easy and pleasurable. Set up a forest fayre, bring instruments, serve elderflower cordial and share in the fun and joy of summer.

Here are some ideas of country games and activities for all ages. Allow the children to create stalls and games of their own. Use leaf-money. Different leaves can represent different coins, for example oak leaves can be larger coins, while silver birch leaves could be the smaller ones.

Hoopla
Drive several sticks upright into the ground. Weave hoops from woodland materials (for example ivy, stripped bramble, hazel or willow). Take turns throwing the hoops to catch them on the sticks. You could give a leaf-money prize.

Welly Wanging
You will need an open space for this stall! Take turns and, from a starting line, 'wang' your welly as far as you can. Mark the distance with a stick.

Pin the Tail on the Fox
Draw a fox on a large piece of cardboard and pin it to a tree. Cut out a separate tail shape then take turns to pin the tail on the fox whilst wearing a blindfold.

Ten Pin Bowling
Use small sawn branches that will stand up as pins. Use conkers or wooden balls to knock them over.

A Summer Treasure for Your Magic Pouch – A 'Touch-Wood' Ogham Stick

The time of flowering is when the spirit of the trees and plants are the most present in our world above the earth. Trees are alive and have a deep awareness, which is understood by people who live close to nature and has now also been confirmed by modern science. As children get to know the different kinds of trees and their characters, they may feel a particular friendship with one they find especially beautiful or strong.

ᴥ Tress have gifts to offer and can be a source of strength and support. Approach the tree with respect, asking out loud if it would share a piece of its wood with its blessing.

ᴥ Ask the child to listen to their feelings for a yes or a no, for example a warm glowy smile inside for yes, or a closed feeling for no.

ᴥ If the answer is yes, offer a small pinch of oats with a thank you, and cut a small branch approx 1–2cm ($^3/_{64}$ –¾in) diameter, using loppers or secateurs just above the collar. (See Elder Fire Blowing Sticks, p 95.)

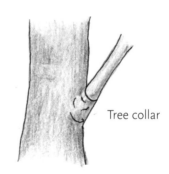

Tree collar

ᴥ This lucky wood may be marked with the Ogham symbol for the particular tree, by either drawing or burning using a pyrography tool. Your Ogham stick can be kept in your magic pouch or threaded so that it can be worn around your neck in times of need.

Please see p 323 for the Ogham alphabet.

Sense Awareness Activity – Tasty Teas

Make three flasks of different herbal teas. These can be made from forest plants if you know safe ones to use. Good ones for this time of year could be elderflower, pine needle and linden blossom.

- Let them brew well and then pour into three different cups.

- Allow the teas to cool a little. Ask the children to open their taste buds and try each one.

- What do their taste buds feel about the flavours?

- Can they feel the effect of the tea in other parts of their body?

- Do they recognize the teas and know which plants they are made from?

- You can then discuss the herbs if you wish, but the most important part of this activity is allowing the sense of taste to be in charge.

Honeybees Waggle Dance Game

Honeybees have an extraordinary way of communicating and working as a team. Special eyes, which can see ultra violet light, help them to see the position of the sun even on a cloudy day, and make the colours of the flowers much brighter. You can use polarized film to show the children how this works. The bees have an internal clock that allows them to know the time of day and the season, even in the dark hive.

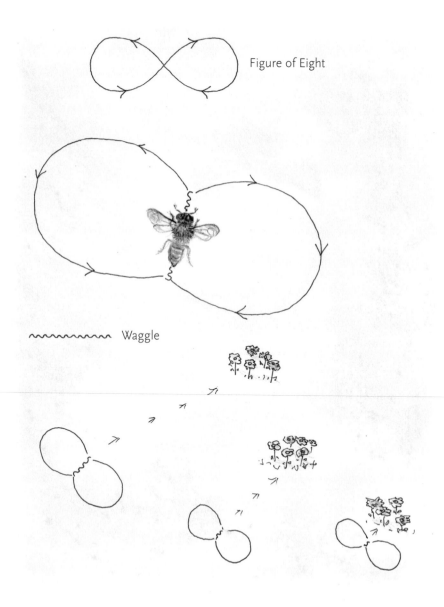

Figure of Eight

Waggle

On sunny days, the bees take it in turns to go foraging for nectar, sometimes flying for miles. When they find a source of nectar-rich flowers, they feed and then fly back to the hive. On their return, they do a dance to show the others where they discovered the flowers. We call this the 'waggle dance'. It shows both the direction the flowers are in and the distance. The bee dances in a figure-of-eight pattern – the angle of the 8 shows the other bees the direction of the flowers. In the middle of the figure of eight the bee waggles. The length and duration of the waggle show how far away the flowers are. In the real bee world the bees dance in relation to the sun. In this game the bee-children are simply dancing the waggle in relation to the flowers.

This game is a fun way to experience the teamwork of the honeybees. Before playing, set up a central hive area and position some coloured bowls representing flowers in the forest. Practise the waggle dance.

The aim of the game is for the children to gather as much nectar as they can in a certain time. In the centre of the hive area is a large bowl or jug for gathering the nectar (elderflower honey water). The guardians protect the hive and their queen from invaders, such as wasps, wax moths or mice, while the foragers take cups to gather the nectar.

It's time to work hard, honeybees! Summer is here and the flowers are open and full of nectar.

YOU WILL NEED:
- Coloured bowls filled with elderflower honey water (these will be the flowers)
- Elderflower honey water (use elderflowers, make honey following the honeysuckle honey instructions on p 145)
- Empty bowls (in the hive – these are the chambers that store the nectar in the hive)
- Acorn cups, spoons or small pots for each bee-child
- One large jug (to collect the nectar at the end)

TO PLAY:
1. After practising the waggle dance, together build your hive with a central chair or blanket as a throne for the queen and place the empty bowls around her – these are the honey chambers.

2. The bee-children choose a partner to work with. They take it in turns to forage or guard the hive. Depending on the size of the group, choose a few guard bees. All the others can fly and forage.

3. The hive of bee-children gather around the queen with closed eyes, while the adults hide the coloured bowls of nectar (flowers) nearby.

4. Call, 'It is dawn! Time to fly, honey bees!' The game has begun.

5. The bees must fly, forage, gather and dance, working together to bring the nectar back to the hive.

They must pay attention because the adults may become invaders and the guardian bees must drive them away before they take the hard-earned honey!

6. After some time, call, 'The sun is setting. It is time for bed, honeybees!'

7. This game can be played again as a new day – with the coloured flower bowls in new positions.

8. At the end of the game, gather and share the well-earned honey by enjoying the elderflower honey water together.

NB: Honeybees are vital to the lives of many of our important food plants – honeybees pollinate the flowers so that they develop into the fruits that we eat.

Insect World Game

We share this world with millions of insects, most of whom are so tiny we cannot even see them. They play vital roles in the connections between all living beings. There are so many different kinds, each unique and with a special job to do. One of their very important jobs is to pollinate the plants, so that the plants can have young and ensure generations to come. Another job they do is to help rot down the bodies of dead plants and animals, which in turn gives food to the soil for the plants to grow. They are also food for many other creatures, like the birds. Explore the forest with eyes for the tiny ones. Look under fallen wood or in rotting stumps. Mosses are mini forests in their own right with miniature worlds of tiny insects who live and hunt in their damp green shade.

This nature detective game can be played to look for evidence of animals of any kind, and is a fun way to direct children's attention and develop tracking awareness.

TO PLAY:

1. Get down on hands and knees and go exploring in the forest. There are many tiny ones living here. Spiders, worms, slugs... What is it that makes an insect an insect? They have six legs, two antennae and three body parts of different sizes. Who can we find hidden in the moss? In the bark of trees? Under logs?

2. Gather everyone together. Tell the children that you are going to count to 10 and then call, 'Insect detective!' Everyone runs off to find an insect and calls out when they have found one. All go and see.

3. This simple game is a good way of learning to distinguish an insect from other small creatures, and also to develop an instinct for where to look for them. Play as much as holds the children's interest.

Summer Plant Lore

St John's Wort

GAELIC NAME: *Caol aslachan Chalum Chille*
(meaning 'favourite flower of St Columba');
Allas Muire (meaning 'the image of Mary');
Eala bhuidhe (from *bhi* – 'yellow' and *neal* –
'appearance')

LATIN NAME: *Hypericum perforatum*

Character

I am St John's Wort, the Plant of the Light.

Shining gold in the midsummer sun, I lift
your spirits with my radiance. I am sun-fire's
healing power, dispelling the darkness.

Lift my leaf towards the sky and see how
the light shines through pinprick holes like
tiny stars.

I am medicine of old, from times of battle and
long before, healing puncture wounds or stab-
bing pains.

See me grow in the open places where few
shadows fall by day, delicate golden flowers
shining in summer light.

Be careful not to confuse me with the yellow
ragwort, my handsome summer companion
who has a poisonous juice. Look for my petals
of five and leaves with bright stars.

Gifts

Gather my stems of leaf and flower at midsummer, when the sun is highest in the sky at
midday, filled with sun's power.

Drink my tea and feel the light warm you in
the dark months of winter, or bring the return of your inner sun when all feels dark and
bleak. Shine your light.

*NB: St John's wort is named after St John the
Baptist, who was said to have his day of birth at
midsummer.* Wort *is the old English word for
'plant', usually used for medicinal plants.*

Summer Wild Plant Song

By Noola Gould

St John's Wort Song

Pentatonic

Drone accompaniment

Hy - per - i - cum per - for - at - um.

Summer

St John he went to the Sun on high, all on a mid - sum - mer's day.

He bears the light and the life in his blood and his gold-en flow-ers shin-ing bright and gay.

Winter

In win - ter time when all seems dark when we're feel - ing cold and sad,

St John he brings the light to our hearts, that

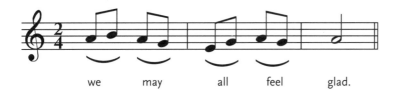

we may all feel glad.

St John's Wort Oil

An oil from St John's wort flowers is a powerful healer, helping your body mend burns, wounds and pains. People have made this medicine for many an age.

YOU WILL NEED:
- St John's wort flowers
- A clear glass jar and lid
- Olive oil

TO MAKE:

1. Pick the golden flowers carefully at midsummer when the sun is high and at its full strength. If the flowers are damp, the medicine will go rancid.

2. Put the flowers in a jar and cover generously with good cold-pressed olive oil. Place this jar on a sunny windowsill or outside in a sunny spot.

3. Shake daily to infuse the flowers, oil and sunshine. See how the oil magically turns blood red. St John's wort heals through love and light.

NB: St John's wort is a powerful healing plant, so take care if you are taking other medicines. It may cleanse the other medicines out of your body and therefore stopping them working.

Its medicine can also make animals sensitive to sunlight (photosensitivity) when they eat the plant. You can safely make St John's wort healing oil and use when needed. To be on the safe side, simply do not apply to skin that may be exposed to strong sunlight.

Summer Wild Plant Song

By Jill Parsons

Wild Rose

Rose, rose, belle of the hedge,

Prick - les of sil - ver and hips burn - ished red.

Heart - shaped, your pet - als that flut - ter like snow,

Danc - ing to the breeze of su - mmer mea - dows,

Dance in the breeze where the sum - mer winds blow.

Honeysuckle

GAELIC NAME: *Lus na Meala*
(meaning 'the honey plant')

LATIN NAME: *Lonicera periclymenum*

Character

I am Honeysuckle, Sweet Woodbine, climbing one of the forest.

See me grow among the trees, weaving and binding on my way.

Smell the honey-scent from my pale yellow trumpets on the summer breeze, my faery goblets full of sweet nectar for a simple summer feast.

Gifts

You too can suckle my nectar; it can be drunk straight from my flower.

Pinch off the green base of my flower to suck out the sweet juice.

Make a tea to soothe a cough – my honey will help heal your throat.

I will ease your pain with leaf or flower and help with summer sunstroke to cool you with my healing power.

Remember me in winter, for I will give you tinder for your fire.

Honeysuckle Honey

YOU WILL NEED:
- Honeysuckle flowers
- Honey
- A clear glass jar and lid

TO MAKE:

1. Pick honeysuckle blossom and opening buds on a warm, dry day. Put them in a jar and cover with runny honey – local is best, as it contains nectar from the flowers of your own place, which makes a stronger medicine.

2. Put the jar on a windowsill or outside in a sunny spot, where it can infuse in the sun. Stir it every few days to mix the flowers with the honey.

3. After one cycle of the moon, strain, bottle and label. The honeysuckle honey can be added to herbal teas or taken, one teaspoon one to three times a day, to help sore throats, colds and coughs or headaches.

Summer Tree Lore

Oak

GAELIC NAME: *Dùr* (from which come our words 'door' and 'durable')
HIGHLAND NAME: *Righ na Coille* ('king of the wood')
LATIN NAME: *Quercus rober* (from which comes the word 'robust')
Quercus petraea (this is the sessile oak, also native and so called because, unlike English oak, its acorns are not carried on stalks but directly on the outer twigs, called 'sessiles')

OGHAM: *Duir* (the letter D)

Essence
Guardianship ~ Strength ~ Centre

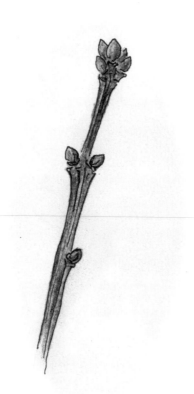

Character

I am Oak, the Tree of Strength.

I am the king of the forest, the guardian and protector of many lives in this land.

My spring leaves are golden-green and I will wear my golden crown once again in autumn, burnished orange-gold.

From my wooden cradles my acorns grow, slow and steady. Many are planted by Jay and Squirrel, my allies of old.

My roots grow deep and wide, my tap root reaching far into the earth, anchoring my broad, strong branches.

Over the years my branches die and I carry them as antlers where the heartwood remains. Strong of heart I grow, enduring and persevering. Seasons, storms and stars turn and dance while I hold fast. I may live and grow a thousand years, steadfast and true.

My oldest trees support thousands of lives, from tiny lichens, mosses and insects to birds and mammals, sheltered and nourished in the home I provide.

I am shelter for people too; timbers for your buildings, which I support for a thousand years or more. I am the wood of your doors, standing guard at the threshold. My old name *Duir* is the source of your word 'door'. In ancient times I was revered as the doorway to the unseen worlds.

My acorns hold all my strength and power and feed many in the forest. Generations ago, people also gathered them, singing and celebrating together. I provided important food that sustained them and kept them close to the heart of the land. As a true king, I am generous to all.

Spend time in my presence and slow down. Lean against my mighty trunk. Feel peace and stillness.From this comes deep strength.

My roots are the deepest of all the trees in the forest. Feel the ground beneath you; my strength will help you to endure with a strong heart.

Gifts

My wood is dense and immensely strong and durable, providing timbers for the framework of your buildings and for long-lasting doors and furniture.

My wood burns slowest and hottest of all the trees. You can feel the many cycles of sunlight released in my warmth and light.

It is traditional to burn my wood on the summer solstice, as I hold the power of the sun in my heart.

My bark is used to tan leather to make it last. My leaves are made into dye and wine. My acorns are rich in all the goodness you need from a staple food and provide long-lasting energy to sustain you. I offer deep, inner strength.

Summer Tree Song

By Anna Richardson,
Oran Ash and River Jones

The Oak Tree Song

Solid and stately

Oak, Oak, Oak of old, King of trees in your crown of go - ld, You

are the do - o - r to worlds un - se - en, In win - ter bare and in su - mmer green.

From gold to gre - en and gold once more, Your leaves will tu - rn be - fore they fall. When

twice you've worn your gold - en cro - wn, Each sea - son's har - vest comes tumb - ling do - wn.

CHORUS

And when you wear your autumn crown,
Blue-feathered Jay from your branches sounds.
From cradles high your acorns fall
So young may grow or feast for all.

CHORUS

Five hundred years to grow and thrive,
Five hundred more you may remain alive,
Shelter for all throughout your reign,
And many thousand lives sustains.

CHORUS

When dark clouds roll across the sky
When thunder roars and storm winds fly,
All must beware you mighty Oak,
For you may court the lightening stroke.

CHORUS

Your roots grow deep, your heart so strong;
Power of the sun to you belongs.
Generous to all as king you stand;
With peace and strength you guard this land.

Elder

GAELIC NAME: *Druman* (meaning 'wood')

ANGLO-SAXON: *Aeld* meaning 'fire' and *Eller* meaning 'kindler of fire'

LATIN NAME: *Sambucus nigra (sambucus* means 'pipe' and indicates elder was used for making musical pipes and fire-blowing sticks)

OGHAM: *Ruis* (the letter R)

Essence

Pathways ~ Healing ~ Wisdom

Character

I am Elder, the Tree of Healing.

I am known in many lands as the wise Elder Mother. My tree is small and fast to grow, my spirit strong and ancient.

I have much to give in my medicine chest and I ask for love and respect in return.

My fresh, young leaves are the first of the trees to emerge in the forest while others sleep. Blackthorn and I awaken together when Brigit walks the land and we brave the cold breath of the Cailleach.

Come summer's fiery sun, my blossoms hang like creamy white clouds, golden with pollen, medicine for hay fever and sunstroke, the ailments of the season.

As the insects dance and hum in the summer sun, my leaves, when rubbed, deter their bite.

Drink my refreshing elderflower at summer picnics and celebrations, delicate and delicious.

As autumn brings the cold air and chills of the season, my berries ripen to shining pur-ple-black, hanging in clusters on red stems, looking like the lungs they help to mend, and providing food for the busy birds need-ing strength to fly south or to weather the cold months ahead with health.

My small trees' branches are like pipes, with a soft pithy core.

I am a tree of pathways, for music, for dream-ing, for gateways to the realm of the Fey, for clearing the passageways so you may breathe clear or open the pores of your skin to help heal a fever.

Pipes made with my wood carry music on the wind, or may be blown to help kindle the fire.

I am like a wise old grandmother – come visit me and tell me your ills and sorrows. I will listen well and look in my medicine chest to guide your return to the pathway of health and wellbeing. Maybe in a tea or in dreams or in a faraway music carried on the wind.

Gifts

My wood is good for pipes for music and fire, though not for burning.

Many people hold my tree as sacred, for all the gifts I carry, and through their respect for my spirit they do not burn me.

I appreciate an offering when asked for my medicine; I like oats and barley. In days gone by, your people asked for my wood with a chant: 'Old girl, give me some of thy wood, and I will give thee some of mine when I grow into a tree.'

My leaves are best for the outside of your body (as they can make you sick if eaten). Chew, stew or make into salve to heal bruises, sprains, aches and pains.

My flowers, when made into tea and allowed to cool, may soothe burns, heal eye infections and can be drunk to help sunstroke. They can also, when removed from the stalks, make elderflower honey (see Honeysuckle Honey, p 145). Drink my flower tea as hot as you can and tuck up warm in bed to help a fever or cold.

My berries should be cooked, as they can make you sick if you eat them raw. Make tea or syrup to strengthen your resilience to flu and colds and to help heal a cough.

My syrup is delicious cooked with apple and blackberries.

My bark, pith and roots are all used too, but only by the wise herbalists, as they are strong medicines. These are a few of the gifts I share and I wish you well.

Elder Mother

By Dawn Casey and Anna Richardson

El - der Mo - ther wi - se and old,

I - n your mo - ther's ar - ms you hold

Fi - re bright and mu - sic clear,

Win - ter warmth and sum - mer cheer.

Elderberries, round and ripe,
Soothe us through the winter night.
Elder blossom, bubbling white,
Cheer us in the summer light.

Elder whistle, music clear,
Play your song for all to hear.
Elder pipe, at the hearth
Feed the flames that warm our hearts.

NB: This song goes well with a drum playing a 'heartbeat' on the first and third beats. It has a stately feeling and medieval quality. A beautiful melody to be played on recorder and harp.

Summer Animals

Wren

I am Jenny Wren. Though I am small and shy, rarely seen, my song soars and trills through the forest, clear and strong. Hear me warning creatures one and all of danger, with my loud rapid call, 'Tik tik tik tik tik!'

Know me from other small brown birds by my round shape and upright tail, which I lift and flick as I hop here and there. I have a band of pale gold above my bright eyes. In many old languages, my name Wren means 'king'. An old tale from Wales tells how one of my kind flew highest of all the birds by hiding in the feathers of the eagle, becoming king of the birds.

I love nesting in nooks and crevices, caves and hollows. Male wrens make a few ball-shaped nests, and I choose the one to my liking, which I line with moss, leaves and feathers, ready for my tiny white eggs, which are speckled with red-brown spots.

Both my partner and I feed our chicks when they hatch. We catch spiders and insects while we hop along the ground and probe into crevices with our long thin bills.

My kind thrive everywhere in this land: on sea-cliffs and islands, moorlands and mountaintops, gardens and forests. I live close to the earth, humble and hidden.

The Welsh word *dryw* means both 'Druid' and 'wren'. To see me is a blessing and an omen of good luck.

Red Admiral Butterfly

I am the Red Admiral. I am named after the band of vivid orange-red upon my black wings. See the bright splashes of white at my wing-tips as I dance by. When I rest and close my wings, I am camouflaged like bark.

I flutter and fly on sunny days, feeding on nectar in hedgerow and garden. I love the sweet bramble flowers. In the early autumn months, I seek the honey-scented ivy flowers, which give me strength in the cold before I seek a place to rest and sleep till spring. You may find me hibernating in your home. Be careful not to wake me. In winters long ago I often shared the homes of your ancestors in their roundhouses and cave dwellings. Perhaps I will find a hollow tree in the forest or a rocky crevice? Somewhere dark, safe and dry to sleep till the warm sun returns.

I love to lay my eggs on the nettles, and when my caterpillar babies hatch they will have their favourite food to eat so they can grow big and strong. When they are ready, they make a tent by folding the leaf edges together with some silky thread. Can you see them in the nettle patch?

Now is the time I go through a metamorphosis, a magical change so complete it transforms my whole being. Inside my cocoon I liquefy and then begin to grow into the ethereal flying one you call 'butterfly'. When I am made whole and ready, I emerge in the warm sun, rest awhile and pump my wings till they are strong ...and off I fly!

Honeybee

In a far-distant time, even before your people knew fire, our ancestors and yours lived alongside each other. Your lives depended on us then, as they do now. We pollinate your flowers so they grow into the food you eat.

You can tell us honeybees from our cousins the bumblebees – we honeybees are smaller and slimmer, like a wasp, while our cousins, the bumblebees, are fat and fuzzy.

You will find me in a hive. I am one of many house bees that work in our nest. We have many special jobs. We make beeswax combs, row upon row of tiny six-sided rooms. Our queen lays an egg in each empty bed – every day she lays as many eggs as there are grains of pollen in a flower! Inside their beds, the eggs hatch into snowy-white grubs. We feed our babies with bee milk and bee bread and the larvae grow and grow. Each spins itself a cocoon and inside it they grow into bees.

I am a house bee for nearly one whole moon. And then, after I have had my time helping in the hive, I fly outside – I am now a field bee. I visit sweet-scented flowers to gather nectar. I do a special dance to show other bees where to find the best nectar. We honeybees have two tummies – one for eating and one to store nectar in. At our hive, field bees fill empty beeswax rooms with nectar and house bees fan the watery liquid with their wings, until it thickens into golden honey.

To make enough honey to fill one of your spoons is 12 lifetimes of work. Your people have always revered our gifts: honey, sacred elixir, potent healer, food of the gods; and our wax, for candles to help you see. Treasure our gifts of gold.

NB: We need bees, and they need our help. Create spaces for bees to use for nesting sites by leaving patches of bare earth in warm, sheltered places and by leaving undisturbed areas with piles of natural materials. We can share our space with the wild creatures; bumblebees will not sting unless their nest is disturbed.

Leave piles of stones, dead plant stems, fallen leaves and log piles for bumblebee queens to hibernate in over winter.

Fox Cub

I am Fox Cub. I was born in an earth, in the springtime. For one whole moon I stayed in the ground, suckling from my mother. Then I came out to play! I like chasing, chewing and tug-of-war! I like catching worms and insects, pouncing on bracken and tumbling with my brothers and sisters. We live with my grown-up brothers and sisters as well as our parents.

My thick fur is rusty red, my eyes are bright amber and my fluffy tail is tipped with white. My parents bring me good things to eat – birds and rabbits and squirrels. I practise hunting as well – I can catch mice and voles all by myself!

In the summertime, I come out of our earth to live above ground. But you will need keen eyes to spot me hiding in the bramble thickets.

Summer Solstice Celebration

It is the time to celebrate the sun! The outward-moving energy of growth and light has reached its full expression. The sun is at its zenith. We know that the sun's presence is vital to all life. We also celebrate the sun within us, the place where we shine and share our gifts with the world. The energy of this celebration is light-hearted and playful.

Sun-Spears

TO MAKE:
1. Ask everyone to find a stick, as straight as can be, in the woods. Bind the stick with yellow wool. This is now a simple sun-spear.

TO CELEBRATE:
1. Light the candle or small fire and stand in a circle, placing the sun-spears on the ground in a pattern radiating from the central candle out towards the children, like the rays of the sun.

2. Hold hands in a circle and take turns to share one thing you love about the summer. Sing 'The Blessings of Light' (see p 159).

3. Look up and see the light of the sun shining all around. Close your eyes and imagine a warm, bright sun inside your heart.

4. Spend a moment thinking about what you love in life... to laugh, to play, to paint, to run? Take a moment to imagine your gifts and the light you have to share. The sun shines, sharing its gift of life unconditionally with us all. We too have our own light to share in the world.

5. Now open your eyes and pick up your sun-spears and together hold them to the middle of the circle and upwards towards the light of the sky. Ask the sun to charge up our sun-spears with power and light. After a moment, the children can bring the spears into an upright position in front of their chests and turn to face the outside of the circle.

6. Say aloud, 'Power of the sun, help us to shine our light!' And, altogether, throw the sun-spears, like rays of light, out into the world.

7. Go and gather the sun-spears and finish the celebration by placing them again around the candle as rays of sunshine. Each child stands behind their ray. Hold hands and together call out, 'Thank you, sun!'

You could hold a Celebratory Summer Forest Fayre (p 134). Feast on fresh fruits, make music and play games to celebrate the summer!

> **YOU WILL NEED:**
> - Yellow woollen yarn
> - Sticks (one per person)
> - Summer fruits
> - A candle or small fire

Summer Celebration Song

The Blessings of Light

Traditional Celtic blessing
adapted by Anna Richardson

Steady and bright

May the bless - ings of light be u - pon you,

li - ght with - out and li - ght with - in. May the

bless - éd sun - shine shi - ne on you, and

war - m your heart till it glo - ws.

Lughnasa

Lughnasa is a late summer festival, halfway between the summer solstice and the autumn equinox, around 1 August . In the cycle of day and night, Lughnasa is akin to mid-afternoon, a time when there is a lull in the activity of the day, a time to rest, play or wander the land. It is the time of ripening in the forest and the first harvest in the fields.

Lughnasa is named after the Irish hero Lugh, who many think of as a sun god. The myths of Old Ireland tell that the festival was begun by him, to honor his foster-mother Tailtiu, and it was held on the land that still bears her name – Teltown in County Meath. It is mentioned in the earliest Irish manuscripts and is a truly ancient festival, celebrated all the way into the 20th century.

In later times, Lughnasa was named Lammas – 'loaf-mass' – a time to bless the newly baked bread and give thanks for the harvest of grain.

The Forest at Lughnasa

It is late summer. There is a lull in the forest. The leaves are rich, dark green, providing welcome shade from the bright sun. Hear the sounds of grain harvesting in the fields. In the meadows, wild grasses are golden, shedding their seeds. In the hedgerows, you may notice ripening berries, still small and green – hawthorn, sloe and rosehip. In sunny spots, the first blackberries may be ripe.

Here in the forest, there is a stillness. It's ripening time; see the nuts forming on hazel, oak, beech and chestnut. The trees are silently pouring their energy into their seeds. High above the canopy, buzzards circle and call their shrill whistle. In the shade, deer move slowly and rest often. There is peace in the ripening woods.

A Story for Lughnasa

The Coming of Lugh
A myth from Ireland

Once in Old Ireland, there was a king who did not rule well. King Bres was strong and he was beautiful, but when chieftains visited, he gave them neither bed nor fire.

Guests had no butter on their bread nor ale in their cups. There were never any poets or pipers, harpers or horn-blowers, jugglers or fools to give pleasure to the people.

Worse still, King Bres demanded a third of the food from every table in the land and a third of the milk from every cow. Wherever smoke rose from a hearth, Bres took tax.

If anyone dared refuse to pay, Bres sent his fiercest warriors to crush them. And the fiercest of them all was Balor, the mighty giant, with a single eye in the centre of his forehead. Whatever Balor looked upon with his poison eye shrivelled and died. In his gaze, flowers withered, bees fell silent, rocks split clean in two. So powerful was Balor's eye, it took four strong men to lift his great eyelid, and on the battlefield, his glare could fell an army.

They were dark days. The people of Ireland, the Tuatha Dé Danann, longed to be free. But the only way to overturn the rule of Bres was to defeat Balor.

A prophecy foretold that one man alone could triumph over Balor – his own grandson. So when Balor's daughter Ethlinn came of age, Balor took her to a tiny island to live alone in a high tower. There she would never meet a husband to father a child.

But Ethlinn's spirit could not be bridled, nor her dreams. She often dreamt of the same young man, a man with hair the colour of sun-kissed barley. And one day, at the edge of the shore of the distant mainland, a young man did come walking. His name was Cian and his hair was the colour of sun-kissed barley. Cian saw the island and caught a glimpse of Ethlinn. The moment he saw he, he loved her.

The old Druid woman, Birog of the Mountain, saw Cian too. She saw the hope in his heart and the light in his eyes, and as she looked upon him she knew that she must help. Birog was wise in the ways of the weather. She knew how to read the clouds and the birds shared the secrets of the wind with her. Birog prepared a charm for Cian – a cord tied with three knots.

Cian stood on the shore. He untied the first knot and a breeze began to blow. He untied the second knot and the wind began to howl. Cian untied the third knot and a wild wind carried him over the water to Ethlinn.

When Ethlinn saw Cian she gasped. His was the face she knew from her dreams.

And while they talked and laughed and fell in love, Birog worked her magic. Not a single tree grew on that wind-scoured island, but with Birog's blessing, a rowan tree sprung up outside the tower – a guardian tree, protecting Ethlinn from Balor's keen eye.

Ethlinn was happy with her love. But Birog was afraid that if Balor ever caught sight of Cian, a single glare from the poison eye would destroy him. So again, Birog whistled up her magic wind and Cian was carried away.

Ethlinn grieved, but her sorrow lightened when she found she was with child. When the time came, the baby was born, a child with hair as golden as sun-kissed barley. This child was destined to bring light to the dark days of Ireland. Ethlinn named him Lugh. But when Balor came to the tower, he heard gurgling and giggling, and with a roar of fury, he snatched the child and flung him far out into the sea.

Birog saw the child falling through the sky, like a shaft of late summer sunshine. Again she whistled up the wind and the breeze carried the child safe to his father.

Cian held his golden-haired boy in his arms. His heart glowed with love. In those days in Old Ireland, there was a custom of fosterage. Giving a child to be fostered strengthened the kinship between families and gave the child the chance to gain knowledge and skills. It was a great honour to be part of this sacred bond. Cian knew too that he must find a place for Lugh where he would be safe from Balor. Cian knew of a great tribal queen, Tailtiu, whose husband had died before she had had a child of her own. Cian went to her. 'Tailtiu, your heart is true and your wisdom is great. Will you share your wisdom with my son? I offer you a privilege beyond price.'

Cian held out his child. Sunlight lit his golden curls. The baby gurgled and chuckled and reached out his chubby arms. Tailtiu took the baby and her eyes shone with tears.

And what of Cian, and of Ethlinn? Well, that is another story altogether.

Tailtiu devoted herself to raising her foster son. With all her heart, she tended him and cared for him. At the same time, she devoted herself to the land, tending and caring for the earth. For in those days of King Bres's rule, the land was neglected, the earth dishonoured.

When Lugh was a little boy, Tailtiu let him play while she worked the land.

He leapt with the grasshoppers in the long grass and chased thistledown on the breeze. He ate bilberries straight from the bush and slept wrapped in the scent of meadow sweet. A deep love of the land grew in Lugh's heart.

With willing hands, Tailtiu cleared the ground, preparing the earth for planting. 'Lugh, Ireland needs its people to be strong. Help me...' Lugh helped his mother heave heavy stones. He even pulled the plough, straight over the muck heap, feeding the earth with dung and ash. Lugh's young limbs grew strong.

Lugh brought water from the river and pocketed smooth pebbles for his slingshot, to practise his aim. From the wood Tailtiu cleared, Lugh took long sticks and sharpened their tips. He practised throwing far and fast, hunting partridge and pheasant for the pot.

After twice seven years, Tailtiu placed Lugh in the care of his uncle, the master smith, to learn every manner of craft and handwork. And after three times seven years, Lugh was a grown man. He felt his destiny calling him and went out into the world.

He went straight to the hill of Tara, seat of the Tuatha Dé Danann, the tribes who were longing to be free from the rule of Bres. Lugh's knock echoed through the hall.

'Open the door,' Lugh called. 'My name is Lugh, I come to serve your leader.'

'What art do you practise?' called the door-keeper. 'No one enters Tara without an art.'

'I am a smith,' replied Lugh. 'Open the door.'

'We have a smith already.' The door stayed shut.

'I am a carpenter.'

'We have a carpenter.'

'Well then, I am a champion.'

'We have a warrior, the mighty Ogma himself.'

'I am not just a man of strength. I am also a harper.'

'That is no use to us. We have a harper.'

'I am a poet and a teller of tales.'

'We have a bard.'

'I am a healer. I am skilled in the arts of magic.'

'We have plenty of people of power.'

Then Lugh said, 'Go, ask your leader if he has any one man who is a master in all these arts?'

When the chief, Nuada, heard Lugh's words, he called, 'Come.'

Ogma, the mighty warrior, looked at Lugh's youthful face. He snorted. There was a great flagstone in the floor, which could hardly be moved by eighty oxen. Ogma heaved up the great stone slab. He hurled it so hard it hurtled through the wall – CRASH!

Ogma looked to Lugh. It was a challenge.

Lugh went out of the hall and he lifted the slab and cast it back through the hole. It landed in the same spot from which it had come. Then Lugh picked up the broken piece of wall and threw it back into the hole. The floor and the wall were both made whole again by Lugh.

Nuada smiled. He bade Lugh play the harp.

Lugh played a silver lament so melancholy even the mighty Ogma wept. Then Lugh played a tune so merry and light that no one could help but lift up their knees and dance.

Lastly, Lugh played a lullaby so soft and so sweet that it lulled them all to sleep.

Nuada rubbed his eyes. He laughed. 'Well, Lugh, you have many skills indeed. So I honour you with a new name: Lugh, the Master of All Arts. Come, be seated in the Seat of the Sage. Your like has never before come to our hall.' He turned to his men. 'Now we have a champion to match Balor of the Poison Eye.'

So it was that Nuada's men prepared to face the army of Bres and his champion Balor. With a blast of the battle trumpet, the two armies charged to meet each other. The plain resounded with the harsh thunder of battle, the whirring and whistling of spears and darts and the clash and clang of sword and shield.

In the midst of it all, a shout went up, 'Balor! Balor of the Poison Eye!' Out onto the battlefield came the mighty giant Balor, with four strong warriors, the ground trembling beneath his feet.

Lugh stepped up to face him. His helmet of burnished bronze shone with living light. Bres saw him from afar and marvelled. 'It seems wonderful,' said Bres to his Druid, 'that the sun should rise in the west today, when every other day it rises in the east.'

'It would be better for us if that were so,' said the Druid.

'What else can it be then?'

'It is Lugh, the Shining One.'

Lugh and Balor came face to face. The two armies stood watching, silent and still.

'Bow before your masters,' Balor cried.

'We will not bow before you,' shouted Lugh. 'You are lords of neither our people nor our land. We will protect our land and we will be free!'

'Who is this babbler?'

'I am Lugh, and I challenge you, Balor.'

'Lift my eyelid!' Balor commanded. 'Let me look upon this babbler and strike him dead!'

The four men began to heave open Balor's deadly eye. But before Balor could unleash the power of his poison eye, Lugh took aim and hurled his spear. It flew like fire. Lugh's aim was true. Balor's eye was torn from his head. Balor's massive bulk thudded to the ground, dead.

The army of Bres was driven to the sea and King Bres himself was brought before Lugh. 'Spare me,' he begged.

Lugh was a merciful man, he let the old king go.

So on the gorse-gold hill of Tara a new king was crowned – King Lugh, the Shining One. Lugh's foster mother, Tailtiu, stood by his side, smiling with pride. The land Tailtiu had cleared now lay transformed – a fair plain sweet with clover. The soil was rich and fertile; it would give a golden harvest of grain.

But Tailtiu was tired from her labours. 'My time has come, Lugh,' she whispered. 'I leave this world knowing that our people have a good king to guide them and good land to sustain them.'

Lugh sang loud laments at the death of his foster mother. He buried Tailtiu on the land that she had loved. Lugh raised a mound over her resting place, which can still be seen to this day.

Then Lugh made a declaration. 'Tailtiu has given her life to tending this land so that we may receive its gift of grain. My foster mother gave up her life. My birth mother gave up her son. I honour the sacrifice of my mothers, Ethlinn and Tailtiu. From this day on, every year, when the grain is gold, we will hold a great gathering, out of respect, and in gratitude.'

And so it is that every year, when summer has reached its full ripeness, a great gathering takes place high on the hilltop and the festival of Lughnasa is celebrated.

There are games and sports and feats of skill: the high jump, the long jump, wrestling, fencing and archery, horse-riding and chariot-racing. Smiths and jewellers, spinners, weavers and dyers share their arts. And in the evening there is singing and storytelling, music and dancing.

And there is thanksgiving, in gratitude for the harvest of gold.

Pronunciation guide:

Tuatha Dé Danann ('the people of the goddess Danu') – *Too-ha day Dan-an*
Balor – *Bah-lor*
Ethlinn – *Eth-leen*
Cian – *Kee-an*
Birog – *Birr-ogue*
Lugh – *Loo*
Tailtiu – *Tal-too*
Nuada – *Noo-a-ha*

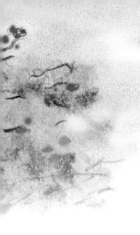

Lughnasa Imaginary Journey

🍂 On a warm day find a sunny glade or meadow and stretch out comfortably. Lick your finger and gently brush it across your eyelashes so they become damp. Now squint and move your gaze till you can see rainbow light and patterns dance in your eyes (be careful not to look directly at the sun). Take a couple of deep breaths. Relax and close your eyes.

🍂 Imagine you are lying on top of a hill with the buzzards circling high above you, calling loudly; the deer are listening, quietly resting in the cool of the forest. The sounds of the tractor bringing in the harvest are far below and the golden sun warms you.

🍂 You are melting into the earth like softening butter, letting go of the need to do anything, just enjoying being on the earth.

🍂 Have a daydream: imagine you could be anything you like. You could be a butterfly dancing across the meadow, or an acorn nestled amongst the oak leaves, swaying in the breeze, with nothing to do but ripen. (Leave time for the daydream.)

🍂 Come back from your daydream, move your fingers and toes, stretch your legs and arms and open your mouth really wide to see if you can yawn to wake yourself up.

🍂 Open your eyes and slowly sit up. If you want to, share your daydream with a friend.

Lughnasa Activities, Crafts and Games

Four Directions Sculptures

It is late summer. There is a pause in the activity in the forest. It is a good time to be creative together. Learning about the directions is useful and helps us to know our world. The sun is in the south at lunchtime. The cold weather comes from the north. The sun moves through the sky from east to west, like writing on the page from left to right.

This activity brings together creativity, trail-making and working as a team. It also helps children to understand the directions north, south, east and west and introduces the idea, common in many indigenous wisdom traditions, that each direction represents an element.

There are many traditions around the world honouring the elements as having relationships to certain directions. They are often different to each other and there is no right or wrong – they are all maps to help us have a deeper connection. In some Celtic wheels, north represents the earth, south represents fire, east represents the air, and west represents water. You could use these elements to inspire the sculptures.

To MAKE:

1. Divide the group into four. Each group is given its direction and the element it represents. Use a compass to find the direction in which each group will be making their sculpture.

2. Instruct the groups to make an environmental sculpture to represent their element in any way they want. It could be a structure or an interactive piece, for example using sound or movement. Ask them to create a trail to their sculpture by means of a set of clues describing the landscape, making them in a poetic style, e.g. left by the giant's knee, through the green tunnel of mystery, etc.

3. Find each other's sculptures by following the clues and participating in their elemental pieces.

You WILL NEED:
- Compass (at least 1 but preferably 4)

Puppets

Creating characters and stories is a perfect woodland activity in the summer months. Although we have given a suggested way to make a simple puppet, the children can have fun creating their own, using forest materials such as sticks and pine cones. The more freedom they have the better, in this imaginative realm. Perhaps tell a story and see if they feel inspired to make some of the characters and play it out.

TO MAKE:

1. Lay out the sticks with the thicker stick for the body in the centre. Tie the string in the middle of its length around the top of the body stick so there are two equal lengths of string on either side. These are the arms. Tie each of these to the top of the arm sticks, leaving a palm's length of string between the body and each arm.

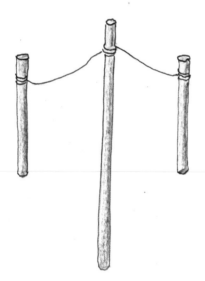

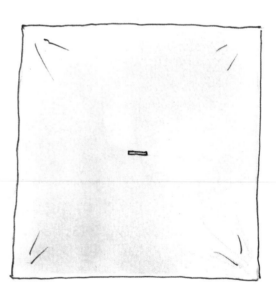

2. Take the cloth rectangle and make a small slit in the centre for the body stick to go through and tie it on with string, leaving room for the head.

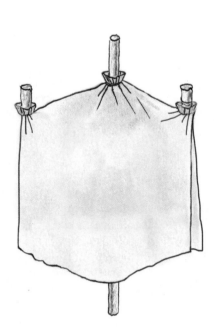

3. Cut smaller slits for the arms to go through at the outer edges of the middle of the cloth.

4. Tie the cloth firmly to the sticks with the string.

5. Add the clay head, firming it onto the stick and tapering the clay down to hold it on, then begin sculpting features and adding found materials such as seeds and moss for eyes and hair or beards.

6. For those with nimble fingers, you could use a needle and thread to sew on leaves to the cloth.

7. When the puppets have been made, give them names and create stories together. Allow the children freedom to play.

Adventurous Wandering

Children love adventures and Lughnasa is a great time to go wandering.

YOU WILL NEED:

- Map
- Compass
- Whistle*
- Water to drink
- Healthy snacks

* The whistle comes in handy if someone is in trouble or you need to re-group quickly

TO PLAY:

1. Agree on an animal or bird call, such as a wolf howl, for gathering the group. Set out the boundaries for your group before you set off.

2. In a large group you can put children with partners who will look out for each other, such as a younger child with an older one, and allocate each adult a small group of children.

3. Along the way, you can stop and spot nests and play games such as chasing, hiding and sneaking. You can follow animal trails, crawling on hands and knees through bracken or into hedgerows, wherever the trail leads...

4. To add to the spirit of adventure, go somewhere you have never been before and/or somewhere the children can have time for free-range adventurous play – climbing trees, leaping streams, making dams and sliding down banks – free from adult direction.

Plaited Grass Dolly

In farmlands all over Europe, it was believed that the spirit of the corn* lived amongst the crop, and so was made homeless by the harvest. It was the custom to fashion the last sheaf of wheat into a corn 'dolly', so that the spirit of the corn could spend the winter in this home, until the 'dolly' was ploughed back into the land in the new season.

In forest glades and edge-lands, wild grass, rather than cultivated grain, is in seed, and can be used to make a simple 'dolly.' Sweet grass is especially pleasing, as the scent of the dry grass is musty and warm – like vanilla-hay.

YOU WILL NEED:
- 3 long stalks of grass, with pleasing seed heads
- Elastic band
- A length of red ribbon (optional)

In European cultures, the word 'corn' often refers to grain grasses, such as wheat, barley and rye, whereas in American culture it refers to maize.

TO MAKE:

1. Tie the three straws together under the seed-heads with an elastic band. The three stalks will be plaited together using the same type of plait you would use to plait hair. Spread out the straws so that one straw is on the left and two are on the right.

2. From the group of two, bring the outer straw and lay it on the inside of the straw on the left.

3. Repeat this rhythm, bringing the outer straw from the group of two over the middle straw, to the inside.

4. When you have completed the plait, hold the ends of all three straws together, and loop the plait around and down

5. Secure the ends into the elastic band, to create a loop of plaited grass stalks above the bunch of seed-heads.

6. If you wish to, on top of the elastic band you can tie a red ribbon in a bow.

(Further information and inspiration on this traditional harvest craft can be found at the website of the Guild of Straw Craftsmen: strawcraftsmen. co.uk)

A Lughnasa Treasure for your Magic Pouch – Rowan Berries for Protection

The rowan is a tree of great beauty and of magical protection. In Celtic areas, and throughout Britain, rowan berries were used as a powerful amulet against dark enchantments of all kinds.

The berries are ripe from early August onwards and are a gorgeous, glowing orange-red. Ask respectfully for the tree to share some of its berries, which are full of the tree's magic. Wait for a feeling in response. Offer some grains of oats or barley, or a song in exchange. Feel the clear presence of the tree as you gather the berries and remember to leave plenty for the birds. Rowan berries are great for this activity because they are non-toxic and do not have a stone in the middle.

YOU WILL NEED:
- Rowan berries
- Strong thread, preferably red
- Needles suitable for the thread
- Scissors

TO MAKE:

1. Cut a length of thread long enough to make a necklace that easily fits over your head with extra for tying off at the end.

2. Tie a knot towards one end and thread the needle at the other end.

3. Sew the berries on carefully. It works well to pierce the tiny end star of the berry and leave via the stalk end; this gives children an easy central way to thread the berries.

4. When the child feels there are just the right amount of berries on the thread, which may not be full, remove the needle, join the ends together and tie a knot to complete.

5. Find an open glade in the forest to scatter some of the berries where birds may see them and enjoy a rowan feast. This helps to carry their seeds across the land too.

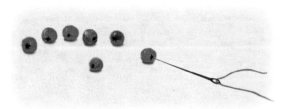

Sense Awareness Game – Who Is Watching Us?

The animals can often see us when we cannot see them. There is so much that we do not see. Let us open our eyes and take in our surroundings with a fresh perspective. Where is the little mouse who is watching us? You can use hazelnut mice to play 'Who Is Watching Us?' (see below). Or mould a clay mouse or make one from felt.

Clay Mouse

YOU WILL NEED:
- Clay
- Pine cone scales
- Charcoal
- Small sticks

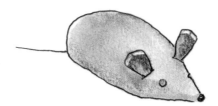

TO MAKE:

1. Mould a small clay body, squeeze one end for the face and add two pine cone scales for ears and a tiny bit of charcoal for a nose.

2. Poke two eyes with a small stick in front of the ears and add a thin stick tail.

TO PLAY 'WHO IS WATCHING US?':

1. Secretly hide the mouse so that it is partially visible from where the group will be sitting. Call everyone over to sit in a circle.

2. Ask them to close their eyes and imagine all the creatures that may be hiding from us in the woods, quietly watching us.

3. Ask the children to open their eyes and look really carefully to see if they can spot a tiny wood mouse watching us. If they spot it they can go and collect it. This can be the springboard to make their own.

Felted Wood Mice

It is simple to make little wood mice finger puppets, which can be used for all kinds of woodland play.

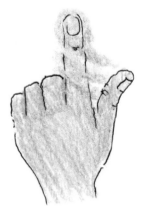

YOU WILL NEED:
- Carded wool (golden brown)
- Small bowls of warm water
- Cold water
- Soap, e.g. washing-up liquid
- Scraps of felt
- Yarn
- Craft glue/needle and thread
- Vinegar (optional)

TO MAKE:

1. Each child wraps some carded wool (quite tightly) around their pointer finger until it's nice and thick. To help the fibres felt together, you could lay some pieces in different directions as you go.

2. Put some washing-up liquid into the bowls of warm water and give them to the children to dip their wool-wrapped fingers into. Ask them to rub the wool with their other hand. They can twist, squeeze and press until the wool felts snug over their fingers.

3. With the wool still wrapped around their pointer finger, the children rinse their wool piece in cold water. (A couple or drops of vinegar can also be added to the cold water to help remove the soap.) Any excess water can be squeezed out.

4. Put the little mice out in the sun to dry. (Make sure the finger holes are open; you could stand them up with the open end down.) They may need to dry overnight.

5. When they are dry, glue or sew on scraps of felt for ears and a length of yarn for a tail.

Lughnasa Game – Woodland Olympics

In Ireland, Lughnasa was traditionally the time for playing games and friendly competing, so how about holding a woodland Olympics? Create your own ideas for woodland sports.

Animal Races

Represent the animals by finding ways to move like them. Rabbits run by moving their hind legs forward together in front of their forelegs. Badgers move with right front and back legs together, then left legs together, in a rolling gait. Foxes run with opposing front and back legs, just as we run with opposing arms and legs.

Balancing Beam Gymnastics

Use fallen trees to walk along or make poses while balancing on them.

Climbing Challenge

Use a secured rope to climb up the roots of a fallen tree or other steep incline.

Stream Leap Long Jump

Leap over a stream onto the other side.

Javelin Throwing

Find the straightest sticks you can find and set up a safe place to do javelin throwing. It is fun to make hoops and hang them from trees. See who can throw their javelin through the hoops. Be careful to have a throwing line that children stand behind, taking turn to throw.

Cloud Racing

Look up and watch the clouds in all their shapes and moods, racing or gliding across the sky. Lie on your back and spot animals, faces and castles in their ever-changing dance.

Or be the wind and race the clouds: set up a starting and finishing line. Give each child a handful of white sheep's wool and a sheet of stiff cardboard for 'wafting'. Children can tease the wool to make whatever cloud shape they like. Consider the prevailing wind and set up the race to follow its course.

Lughnasa Plant Lore

Meadowsweet

GAELIC NAME: *Rios Cuchulain* (named after the legendary warrior who was treated with baths of meadowsweet to calm his rage and cure fever)

LATIN NAMES: *Filipendula ulmaria, Spirea Ulmaria*

COMMON NAMES: Queen of the Meadows, Bridewort (it was traditional to strew the flowers under the feet of the bride at handfasting – an old tradition of marriage. Also, it was traditional at Lughnasa for women to wear garlands of meadowsweet in celebration of Bride – the goddess Brigit.)

Character

I am Meadowsweet, Queen of the Meadows.

With creamy blossoms of late summer, I bring beauty to the wetlands, ditches and river banks.

See my red stems and leaves with their silvery undercoat.

Smell my dreamy scent drift on the breeze.

Gifts

I am a healer, a gentle helper, to soothe your aches and pains, relieve sore tummies, headaches and fever.

My roots like the damp places, and those of you who suffer with joints that ache in the damp weather may seek my comfort.

I am blessed of Brigit... sing to me, sit with me, dance with me, gather my dreamy flowers and leaves on a sunny day and in tea I will soothe you.

Meadowsweet Rub

This magic meadowsweet rub is a warming ointment that can have amazing pain-relieving effects and smells dreamy. It is wonderful for treating growing pains and achy joints and muscles. Simply rub on and enjoy the magic.

YOU WILL NEED:
- A packet of butter
- 6–8 flower heads (picked when the weather is warm and dry)
- Pan
- Sieve
- Jars and labels

TO MAKE:

1. First make a ghee, which is clarified butter. This is an interesting process to do with children. Ghee is often used in Indian cooking. Making it is a good way of creating a pure fat that lasts much longer than butter. It is easily absorbed into the skin and this medicine can also be eaten. An alternative way of making this medicine dairy-free is to use coconut oil – simply add the flowers and heat.

2. Melt the butter in a pan. When it has melted, use a spoon to remove the foam from the top of the golden liquid by skimming it off. When this has been done, carefully pour off the golden ghee, leaving behind the whitish globules (the milk solids) at the bottom of the pan. The golden liquid is pure ghee.

3. Clean the pan and have help from the children taking the meadowsweet flowers off the stems and putting them into the ghee. Heat the flowers in the ghee on a gentle heat while stirring, for about 20 minutes. Strain, pour into small jars and allow to set.

4. Clarifed butter will go off after a month or so and is best stored in the fridge. To make a longer-lasting magic rub, use coconut oil or use the same recipe as for the daisy ointment (p 107), replacing the daisy flowers with meadowsweet flowers.

The Meadowsweet Song

By Lucinda Warner

Slow jig

Mead - ow sweet Mead - ow sweet, Queen of the mead - ows, Queen of the dit - ches,

Queen of the lakes. Mead - ow sweet Mead - ow sweet, Bring - ing us heal - ing,

Help - ing us with all our ach - es and pains. Mead - ow - sweet oh

Mead - ow - sweet, The prett - i - est flow - er you ev - er could meet.

Meadowsweet Meadowsweet,
Cooling our fevers,
Soothing our tummies,
Healing our woes.
Meadowsweet Meadowsweet,
Growing so freely,
We're pleased to see you
Wherever we go.

Meadowsweet oh Meadowsweet,
The prettiest flower you ever could meet.

Harvest Herb Chapattis

In Christian times, the Celtic festival of Lughnasa became known as Lammas, meaning 'loaf-mass'. Here we honour the harvest of wheat and combine it with some wild seeds and herbs. Chapatti is a staple Indian unleavened bread recipe, though wheat and water cooked simply in this kind of way is a primitive and universal form of bread. Ash bread is a dough of flour and water cooked directly on the embers in little patties. This recipe could be used in that way too.

TO MAKE:

1. First the children wash their hands. Set aside a cupful of flour for kneading and rolling later. Place the remaining flour, the salt, wild seeds and finely chopped herbs in the bowl and stir. Add water bit by bit, stirring and kneading into a soft elastic dough.

2. Take a small handful of dough and roll into a ball. Heat the frying pan. No oil is needed for this bread. On the floured board, roll the ball out flat, until it is as thin as a tortilla.

3. When the pan is hot, put the chapatti on to cook. Use the spatula or tongs to check the underside. It should take about 30 seconds for small brown spots to appear.

4. Then turn and cook the other side, which takes about the same amount of time.

5. Once all the chapattis are cooked, serve with butter and enjoy as a forest treat.

YOU WILL NEED:

- 4 cups plain flour
- 1.5 cups water (or as needed)
- 1 teaspoon salt (optional)
- Herbs such as parsley, thyme and oregano
- Large bowl
- Spoon
- Board
- Rolling pin (or freshly peeled willow or hazel stick)
- Frying pan
- Fire or heat source
- Spatula or tongs for turning
- Optional wild additions (e.g. 'wild greens' such as ground ivy, linden leaves, wild marjoram, wild thyme or nettle seeds)

Lughnasa Tree Lore

Rowan

GAELIC NAMES: *Craobh chaoran (coaran,* or, as the Rowan is also known, *fuinnseach coille,* means 'the wood enchantress')
LATIN NAME: *Sorbus aucuparia*

OGHAM: *Luis* (the letter L)

Essence
Resilience ~ Magical Protection ~ Brightness

Character

I am red-berried Rowan, the bright tree of the high places.

I love the wild mountains, where the air is clear and waters flow through rock and heather.

Some call me the Mountain Ash, though the ash tree and I are from different tribes.

The Norse people say that I bore the first woman and ash the first man. Our leaves are similar, it is true, but he bears the key and I the berry.

Red deer and mountain hare love my leaves and my bark too when snows are deep.

My berries ripen in perfect time for birds arriving after long flights from the lands of the northeast. I offer them a feast of red berries to gather their strength to travel south for the winter. In return, they carry my seeds and sow my young on their way.

I grow in many lands but can thrive in places higher than any other tree of the north. I stand strong and resilient in all the elements – wind and snow, rain and hail.

My winter buds are pointed and strong, protected from the mountain wind by a coat of downy white fur.

Growing in the light, I cling to rocks where ravens roost, or grow in the tiniest crevice, wild and free.

I shine clear and bright and no darkness threatens me. I am haven for the little folk of rock, stream and hill.

I can remind you to hold strong to your own true nature, not to give up, and to always find your way. If dark forces threaten, calm your mind and call on the protection of my strong bright presence.

My berries, favourite of the birds, are very bitter and sour. They have been traditionally used for making into a jelly with crab apples, to have with meat. Dried they are like bitter raisins and some say they should not be eaten.

A tea of my simmered berries, sweetened with honey, may be used to treat sore throats, to protect your body against the ailments of the cold winds of the north.

Gifts

Throughout time, people have used my wood for magical and sacred purposes, such as talismans, amulets, staffs and wands.

My berries can be sewn into necklaces or charms.

I am imbued with light and protection against unseen perils. People often plant me near their homes for the bright protection I offer.

Like hazel, my wood has been used for divination, to find underground waterways and minerals.

My wood is yellow-grey and is strong yet flexible, so can be used for making baskets, bows, tool handles and for carving.

A black dye can be made from my bark.

The Rowan Tree Song

Lyrics by Anna Richardson
Melody by River Jones

Dancing and bright

High on the hills, the red - berr - ied Ro - w - an, Roots a - mong the rocks where the

mount - ain streams are flow - ing. There she grows, the red - ber - ried Row - an,

Danc - ing in the wind u - pon the wild hi - gh hills. Oh the bright, the

red - berr - ied Row - an, Shin - ing in the light, where the pur - ple heath - er's grow - ing.

Oh the bright, the red - berr - ied Row - an,

Danc - ing in the sun u - pon the wild hi - gh hills.

Linden

GAELIC NAME: *Craobh theile*
ANGLO-SAXON NAME: *Lynde* or *Linde*
LATIN NAME: *Tilia spp.*

Character

I am Linden, the sweet, gentle Tilia.

Some know me as the lime tree, though I am from a different tribe to the green citrus fruit.

For a long age I was the most common tree in the ancient forests, before farming came to these lands.

Your ancestors, with deft hands, wove my inner bark into baskets, rope and clothing.

Imagine the sweet perfume of my abundant blossoms, wafting on the summer breeze in those forests.

I am a tree of music; hear the hum of the insects in my branches and the fine music from instruments made of my golden wood.

In Europe people held councils and court beneath my tree. I am a tree of love and truth, and some people upheld the belief that you could not tell a lie under my boughs.

Come and find me in the forests; I am still here. Though rare in wild places now, I am in the parks and gardens where you wander.

In winter, my buds are distinctive, like red mittens.

In spring, my tender leaves are translucent hearts. In summer, smell my fragrance when my winged flowers open, glistening with nectar.

Watch ants farming the aphids for the honeydew I give.

Listen to the humming bees in my branches and smell the sweet fragrance.

See my heart-shaped leaves shine gold-green in the summer sun.

Feel the warmth and peace within you as you rest beneath me.

Gifts

My golden wood is excellent for carving. I have been used in many great carvings in cathedrals and mansions, as well as for making musical instruments.

My wood is one of the best for making fire by friction.

My inner bark is sometimes called 'bast' and has long, strong fibres for making into rope, nets, baskets and clothes. I make good charcoal too.

My buds, leaves and blossom are all good to eat, with a soft, soothing flavour.

The blossoms are especially good for making tea and I can help calm anxiety and stress, supporting your heart and relaxing tension.

I can help bring restful sleep and calm a fever. I have good medicine for you, especially in these troubled times.

I am strong but gentle. I can help you to slow down, relax and be at peace.

The Linden Song

By Noola Gould

Gentle and soft

Lin - den tree, Ti - li - a cord - at - a, sma - ll - lea - ved lime. Gold - en wood,

beaut - i - ful and strong for in - stru - ments so fine. A sa - lad from your ten - der heart-shaped

lea - ves, Sweet bloss - om for the ho - ney bees and gen - tle sooth - ing tea.

Linden tree, Tilia cordata, small-leaved lime.
Inner bark, fibres long and strong, twist them into line.
Haul the ropes to sail across the sea,
And string the bow to spin the wood
And set the fire free.

Linden tree, Tilia cordata, small-leaved lime.
Linden tree, Tilia cordata, small-leaved lime.

Lughnasa Animals

Great Spotted Woodpecker

I am Great Spotted Woodpecker, handsome in my black and white coat and merry red crown and tail feathers. I am about the same size as the sweet singing blackbird and easier to see than my rarer relative, the lesser spotted woodpecker.

Hear me drumming in the forest from a long way off. I tell the other males where I live, and, perhaps, a beautiful female will hear my powerful drumbeat. Maybe I am hollowing out a cosy tree nook for my nest, to raise a family? Perhaps it is autumn and I am making holes in the tree trunk to stash my hazelnuts? Am I digging into the bark to find insects for a tasty snack, retrieving them with my long sticky tongue? Sometimes you must dig and dig for what you need and let the whole world know, beating your own rhythm.

See me fly by with an undulating flight, down and up, down and up. And when I sing I laugh and laugh, 'Ha, ha, ha, ha, ha!' brightening your day with my merry ways.

Wood Mouse

I am Wood Mouse, small and bright-eyed, with golden fur and a soft white belly. I am usually asleep during the sun-hours. My eyes are able to see sharply and my keen ears and nose tell me all about the world in the shadows of night. I can climb and swim and leap far with my strong back feet.

I need all my skills to stay alive, for many in the forest like to eat me – owl and weasel, stoat and fox. I must keep alert during my gathering hours. Oh, there is much to do, much to do, seeds to gather, nests to make... Mmm... is that a wild strawberry? My favourite! Careful though, I must move as quiet... as a mouse.

I am organized too, paying attention to tiny details. In my burrows I have rooms for storage and chambers lined with moss and grass for my nests, where I have my babies and feed them on my mouse milk. I have made special escape tunnels, which I share with other mice. I mark them with sticks and leaves so I always know where they are.

Lughnasa Celebration

It is Lughnasa, the harvest time of the grasses and grains and the ripening time amongst the trees. The late summer sun is blessing the land and we hope also for the life-giving rains, without which there will be no harvest to come. We thank and celebrate the weather beings. The sun, sea, wind and clouds all bring the rain so that the plants will grow and the fruits ripen. It is the gift of the rain and sun that gives us life and makes our lands so green. It was traditional in Ireland to take offerings of bread and early berries onto the hilltops at this time, in hope of the blessing of the gods for the harvest to come.

TO PREPARE:

1. Everyone makes a dancing stick, wrapping coloured wool and threads for the handle and attaching little bells at the top of the stick.

2. As a group, create a simple dance.
Here is an example: form a circle and hold your sticks in your right hands, pointed to the middle like the rays of the sun. Dance or skip around the circle clockwise. Change direction and repeat anticlockwise. Partner up with the person to your right. While the right-hand partners stay still, the left-hand partners move out four steps to form a second larger outer circle. Partners face each other. In rhythm to the music, they skip towards each other and strike the tops of their sticks together. They swap positions, from inner to outer circle, turn to face each other and move together to strike sticks again. Complete with another circle together with sticks pointed towards the centre. The mood is fun and light-hearted.

3. Light the fire. Then create a simple shrine with the candle and place the empty basket in front of it. Each person has a piece of fruit or bread for the Lughnasa basket. You may wish to sing the 'Weather Thanksgiving Song'. Circle round and in turn give thanks for the season – the warm sun, the blessing of the wind and clouds bringing the gift of rain so plants may grow, the ripening trees, the fruit and nuts to come, the harvest of the grain. Place the gifts of nature into the basket.

4. Move to a clearing and dance your Lughnasa dance, celebrating the gift of life and the hope for the good harvest yet to come.

5. Close the celebration around the fire, feasting on warm herb chapattis.

YOU WILL NEED:
- 1 freshly cut stick each, about finger-tip-to-elbow in length.
- Assorted coloured wool or threads
- Little bells, at least 1 each
- A basket
- Seasonal fruits such as bilberries, raspberries and early blackberries
- Home-made bread, e.g. Harvest Herb Chapattis (p 181)
- Candle
- Fire
- A musician to play for the dance, or a merry seasonal song

Weather Thanksgiving

By Anna Richardson

Slow and broad

Thank you Sun. Thank you Sea. Thank you Clouds. Thank you Wind.

Thank you Rain. Thank you Thun - der. Thank you weath - er for al - l you bring.

NB: This song is intended as a call and response in which the caller continues the long note while the other singers echo the response. Harmonies are lovely as an addition.

The Water Song

By River Jones

Slow and broad

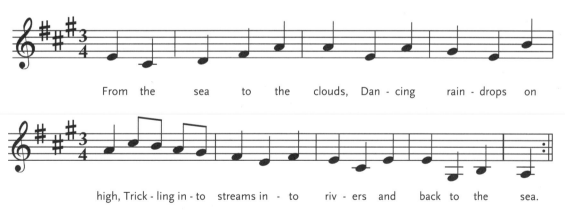

From the sea to the clouds, Dan - cing rain - drops on

high, Trick - ling in - to streams in - to riv - ers and back to the sea.

NB: This song is cyclical, as are the cycles of water, to be sung round and round.

Autumn

Autumn is harvest time. The autumn equinox is a point of perfect balance in the year, when the length of the day is exactly equal to the length of the night. It is a turning point: from now on, the nights will grow longer as we move towards winter.

The Forest in Autumn

Autumn mornings bring cool fresh air, mist-filled valleys and dew
drops glistening on spiders' webs. It is the sunset of the year and
the leaves begin to blaze in flaming colours – red, amber and gold.
See the trees transform, each in turn. Who will be the first to lead
the glorious procession? Catch a falling leaf and make a wish.

Fruits, nuts and berries are full and ripe, shining in the hedgerows. Birds are feasting on the abundant harvest. Animals are
busy in the forest, gathering seeds and nuts of all kinds, creating
stores for the cold months ahead. Apples shine, ripe and round,
in the orchards. Nature provides abundantly to give us all strength
and resilience for the winter to come.

It is time to give thanks and celebrate.

An Autumn Story

The Apple Tree Man

A folktale from Somerset, England

Once upon a time, there was a man who was the eldest of a long line of brothers. He'd been out in the world, working, since he was a lad.

Well, his father died, and everything he owned was passed to the youngest son, as was the custom in those parts. The youngest brother doled out bits and pieces to all his family, but, when it came to the eldest, all he let him have was their father's bony old donkey and the ox that was lame in the leg. The youngest brother inherited an old tumbledown cottage, where their grandfather used to live, with a couple of ancient apple trees standing round it. The walls creaked and the roof leaked. The apple trees never gave any fruit. 'I'm going to buy myself a grand house in town,' said the youngest brother. 'You can live in Granfer's old cottage – you can pay me rent for it. I'll have it every month, on the dot.'

Well, the eldest brother didn't grumble. He just set to work to make the best of it. He got up early, when the morning's all mist and sparkling spiderwebs, and went out along the lane. The edge of the lane was patterned with seed-heads, cow parsley and teasel, and rust-red dock. Along he went, cutting the grass and foraging the hedges. And by the time the sun was out, the donkey was munching on good grasses, full of wild herbs, and enjoying handfuls of hips and haws to ease his stiff legs and strengthen his old heart. The eldest brother picked meadowsweet and made an ointment. He rubbed the ox's sore leg with the balm every day, and it began to heal.

That skinny old donkey began to fatten up, and that lame old ox, he picked himself up and began to walk again.

The eldest brother patched up the stable to keep the animals warm against the evening chill, and in the daytime, when the sun shone low and mellow, he let them graze in the orchard and manure the ground.

Well, the apple trees liked that! They perked right up. 'Bless you!' the eldest brother said to the trees. 'You're flourishing a marvel.' And he almost thought he heard the trees respond. Perhaps it was just the autumn wind.

When Twelfth Night came around, the eldest brother went out into the shivering orchard to wassail the trees. Their boughs were silver in the moonlight. He went to the very oldest tree, where the spirit of the orchard lives, and poured warm spiced cider over the roots, and hung sopping cider-toast in the branches for the robins. He stamped and hollered, and banged and clanged pots and pans, to scare off any impish spirits.

And he sang to the old tree:

Here's to thee, Old Apple Tree,
Whence thou mayest bud,
And whence thou mayest blow,
And whence thou mayest
Bear apples enow.
Hats full, caps full,
Bushels full and sacks full,
And our pockets full too.
And our pockets full too.
Hurrah! Hurrah!

The trees liked that. Their moon-silver branches quivered.

As winter tightened its white grip, shrill winds blew through the cottage, rattling windows, banging doors. The eldest brother's nose was red, his fingers raw. His youngest brother said, 'I don't know why you bother with those old trees. Chop 'em down, I say. Burn 'em for firewood!'

But the eldest brother cut only the dead wood and the broken branches to give the tree room to stretch.

Spring came, bringing warm sun and soft rain, and the apple trees opened delicate pink-white blossoms. Soon the leaves were abuzz with bees. Over the summer, hard little apples grew and ripened in the sun. Come autumn, the fields were stubbled pale gold and ploughed velvet brown. The bracken was turning yellow and the leaves were lighting their inner fires. The harvest moon polished the apples red-gold.

The boughs were bright with clusters of apples. The eldest brother could hear them calling to him from the other side of the lane, as clear as bells ringing.

All around the cottage, the trees were shining with Red-streak and Russet Coat, Golden Pippin and Crimson King – a treasure-trove of apples.

The eldest brother patted the dappled trunk of the old apple tree. 'Thank you, old man,' he said. And the tree bowed and bent low so he could pluck a round rosy apple.

The eldest brother took out his pocketknife and cut a slice. At the centre was a perfect star. He smiled and took a bite. It was crunchy and crisp, juicy and sweet. 'Mmm...' He loved apples!

But, though working with the animals and the trees made the eldest brother's heart happy, it didn't pay the rent. Oh yes, the youngest brother would have his rent, on the dot!

Well, one day, the youngest brother came to the orchard and said, 'Tomorrow's Christmas Eve, and come midnight, beasts do talk, so they say. There's treasure buried hereabouts, we've all heard tell, and I'm set to ask that old donkey. He's bound to tell me. So, you wake me up just afore twelve, and I'll tell you what I'll do: I'll take sixpence off your rent.' And off he went, quite pleased with himself.

Next day was Christmas Eve. The eldest brother got up early and did a grand clean of the whole place. He filled the mangers with a double feed of hay and hung holly and ivy in the stable. He led the donkey and the ox in early, through the blue-grey dusk, their warm breath steaming in the freezing air. He stroked their soft noses and tickled their velvet ears.

Then he lit the Yule log and he took his last little drop of cider from the autumn apples, and warmed it over the flames. It was spicy-sweet, mulled with honey and cinnamon, ginger and nutmeg. He curled his cold hands round the warm mug. And he outs to the orchard to give it to the apple tree.

He went to the very oldest tree and poured his cider over the roots.

And he sang:

Here's to thee, Old Apple Tree,
Whence thou mayest bud,
And whence thou mayest blow,
And whence thou mayest
Bear apples enow.
Hats full, caps full,
Bushels full and sacks full,
And our pockets full too.
And our pockets full too.
Hurrah! Hurrah!

Out in the silent night, the eldest brother was listening so closely he heard the Apple Tree Man answer. He heard a voice call out to him from inside the tree. 'You take your spade, and dig down under this here root, and see what you can see.'

So the eldest brother fetched his spade and he dug, through the crumbling loam and round the knuckles of flints. There, he found a wooden box.

And inside the box, gold. Treasure as golden and overflowing as a harvest of autumn apples. 'You take it,' said the Apple Tree Man. 'Take it and keep it. It's yours.' So the eldest brother did just that. 'Now,' says the Apple Tree Man, 'you can go and call your brother. Midnight is close by.'

The bells in the church tower tolled twelve. Out came the youngest brother in a terrible hurry-push. He saw light coming from the stable and sure enough the donkey was talking to the ox. 'Do you know,' the donkey was saying, 'someone is eavesdropping on us?'

'How unmannerly!'

'He's wanting us to tell where the treasure is.'

The youngest brother's eyes gleamed. He clenched his fists and held his breath.

'But he'll never get it,' said the ox. 'Someone else has already took it.'

And that was all the youngest brother ever heard of the treasure.

As for the eldest brother, the donkey, the ox and the old apple trees, they all lived happily ever after.

Autumn Imaginary Journey

The light and dark are in balance; day and night stand equal. Wrap up warm and lie in the forest beneath the trees. Breathe the fresh autumn air. Feel the sacredness of this time. In the following imaginary journey, give time and space between each breath.

- Close your eyes and relax. Notice your breath. As you breathe in through your nose, it is cooler on the way in, and warmer on the way out. (Pause.) Feel the earth beneath you and the sky above. Breathe in the sky, and breathe out into the earth. Feel held in perfect balance by the earth and the sky, without needing to do anything.

- Breathe in the last of the summer days. Breathe out the frosty nights to come.

- Breathe in the misty, fresh mornings. Breathe out the fiery red glow of autumn sunsets.

- Breathe in the starry nights, dark and peaceful. Breathe out the golden light of autumn shining on the ripe fruits and berries.

- Breathe in and remember your inner world, full of forests and seasons, weather, wildlife and wonder. Give thanks for your inner world.

- Breathe out and gently open your eyes to the forest all around you. Notice the trees. Listen to the wind. Feel the earth. Smell the arrival of autumn. Give thanks for this world.

- Feel your breath rising and falling without any effort at all. The breath of life. Like day and night, like the tides, like the seasons, in and out, in and out...

- All is in balance.

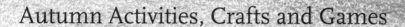

Autumn Activities, Crafts and Games

Apple Flags

Apples have a secret deep inside: they contain a beautiful five-pointed star. Cut the fruit open and have a look at the chambers where the seeds live. Apple belongs to the rose family, along with many others of the fruits and berries. You can see five-petalled spring blossoms on the blackberry, the wild rose and the blackthorn. Find the secret star on the hawthorn berry too. Celebrate the apple, generous fruit, gathered since times of old.

TO MAKE:

1. Cut the cloth into the shapes you would like for flags. To cut the apple and reveal the star, imagine the apple is the earth, with the stalk as the North Pole and the brown-black base star as the South Pole. Cut the apple along the equator. Carefully remove any pips with the tip of the knife.

YOU WILL NEED:
- Apples
- Plain cloth, white or cream
- Sticks for handles
- Poster paint
- Sponges and bowls to apply the paint
- Scissors
- Knife

2. Use the sponge to thinly apply the paint to the inside of the apple. Then print the apple onto the cloth. It is important to do this on a hard surface for the best effect. Each flag can have as many prints as the artist wants.

3. The simplest way to attach the flag is to cut horizontal slots along one side of the cloth and insert a stick. Glue or stitches can be used for longer-lasting options.

4. Make an apple parade through an orchard or through the forest, waving the flags. 'The Apple Star Song' (p 203) can be sung to celebrate.

Cut some thin slices of apples with stars in the middle for the children to eat while you read 'The Apple Tree Man' (p 196).

Autumn Tree Song

The Apple Star Song

By Anna Richardson

Lively

Hey hey it's time to play,

Gath - er - ing the fruit in the good old way.

Ripe ro - sy app - les, one, two, three, A

star in - side for you and me.

Woollen Apples

Woollen apples are simple to make. They can be hung in the autumn branches or tied on a string to make an apple garland in celebration of the apple tree.

TO MAKE:

1. Slightly bend the card in half lengthways. This helps the yarn to slide off easily after it has been wrapped. Wrap yarn around the cardboard around 80–100 times. The more you wrap, the rounder and fuller your apple will be.

YOU WILL NEED:
- Red/green/yellow yarn (wool is best, as it is biodegradable)
- Brown cotton pipe cleaner, cut in half
- A leaf (optional)
- A rectangle of cardboard, e.g. 5 x 10cm (2 x 4ins)
- Scissors

2. Cut the yarn from the ball of wool when you have finished weaving.

3. Slide the pipe cleaner piece under the loops of yarn. Bring the ends to meet each other and twist together to make a stem. If you like, you can add in a real leaf.

4. Take the second half of the piece of pipe cleaner, and again pass it through the loops of yarn. This time twist the two ends together at the opposite side of the yarn – the base of the apple – to create a rounded apple shape. Trim off the long ends.

Hazelnut Mice and Ladybirds

In autumn, wood mice are gathering food to store in their underground burrows over winter. Ladybirds are looking for a place to hibernate during the cold days ahead.

Mice

To make:

1. On its round base, the hazelnut is a lighter colour, which lends itself to the face of the mouse. Paint on eyes, nose and whiskers for a simple but pleasing effect.

2. You can add a tail of wool or string by rolling a small ball of beeswax until it is warm and sticky. Use this to attach the tail.

Ladybirds

To make:

1. Paint the nut red, leaving the lighter round base unpainted for the eyes. When the paint is dry, paint a black line along the middle of the back and add dots on either side.

Leaf Art

The autumn leaves are one of nature's great works of art. Our world is transformed in these months. Gather the fallen leaves and, with the inspiration they offer, create art of all kinds. Here are just a few ideas.

Leaf Snakes or Crowns

TO MAKE:

1. Pin leaves together with thin sticks or thorns to make a long snake, or to make an autumn leaf crown to wear. Overlap the leaves, and use a short thin stick to make a stitch, in and out.

YOU WILL NEED:
- Leaves
- Sticks
- Large-eyed sewing needle
- Strong thread or wool
- Beeswax and saucepan

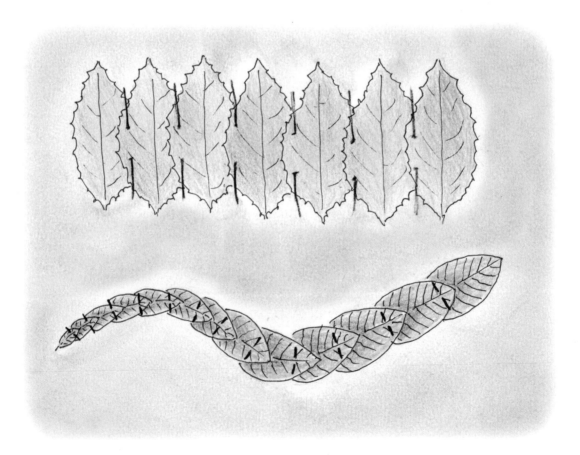

Leaf Sewing

TO MAKE:

1. Use a needle and strong thread, or wool, to stitch leaves together. Sew autumn leaf mini patchwork quilts or clothes for puppets and elves.

2. For younger children, instead of a needle, use a thin but strong stick. Tie the thread to one end, and use the stick as a needle. They may need help securing the first two stitches.

Leaf Bunting/Mobiles

TO MAKE:

1. Leaves can be stitched to create beautiful bunting and mobiles. In order to keep the autumn colours for longer, first press the autumn leaves for a few days until flat and dry.

2. In a saucepan, warm the beeswax gently over the fire. When it has melted, hold the stem of the leaf and dip the leaf into the beeswax.

3. Use a needle and thread to sew into bunting or mobiles. You may also wish to add other woodland treasures, such as acorns, berries and alder cones.

Leaf Spiral

TO MAKE:

1. Throughout the world, day and night are equal at equinox. As the nights get longer and winter approaches, we are moving into the dark time of the year and our journey inwards.

2. Gather leaves of different colours and grade them from light to dark in piles. Clear a space on the forest floor and create a spiral with the darkest leaves at the centre moving out to the lightest.

3. When complete, stand back and see how our spiral shows the movement of our season, moving inwards towards the darkness.

Clay Spiders and String Webs

Spiders are the web weavers, the spinners, the expert rope makers, and in autumn they are busy. Go into your gardens or through a park in the misty mornings to see the cobwebs glistening with dew. The spiders have cast their silver threads of light all over the land, across the wide hilltops and into the smallest bushes. The spider's web has mysterious healing powers and can be gathered and applied to cuts to stop bleeding and heal the skin – a well-known folk remedy. Watch a spider spin a web; see the beautiful nets they make. Can you find their webbed nurseries full of tiny babies, their spiderlings? Notice the spiders, their patterned bodies and jointed legs; there are so many of them in all colours, shapes and sizes. Give thanks for their place in the world and their miraculous talents.

The Spider

To make:

1. Pointing out that spiders have two main body parts, give everyone two blobs of clay. Roll them into egg shapes and stick them together (a small stick in the middle helps).

2. Notice how many legs spiders have and where they join the body. Find sticks and add the legs to the clay.

3. The basic spider is made – add detail as you wish.

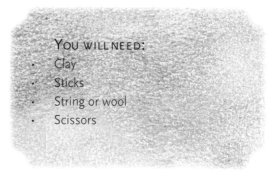

You will need:
- Clay
- Sticks
- String or wool
- Scissors

The Web

To make:

1. Give the children a decent length of string. This can be bound onto a small stick like a cotton reel. Now send them out to weave a web. They will have fun experimenting and gain respect for spiders.

2. You can follow this activity by playing the Spiders and Flies game (p 211).

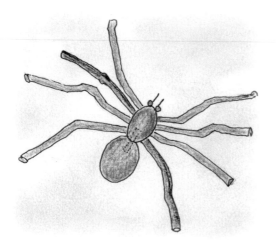

Acorn Cup Dew Medicine

Collect water pearls of dew or rain from the leaves of trees and plants in acorn cups. Water has always been revered – it is one of the vital elements for all life. It can dissolve minerals, and moving water picks up and carries microscopic particles. This is why in certain areas tap water tastes 'hard' – the water has picked up minerals on its journey. Imagine that the water resting upon an oak leaf is carrying the energy of the oak tree. With our acorn cups, we can gather precious dew medicine: oak dew for strength, birch for cleansing, linden dew for peace. See the pearls of water shimmering with silver light and reflections. Autumn is the time of mists and dew. On a misty autumn morning, go hunting for dew and drink bright droplets of it.

An Autumn Treasure for Your Magic Pouch – Hazelnuts for Knowledge

It is said that the Druids carried hazelnuts and ate them to receive knowledge or connect to their inner knowing. Carry some hazelnuts in your magic pouch as an emergency food or to eat when you need to hear your inner wisdom. You could also use a palm drill to make a hole through the nut, which can then be threaded onto a string and worn so you can connect with the hazel.

Sense Awareness Activity – Mystery Bag Game

Feel the bark of a tree, a leaf, the earth. Notice the texture, the temperature, the weight and shapes. This game is a simple way for young children to explore the sense of touch. You can play it by seating everyone in a circle or you can use it during an exploratory play session. The children's natural curiosity will draw them to the game. It's a great game for inspiring children's careful attention and rich language.

To PLAY:

1. Ask one child to come up and feel an object in the bag and describe it to you so that you can guess what it might be. When you or the other children have guessed what the object is they can pull it out of the bag.

2. Choose another child and repeat the process until all the children have had a go.

3. For older children, gather leaves and nuts or fruit from the same trees, e.g. oak leaf and acorn, conker and horse chestnut leaf. After the children know the pairings, place three or more pairs in the bag and see if they can retrieve a pair by feel.

YOU WILL NEED:
- Bag with drawstring
- Natural objects in the bag, such as a conker, pine cone, sloe berry or beechmast

Spiders and Flies Game

This game works best in a space where there are trees at fairly equal distances from each other, with room to run around. The object of the game is for the spider to catch the flies.

To PLAY:

1. One person is the spider and defends their web – a space between two trees. The flies have to run through the space without the spider catching them. If the spider catches them they become spiders and help to catch the flies.

2. When there are too many spiders in the space, they can spin another web between two trees and the remaining flies can choose which web to run through.

3. The game is over when there are only one or two flies left. You could use the game as an opportunity to share more about spiders and their lives.

Secret Squirrels Game

The squirrels are at their busiest at this time of year. There is so much to do! They must seek and gather, stashing their stores in secret places. Ask the children to imagine being squirrels and to look for nuts or berries. Ask the children to imagine, as squirrels, what they should do if they see a fox. Foxes cannot climb, so they will need to climb to be safe. A sparrowhawk can fly through the trees with great agility; the squirrel's best chance is to be completely still and silent. A pine marten is an excellent climber, but is much larger than a squirrel. The squirrel must find a small place to hide. This is a fun game to play whilst walking to a destination.

TO PLAY:

1. The children are the squirrels. The adults in the group are the predators. The predators are Fox, Pine Marten and Sparrowhawk.

2. The children walk along and the adult calls, 'Fox is prowling!' The adult assumes a foxy prowl and tries to catch the children before they can climb to a safe place off the ground. After passing by, the adult calls, 'Fox has gone!' and the children carry on walking.

3. When the children hear the adult call, 'Pine Marten is about!' they must find a small place to hide. When the adult calls, 'Pine Marten has gone!' they can carry on walking again.

4. When the call, 'Sparrowhawk!' comes, everyone is completely still. The adult spreads out their arms, like wings, and flies among the children, looking to spot any movement. When the adult calls, 'Sparrowhawk has gone!' everyone can carry on walking.

5. These calls can be given in any order and in any frequency. It helps to focus the group and is fun to play on a walk or whilst the squirrel-children gather acorns or nuts from the ground.

Autumn Plant Lore

It is the season for wild fruits. See them hanging from the trees and like jewels in the hedgerows. Nature provides exactly what we need to make our bodies strong and resilient for the winter ahead, and these fruits taste delicious too.

Hawthorn berries can improve our circulation, and blackberries strengthen us to resist the coughs and colds of autumn. Apples are the fruit of good health; as the old saying goes: 'An apple a day keeps the doctor away.'

Bramble

GAELIC NAME: *Dris* (from the root *rys* meaning 'entangle'. In Gaelic the word *dris* is used for both bramble and briar.)

LATIN NAMES: *Rubus fruticosus*

OGHAM: *Muin* (the letter M)

Character

I am Bramble, with blackberries sweet.

I am strong and thorny, growing in hedge and glade.

I grow vigorous and fast in spring and my green tendrils weave sharp thickets.

Leaves of five and tenacious hooks protect my pale, rose-pink flowers.

Some call me the Mother of Oak, for in my thorny shelter tiny trees may grow ungrazed. I protect little ones from hunters too.

I stand my ground, so beware! Those who force their way through me, I will cut and ensnare. I hold strong with tenacious roots.

You may find all my phases still upon my autumn form: bud and flower, berries green, red and black.

With due respect, I am generous too and have many gifts to share.

Gifts

For cuts that I may give, chew my young leaves and apply; I will heal your bleeding skin.

My fresh tendrils, when stripped, weave a basket to hold your wares.

My roots dye cloth a golden hue.

In beautiful procession I offer my ripe blackberries to give you my gift of strength, resilience and protection for the cold months ahead.

The Bramble Dance

Go with the children and take time to look at the bramble and see how it grows. See how its tendrils grow long and strong, weaving their way. Notice the pattern of five in the leaves and blossom. This dance is a fun way to be 'like' the bramble.

To play:

1. In preparation for the dance, reach up, holding hands. Now break the circle in two opposite places by asking the relevant children to let go of each other's hands. Choose one half of the circle to be the 'bramble' and the other to be the 'hedgerow'.

2. Both groups will keep holding hands. Explain that, when the time comes in the song, the hedgerow half will raise their arms up to form archways. The bramble line will then dance in and out of the archways in a clockwise direction until they reach the other end, where they continue round to form the circle again. It's a good idea to practise this.

3. The dance begins with the chorus. Count to four out loud as you get ready to begin:

I am the bramble, see me grow

Circle altogether holding hands for the count of four clockwise.

Weaving thickets as I go

Change direction and circle anticlockwise for the count of our.

Leaves of five and flowers too

Let go of each other's hands and hold hands up with fingers splayed (like the five of the leaves and flowers). Skip into the middle of the circle to the count of three, then clap on the last beat of four.

Blackberries sweet I give to you

Skip back to the circle and prepare to dance the bramble! The hedgerow children raise the archway, while the bramble children prepare to weave.

Tra la la la la, through the hedgerow I grow
Tra la la la la, watch me grow (x 2)

The bramble line weaves in and out of the hedgerow children until it reaches the end and continues back round into the circle.

4. The hedgerow line now holds hands with the end of the bramble line and prepares for the verse, in which the front bramble child will lead the whole group.

5. While the verse is sung, the whole group can weave the dance in a long line, like a giant bramble tendril, in and out of the trees, while staying close enough to hear the song. This is the bramble's wild and free nature.

6. At the end of the verse, play the drum or clap for four beats while the circle reforms for the chorus. Now repeat the dance until it is all sung. The hedgerow and bramble can swap over for each chorus.

Simple version for younger children

1. Only sing the chorus and miss out the verses. Circle around for four beats clockwise then circle round for four anticlockwise. Skip in for three and clap on four. Skip out for four.

2. Dance the bramble–hedgerow as described previously. When the bramble line has completed the weave and reformed as a circle, they become the hedgerow and make an arch. The other half becomes the bramble and begins to weave. You may need to sing the 'Tra la la la la' section twice.

Song of the Bramble

By Anna Richardson

Lively and fast

CHORUS

I am the Bram - ble, see me grow, Weav - ing thick - ets as I go.

Leaves of five and flow - ers too, Black - be - rries sweet, I gi - ve to you.

Tra - la - la - la - la, through the hedge - row I go. Tra - la - la - la - la - la, watch me grow.

Tra - la - la - la - la, through the hedge - row I go, Tra - la - la - la - la - la, watch me grow. In

VERSE 1

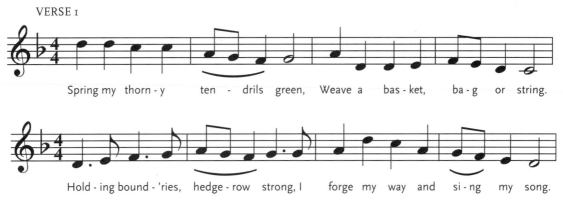

Spring my thorn - y ten - drils green, Weave a bas - ket, ba - g or string.

Hold - ing bound - 'ries, hedge - row strong, I forge my way and si - ng my song.

Verses 2–4 overleaf.

I am the Bram-ble, see me grow,
Weaving thickets as I go.
Leaves of five and flowers too,
Blackberries sweet I give to you.
Tra la la la la, through the hedge-row I go.
Tra la la la la la, watch me grow.
Tra la la la la, through the hedge-row I go.
Tra la la la la la, watch me grow.

1. In spring my thorny tendrils green,
Weave a basket, bag or string.
Holding bound 'ries, hedgerow strong,
I forge my way and sing my song.

CHORUS

2. Blackberry blossom rambling free,
Favoured by the honeybee,
Flowers and leaves a wound to bind,
I dance and grow through summertime.

CHORUS

3. When nights grow cool across the land,
See my berries hand in hand,
Green to red to blackberries sweet,
A hedgerow feast for all to eat.

CHORUS

4. Fairy castle, forest deep,
A hundred years enchanted sleep,
Only those who are true of heart,
Through my thickets a path may part.

Hawthorn and Blackberry Honey

TO MAKE:

1. Gather the berries and de-stalk the haws. Place them in a pan, cover with water, plus a bit extra. Bring to the boil and simmer gently for about 20 minutes until the haws are soft. Check the water levels – the berries need to be just covered by water.

2. Now sieve the whole lot and, using the back of a spoon, squish the fruit pulp through the mesh, as much as possible. Once you have been squishing for a while, it works well to tip the sieve contents back into the pan with the liquid from the jug, mix and sieve again.

3. Now add ample honey to the jammy syrup so that it tastes good. This syrup can also be added to stewed apple.

YOU WILL NEED:
- Hawthorn berries
- Blackberries
- Honey
- Water
- Pan
- Sieve
- Spoon
- Jug
- Fire

Elder Song

Lyrics by Helen d'Ascoli
Traditional melody

'El - der El - der have you got a cure?' 'Yes sir, yes sir,

three or more. Flo - wers for a fe - ver, berr - ies for a cough,

Leaves to keep mos - quit - oes off. Re - mem - ber I am a

fae - ry tree, So please take good care of me.'

Autumn Tree Lore

Apple

GAELIC NAMES: *Craobh ubhal fiadhain* (meaning 'wild apple tree')
LATIN NAME: *Malus sylvestris* and *Malus domestica*

OGHAM: *Quert* (the letter Q)

Essence
Cleansing ~ Generous Heart ~ Health

Character

I am Apple, Tree of Generosity.

I love to share my abundant fruit, my rosy apples. I am in the rose family.

In spring, my rosy pink blossoms bear the pattern of five. Within me is a secret star.

I am Crab Apple, ancient apple of this land. I bear small green fruit and protect my branches with thorns.

A long time ago, people travelled far to the east. They came to the Tian Shan Mountains, known as the Celestial Mountains in China, where my larger, sweeter relations grew in abundance in beautiful valleys. They returned to Britain with the precious seeds and since that time we have grown side by side for many generations, domestic apples grown and tended by people, while my wild thorny crab apple trees grow like hidden treasure in the forests, feeding the animals in autumn. We both have the hidden star inside.

Even today, when much has been lost in these old friendships between people and trees, I have continued to be honoured by the old tradition of wassailing in winter. People thank me with song and dance, cake and cider... blessings to help me grow and give again in seasons to come.

I have been held in high esteem since long ago, and the sacred mistletoe that grows in my boughs has been used for healing. My seeds have been used for divination and I may bestow wisdom and otherworldly gifts.

Gifts

Come and enjoy my trees and fruit. I will cleanse you and bring you gladness and health. I can show you how to give generously and with an open heart, trusting that you will receive all you need in return.

Visit me in autumn and see the great abundance of nourishment the Earth provides. Share my apples with those you love.

My wood is hard and strong, a beautiful pinkish-orange hue, not easy to carve. It is used for the cog teeth in wind and water mills, as well as tools such as engravers' blocks and set squares, for its strength. I lend to the wood a quality of heart which makes it perfect for carving a talisman of friendship and love.

I burn hot and fragrant on the fire. Share my warmth and light.

My bark and leaves can be used to dye wool yellow-green.

My apples are good medicine, full of minerals and vitamins. They help your digestion, cleanse, heal wounds and burns and restore your health. My juice, cider and vinegar are some of the ways my goodness is shared. I store well over winter.

You may also slice my apples and thread them on a string to dry them in rings.

My crab apples are sour but when cooked become sweeter, like sloes. They were cooked by your ancestors on hot rocks by the fire. Stew my apples and bake in pies and crumbles, tarts and cakes. Share with friends and family round the table or the fire.

Crab Apples on Sticks

TO MAKE:

1. Gather crab apples, at least a couple per person. You can use other small apples too.

2. Find or cut one stick per person and whittle one end to a point. Insert the stick into the apple and roast slowly, like a marshmallow, over the embers, turning slowly and constantly. Flame cooking does not work well, so use a well-established fire and create a hot ember bed for the best results.

3. This activity is perfect whilst listening to a seasonal story, as it takes a while for the apples to cook. The skin will become burnt, but the apple inside will be soft and sweet.

4. Once it is cooked, cool it by dipping in a bowl of cold water, then peel off the burnt skin and dip into hawthorn and blackberry honey (see p 218). Enjoy!

YOU WILL NEED:
- Crab (or other) apples
- Sticks
- Fire

Elderberry Syrup

Elderberry syrup is one of most wonderful hedgerow medicines. Elderberries strengthen our body's resistance to illness, especially from colds and flu, and are good for treating a cough. Elderberries can be simmered and made into a tea, adding honey to taste. Here is a delicious, sugar-free alternative to making a cordial:

TO MAKE:

1. Simmer the berries in the water for about half an hour (or until the liquid is reduced by half). As it simmers, you can add extra spices – star anise, cloves and cinnamon are all delicious and warming, and, along with elder, help heal the colds and flus of this time of year.

2. Strain the berries and allow the liquid to cool a little.

3. Return the deep purple liquid to the pan over the fire, and add the honey, stirring for a few minutes until the honey is melted.

4. Remove the pan from the fire and, if desired, mix in the brandy. The brandy acts as a preservative if you intend to store the syrup. When it is diluted with hot water and allowed to sit for a few minutes, the alcohol evaporates, leaving a warming, health-giving, delicious elderberry drink.

YOU WILL NEED:

- 1 cup elderberries (destalked and excluding any green or withered berries)
- 4 cups water
- 1 cup honey
- ½ cup brandy (optional)
- Spices such as cloves, star anise and cinnamon (optional)

Here's to Thee, Old Apple Tree

A traditional wassailing song from Devon.
Published in The Gentleman's Magazine *1791*

Slow and strong

Here's to thee old Ap - ple tree, Whence

th - ou may - est bud. And

whence thou may - est bl - ow, And

whence thou may - est bear ap - ples e - now.

Hats full, caps full,

Bush - els full and sacks full,

And our pock - ets full to - o.

And our pock - ets full to - o.

HOORAH! HOORAH! (shout out at end of song)

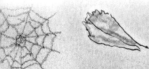

Blackthorn

GAELIC NAMES: *Preas nan airneag* (meaning 'sloe bush')
Droighionn dùbh ('the black piercer', from *druid* – to pierce)
LATIN NAME: *Prunus spinosa*

OGHAM: *Straif* (the letter Z)

Essence
Protection ~ Challenge ~ Respect

Character

I am Blackthorn, who bears the sloe.

I am the Tree of Challenge and Protection.

For many ages I have grown here, calling in the spring with my delicate white blossom.

I am hardy and strong, and bloom even while the ice-cold breath of the Cailleach, Lady of Winter, blows her last across the land and others hide in sleep.

I show you too how to rise to the challenge of life, with acceptance and strength.

After my flowers, my leaves follow, grey-green and oval amongst my sharp and menacing spines. I am Grandmother Blackthorn and I demand respect.

My long thorns can cause you great harm: take care, and if I wound you, you may need medicine to heal you.

I have much to teach you about protection, keeping out those you don't want near you.

I am often planted in hedges with my close companion, Whitethorn, who you may know as Hawthorn. We hold the boundaries.

I am the ancient wild plum and through the ages have been gathered and cooked, giving my nourishment to people and to animals of many kinds.

Come in autumn and gather my purple-black sloes after the first frost. I challenge you to eat one raw!

When the fruits are soft, I will share my hidden sweetness with you.

Gifts

My wood is hard and tough, like my nature. I have been used for fighting sticks and cudgels. I rise to the challenge! I make beautiful polished walking sticks and staffs to help protect you on your journeys.

My sloes, tiny round plums, are well known for making gin these days, but offer far more as food. Cook me with apple as stewed fruit with honey, spitting out the stones of course. I am delicious when cooked – in jams, pies and crumbles, or made into a fruit leather.

Here are a couple of secrets. My sloes are sweeter after the frost. Also, if you roll a sloe for a while in your hands, as you walk along, it becomes bruised and the skin will split slightly. Try eating the sloe – you may be surprised at the secret sweetness I carry beneath my sour appearance.

I help you find the hidden sweetness within difficult situations. You can also cook my sloes on rocks by the fire, as your ancestors once did.

My flowers can be made into tea to treat fevers and as a gentle digestive medicine. My leaves, infused, make a gargle for sore throats, or, cooled, soothe sore eyes.

Take care as you gather me; come in respect and I will share my gifts.

Grandmother Blackthorn

By Lucinda Warner

Lively

Out in the hedge - row the Black - thorn is grow - ing,

Spring time is com - ing and sap is a flow - ing.

Clouds of white bloss - om and soon the leaves fo - llow,

Ripe black sloes in aut - umn will come.

Grand moth - er Black - thorn, we thank you well.

Put on your boots for it's time to go gather,
North wind is blowing and cold grows the weather.
Watch out for thorns as we fill up our baskets with
Ripe black sloes in autumn time.
Grandmother Blackthorn, we thank you well.

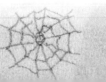

Thorn Trees

A simple rhyme to help children distinguish between blackthorn and hawthorn.

Blackthorn blossoms, white as snow,
Bloom when Hawthorn's green leaves grow.
Hawthorn flowers
In May are cream,
When Blackthorn leaves are oval green.
Blackthorn bears the purple sloe,
As Hawthorns red in hedgerows glow.
Thorn trees rest in wintertime;
Friends of old, with roots entwined.

Autumn Animals

Blackbird

I am Blackbird, with feathers of black and beak of yellow. A golden yellow ring circles my bright eye. My mate has a duller beak and her feathers are not black at all, but speckled brown. Her colours help her to blend in as she sits on our nest, which keeps our babies safe from hungry cats and foxes.

I love to sing from my treetop perch. Hear my fluting song, bright and clear as liquid crystal. I especially like to sing after the rain.

If I see a cat, I will call out, 'Danger! danger!' See how I flick my wings and cry, 'Chip, chip, chip, chip, chip, chip!'

In days of old, we blackbirds lived in the thick of the forests. Our loud, powerful song helped us to communicate through the dense leaf canopy. Now we love to come into your gardens too, and sing our songs from fence posts as well as treetops – we love to feast on the earthworms and insects who live in your lawns. In the autumn, you can watch us eating the ripe red berries of the rowan and the holly and see us feasting on windfall apples.

Red Squirrel

I am Red Squirrel, with tufty ears and fluffy tail. My bushy tail helps me balance and steer as I leap from tree to tree. It keeps my nose warm when I snuggle down to sleep. My fur is russet red and I have a creamy-white tummy.

These days, I am rarely seen in England and Wales; instead you will see my grey cousin, who was brought by your people from America. I still live in Scotland, in the Lake District and on the Isle of Wight. Find me nibbling spruce and pine seeds. I am fond of berries and fungi too. In the autumn I am very busy, storing food for winter in nooks and crannies, in the trunks of trees and below the ground.

Sometimes I hide my seeds in the earth and forget where I hid them, and so I help new plants to grow!

I live in the trees, but I can swim too! I make large, round nests of twigs, lined with moss and grass. Spot them high among the trees, in the forks of branches or against the tree trunk. I make several dreys (nests) as I roam far around the forest. You may find my feasting tables in the woods – look for the nibbled pine cones I leave behind.

Autumn Celebration

An Edible Mandala

Autumn is a special time of balance, when day and night are an equal length. Look with the children at the trees and see how some of the leaves are starting to change colour: the energy of the tree is moving towards the roots for the coming winter. This is the time of gathering, harvest and celebration. We share nature's gifts with the animals.

To prepare:

1. Prepare the fire and feasting area. Come together and share the essence of a mandala; a flower-like pattern created as a form of meditation. Send the children out to find berries, nuts and glowing autumn leaves. This gathering can also be done together on a walk.

2. Create the mandala by clearing a circle in the forest. Place the candle in the middle. Carefully place the berries, nuts, leaves and seeds in a beautiful pattern extending outwards from the light. It is a time for contemplation and working quietly together.

3. When the mandala is complete, each person gives thanks for some aspect of autumn that they love. Form a circle and, holding hands, go round the mandala singing a seasonal song. Children might try closing their eyes for half the circle as they turn, to give a sense of the equal dark and light at this time of year.

4. Finally, make a wish of goodwill for the animals, that they might have enough food to eat in the winter to come. This edible mandala is a gift for them.

5. Afterwards, feast and tell stories by the fire. Remember to blow out the candle and take it with you when you leave.

You will need:
- Gathered autumn treasure, such as chestnuts, acorns and hazelnuts, rosehips, blackberries, apples and hawthorns
- Berry tea and cups
- Food to share (such as crab apples and hawthorn honey)
- Fire
- Beeswax candle

Samhain

Samhain, from the Gaelic word meaning 'summer's end', is half-way between the autumn equinox and the winter solstice. It is akin to bedtime in the cycle of day and night. In Britain, the clocks go back, and the evenings are dark. It is the turning point when autumn moves towards the cold of winter. Jack Frost visits in the night and, as the sun rises, the world is transformed by the sparkle of crystals. Once again, we wear our hats and gloves and scarves, wrapping up warm.

The Forest at Samhain

In the woods, the last of the autumn leaves are falling. The growing season has ended. The trees breathe out, shedding their leaves and their seeds. Death and birth nourish life. All over the land, seeds make their journeys to their new homes in the earth, with thanks to the wind, birds and animals. Only a few will survive. They nestle into the dark beds of soils, under leafy blankets of autumn colour.

Mushrooms appear overnight, their underground webs connecting the roots of the trees. In the hedgerows, see bright berries shine. Taste the pulp of the rosehips. Hear the buzz of bees drinking the last of the year's nectar from the honey-scented ivy flowers. Gather fallen nuts and roast them over warm fires. Summer birds have flown. Hedgehogs and dormice snuggle deep in their cosy dwellings, beginning their long winter sleep. Ladybirds hibernate together in hollows.

The trees take their energy, and their sap, deep down into their roots. The soil they rest in is made of thousands of seasons of leaves, and generations of trees, plants and animals – all those who have lived before.

A Story for Samhain

Vasilisa

A folktale from Russia

In a certain kingdom, in a certain land, there lived a merchant and his wife. They had only one child, a daughter called Vasilisa.

When Vasilisa was only eight years old, her mother died. On her deathbed, her mother took Vasilisa's hands. 'Listen Vasilisushka,' she said. 'Heed my last words. I leave you my blessing, and this..." And from beneath the blankets of the bed, she brought out a little doll and gave it to Vasilisa.

Vasilisa's mother had made the doll herself, stitched it and sewn it and stuffed it with sheep's wool and mother's love. Its boots were black. Its apron white. Its dress was red as a rosehip.

'Keep this doll with you always. If you lose your way, or if you need help, ask the doll what to do. Feed her when she is hungry. She will help you.' The mother kissed her daughter, breathed out, and died.

After her death, Vasilisa and her father grieved for a long time. After a long time, Vasilisa'a father began to think of marrying again. For there was a widow in the village who had two daughters of her own, almost the same age as Vasilisa. 'And surely', thought the merchant, 'she has been a good mother to her own children; she will know how to care for my Vasilisa.'

But the stepmother did not care for Vasilisa. She was jealous of Vasilisa's beauty and her goodness. The stepmother made Vasilisa do all the work, hoping she would grow thin from toil and burnt from wind and sun.

'Weed the garden, Vasilisa. Fire the stove, Vasilisa. Fetch the water, Vasilisa.'

But Vasilisa worked without complaining, and every day grew stronger and more lovely, while the stepmother and her daughters grew thin and pinched from spite, though they never dirtied their hands with work.

At mealtimes, Vasilisa kept the choicest morsels from her dish to give to her doll.

And at the end of the day, Vasilisa laid out the food before her doll, and shared with her the secrets of her heart. She held her doll close and poured out her sorrows. The little doll always listened, and Vasilisa was comforted.

One day, Vasilisa's father went away for a long time, to trade in distant lands. While he was away, the stepmother moved the family to a house at the edge of the deep forest. In the centre of the forest was a clearing. In the centre of the clearing was a fence, built of bones. At the top of each bone was a skull, and inside each skull was a flame. Within this ring of bones, in a little wooden hut, lived Baba Yaga. Baba Yaga Bony-Legs, Baba Yaga the witch! Baba Yaga who ate children as if they were chickens. That's what they said.

The stepmother was forever sending Vasilisa into the forest, hoping she would get lost and be eaten up by Baba Yaga. 'Go into the woods for kindling, Vasilisa. Gather mushrooms in the forest, Vasilisa.'

One evening, Vasilisa did find herself lost in the dark forest. But she always had her doll with her. Vasilisa could feel the doll in her apron pocket. And just holding the doll close made her feel better. Pausing at the fork in the path, Vasilisa almost thought she heard the doll speak, though it was the faintest whisper: 'Vasilisushka...'

Vasilisa found that the more she listened, the clearer the doll's voice grew. The doll always showed Vasilisa the way home.

It was the brown end of autumn. The trees were letting go of their leaves and the evenings were drawing in. The stepmother gave evening work to all three girls. The oldest was to weave lace, the second to knit stockings, and Vasilisa to spin flax into thread.

One night, at the gateway between the light and the dark of the year, the stepmother went around the house, putting out all the lights. She left only one candle, in the room where the girls were working, and she went to bed.

'The candle is smoky,' said the younger stepsister. 'I'll trim the wick,' and as if by accident, she snuffed the light out. 'Oops! The candle has gone out. Someone will have to go and get a light. Someone will have to go out and get a light from Baba Yaga.'

'I won't go,' said the first sister. 'I can see my pins.'

'I won't go,' said the second sister. 'I can see my needles.'

'You go!' they both cried to Vasilisa, and they bundled her out of the door.

Vasilisa stumbled out into the howling night. The wind stung her ears. The trees creaked and groaned. Vasilisa jumped at every leaf rattle, turned at every twig crack.

She clutched her doll. Even though her heart was hammering, she listened.

'Fear not, Vasilisushka,' she heard. 'I am always with you. You will come to no harm

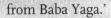

from Baba Yaga.'

Hour after hour, Vasilisa walked through the dark.

What was that noise? Horse's hooves. A man on horseback galloped past. He was all in white: his hair was white, his cloak was white, his horse was white. As he passed, daybreak followed.

Vasilisa walked. Another horseman galloped past, all in red. Red hair, red cloak, red horse. The sun began to rise.

Vasilisa walked the whole day. The light didn't last long. Again, the thunder of hooves. Again, a horseman rode by; black hair, black cloak, black horse. He disappeared like a shadow and night fell.

In the centre of the forest, there was the clearing. In the centre of the clearing, there was the fence of bones. At the top of each fence post was a skull. Inside each skull was a flame. The eyes flickered. And there was the hut, standing on four crooked chicken legs. It danced about, turning round and round, round and round.

Vasilisa was numb with horror. She stood, clutching the doll in her pocket. Then, behind her back, she heard trees crackling, leaves rustling. And out from the forest came Baba Yaga, riding in her mortar, her great grinding pot, driving it along with her pestle. As she flew, she swept away her tracks with her broom.

Baba Yaga rode to the gate and she stopped. Her nostrils quivered. She sucked in the air with her long nose. 'I smell someone. Who's there?'

Vasilisa could hardly speak. She bowed low to Baba Yaga. 'I... I... It is I, Grandmother. My stepsisters sent me to get a light.'

'Hmm... I know them,' said Baba Yaga. 'Very well, I will give you a light, but you will work for it. And if you don't, I'll eat you up.'

Then Baba Yaga turned to the door. 'Bolts, unlock! Gate, open!'

And the door of the hut creaked open. Baba Yaga went in, whistling. Vasilisa followed. Creeeak. Click. The door closed behind her.

Baba Yaga stretched herself out in her chair. She looked at Vasilisa. 'I am hungry. Serve my dinner.' Vasilisa took a glowing skull to light the stove. Inside was enough food for ten men. Baba Yaga ate it all, slurping and crunching and smacking her lips. Vasilisa brought kvass and mead, beer and wine, and Baba Yaga gulped it all down.

All that was left for Vasilisa was a crust of bread. She put the food in her pocket for her doll.

Baba Yaga made ready to go to bed. 'Tomorrow,' said Baba Yaga, 'when I go out, see that you sweep the yard and clean the hut, cook the dinner and wash the linen. Then go to the corn bin and sort out the wheat. Separate the grain from the chaff. Be sure that everything is completed. If it is not complete…' Baba Yaga drew closer. Vasilisa could smell her hot breath. '…I will eat you.'

Then Baba Yaga climbed onto the plank-bed on top of the stove, turned her back on Vasilisa and began to snore.

'What shall I do?' Vasilisa said to her doll. 'How can I sort the wheat from the chaff? There are thousands of grains, millions…'

Vasilisa held her doll close and she listened. And in its own way the doll answered: 'Eat your supper, say your prayers and go to sleep. The morning is wiser than the evening.' So, holding her doll to her heart, Vasilisa slept.

She woke early. She saw the white horseman flash past the window; it was daybreak. Baba Yaga went out into the yard and she whistled. The pestle, mortar and broom appeared before her. The red horseman flashed by, the sun rose and away she swept.

Vasilisa was left alone. She looked about, wondering where to begin. But what was this? Her doll was sitting atop a heap of golden grain, the last husks of chaff on her lap. All the work was done. 'Just cook the dinner, and then rest,' said her doll, 'for the sake of your health.'

When evening came, Vasilisa set the table. She waited. Dusk began to fall, the black horseman flashed by – night came. Only the skulls were shining. Then the trees began to crackle, the leaves to rustle. Baba Yaga was coming.

Vasilisa met her. 'Is everything done?' asked Baba Yaga.

'Please see for yourself, Grandmother.'

Baba Yaga looked. 'Nyah!' There was nothing for her to complain about. Baba Yaga called out, 'My faithful servants, my dear friends, grind the wheat into flour.'

From nowhere, three pairs of hands appeared, took the wheat and carried it away out of sight.

Baba Yaga ate her fill and again gave her orders. 'Tomorrow, do the same work you have done today. And, someone has spoiled my poppy seeds; they are all covered with dust. Take the poppy seed from the bin and sort out the seed from the dust, grain by grain.' The old witch turned to the wall and began to snore.

'What shall I do?' Vasilisa said to her doll. 'How can I sort the seed from the dust? There are millions of seeds, millions of millions…' Vasilisa felt she could cry.

But again she heard her doll: 'Say your prayers and go to sleep. The morning is wiser than the evening. Everything will be done, Vasilisushka.'

Next day, again, Baba Yaga swept away in her mortar, and, with the help of her doll, Vasilisa soon found all the work complete. The old witch looked at everything and called, 'My faithful servants, my dear friends, press the seed into oil.' Again, the three pairs of hands appeared, took the poppy seed, and carried it out of sight.

Baba Yaga sat down to eat. Vasilisa stood silent. 'Why do you not speak to me?' said Baba Yaga.

'I did not dare to speak, Grandmother, but if you will give me leave I'd like to ask a question.'

'Go ahead, but not every question has a good answer. Those who know too much soon grow old.'

'I want to ask you, Grandmother, only of what I have seen. As I was on my way to you I saw three horsemen, one all in white, one in red, one black. Who were they?'

'They are my faithful servants. The red horseman is my red sun, the white horseman is my bright day, and the black horseman is my dark night. Why don't you ask more?'

Vasilisa remembered the three pairs of hands, but she kept silent. 'As you said yourself, Grandmother, one who knows too much soon grows old.'

Baba Yaga smiled a knowing smile. 'It is well you asked me only about what you saw outside my house, and not what you saw inside my house. I do not like my dirty linen washed in public, and I eat the over-curious. Now, I have a question for you: how is it that you complete the tasks I set?'

'Why,' said Vasilisa, 'I am helped by the blessing of my mother.'

'Nyah!' shrieked Baba Yaga. 'I want no blessed ones in my house. Take your light and begone.' Baba Yaga twisted a skull onto a staff and thrust it into Vasilisa's hand. The skull began to blaze with fire.

By the light of the skull, Vasilisa ran homewards. As she came to the gate, she thought to throw the skull away. But the skull ground round on the staff and fixed Vasilisa with its flaming eyes. 'Take me to your stepmother.'

'You!' the stepmother glared at Vasilisa. 'What took you so long? Ever since you left, the candles won't light, the fire won't burn.'

Vasilisa held up the skull, and the fire leapt out, like a living thing. The stepmother and stepsisters were burnt to ashes. In the morning, Vasilisa buried the skull in the earth, and closed the door of the house behind her. And after that, well, I wonder...

Perhaps, while she waited for her father to return, she went to live in the village with one of the old women there. A white-haired old woman with bony legs and a knowing smile. Perhaps she spun cloth so fine her shirts were fit for the Tsar himself. Perhaps she travelled, fell in love, married. After all, anything is possible for a girl with a spark of fire. One thing I do know, Vasilisa carried her doll in her pocket always. For it was the doll who told me this story, when I held her close, and listened.

Samhain Imaginary Journey

🌿 The trees are getting ready for their winter sleep, deep in their roots. It is time to go within. Provided the forest floor is dry, ask the children to clear a little space in the leaf litter, creating a deer bed. Ask them to lie down and curl up in a comfy position. Cover them lightly in an autumn leaf blanket.

🌿 Close your eyes. Breathe deeply and relax. You are safe in your deer bed, ready to dream.

🌿 Imagine before you the hugest tree you have ever seen, reaching up, up into the sky. It is full of life, beautiful to behold. Animals are grazing beneath it and as you look up you see birds, animals and insects of all sizes and colours, flying, moving, singing and humming in the branches. The branches reach up and up, past darting swallows, singing skylarks and the high, circling buzzards and eagles... through the clouds the tree grows. The highest leaves are touching the stars.

🌿 Walk towards the tree and feel the rough bark beneath your fingers. You notice there is an opening in the huge roots. You go through and find yourself on a dimly lit path leading to a stairway made of roots, spiralling down. You follow the roots, down, down into the Earth. You feel safe and guided. You can smell the cool, damp earth and feel it with your fingers on the wall as you pass. You arrive in a cave. The cave of dreams. This is a sacred place. There is a pool of crystal clear water in this cave. The pool contains a message or gift for you. You approach with deep respect. Looking into the water you may see an image or hear a message coming from the pool of dreams, especially for you. (Pause and give time...)

🌿 Give thanks for your gift and ask if there is anything for you to give or do in return. (Pause...) It is time to start climbing back up the stairs of the great tree's roots... up, up, up. Step through the opening into the light. Turn and look once more at the great tree before you go. It lives inside you, the Tree of Life. Breathe in its beauty, life and magic to take with you into the darker time of year. Breathe out, sharing your life breath with the tree. Open your eyes and gently sit up in your deer bed. Feel your roots reaching deep into the earth beneath you. Stretch your arms up, reaching to the stars.

Samhain Activities, Crafts and Games

Seed Treasure

Seeds are tiny cases of living treasure. Within each seed lies the spark of new life. A small acorn holds all the magic inside it to grow into a mighty oak. The tiny seed of birch contains a whole, graceful birch tree. Throughout the autumn, plants send their children, as seeds, into the world on a perilous journey. They travel by wind, by bird or by animal, in the hope that some will find sanctuary in the soil of the earth to bed down until spring. Of tree seeds, less than one in a thousand may grow into an adult to have children of their own.

Seeds come in many shapes, colours and sizes. They have special boxes or cases, designed to protect them until they are ready to grow, just as an egg has a shell. Some have hard shells, like hazelnuts. These seeds have food inside to feed them as they grow. This food is also tasty to other beings such as squirrels. Nature is a dance of give and take. The squirrel buries its nuts for the cold months ahead, and forgets where some are, so helping to plant the trees.

Some seeds are shaped with wings to help them to fly through the air. Sycamore spins like a helicopter. Birch seeds, with their bird-shaped wings, fly in flocks on a gust of wind.

Some plants, like rowan or rose, house their seeds inside a fruit. As the seed ripens, the colour of the fruit changes. When the seed is ripe, the berries become shiny red to attract the birds who love to eat them. The fruit feeds the birds and meanwhile the seed goes on a journey in their tummy, through the air, from place to place, and in time will land in their poo, with a generous helping of nature's finest compost.

In many forms and different ways, the seed children of the plants make their journeys, away from their parents, in the hope of finding all they need to grow.

Seed Hunt

Late autumn is a perfect time to go on a seed hunt. Gather ripe seeds from trees and plants in a leaf cone or pot. Set the children the challenge to notice which tree is the parent of the seeds that they are gathering, and where they like to grow. Hawthorn likes to grow on the edge of a woodland, alder by water. We pay attention so that later we can help plant or disperse the seeds in the places that will help them grow.

When the seeds have been gathered, lay out a plain sheet or cloth and empty the seeds out carefully. Here they can be sorted into different piles. Discussions can be had about how each type of seed is making its journey. By air? Or as tasty food for animals? Use magnifying glasses and eye lenses to look closely at the seeds' beautiful shapes and textures. Here is another world of the plants: intricate and miraculous.

Seed Fun

Invent and play seed games.
Here are some examples:

· Ask people to close their eyes and recognise a seed by feel.

· Give each child a seed in their hand and when you say, 'Ready steady go,' each child runs to the plant or tree their seed could have come from.

· Seed fireworks are fun. Everyone gathers a handful of sycamore seeds. Stand in a bunch facing outwards and count down from 10, then throw the seeds as high as you can.

· Gather the ripe birch seed catkins and rub them to separate the seeds. Give a friend a birch seed shower.

· Play boules with conkers.

Seed Bedtime

It is the turning in of the year. The trees take their energy down into their roots and the seeds make their journeys to bed in the earth.

Gather a selection of seeds in a leaf cone or pot and find places they might like to grow. Acorns like to be buried. Sycamore and ash seeds can be placed on the soil's surface, tucked up under some autumn leaves. Hawthorn and rowan berries need to be placed somewhere visible for the birds or animals, or take some home to place on a bird table.

For younger children, engage their imagination in putting the seeds to bed. The gnomes are Mother Nature's helpers. Make clay or felt gnomes and go with them to gather seeds and to find places to put the seeds to bed, tucking them up under leafy blankets. The children can also imagine being seeds themselves. They could be a swirling sycamore seed or an acorn. Ask them, as a seed, to tumble and swirl and to find a nice place to land on the woodland floor. There they can lie down or curl up. Ask them to close their eyes and imagine going to sleep. Visit each child and sprinkle some autumn leaves over them as a blanket. You may like to sing 'Goodnight Little Seeds' (see p 244).

Goodnight Little Seeds

By Anna Richardson

Gentle and quiet

Good - night   lit - tle seeds, good - night.   Sleep well, your jour - ney's at an   end.

Moth - er Earth will   hold   yo - u   as   you   rest.   Dream

now   till   the   spring re   -   turns a   -   gain.

Leaf Cones

This simple leaf container is perfect for gathering forest treasures such as seeds.

To make:

1. Take off the stalk and keep it safe. Hold onto the bottom of the leaf and roll one side around, pulling the other side tightly round to meet it, keeping it closed at the bottom, whilst helping the top of the leaf to make a cone-like shape, as wide as possible. Making a cone shape may take a bit of practice!

2. When you have made a cone, pin it together with the stalk, or a thin stick such as a birch twig, by weaving it in and out of the leaf join, like a stitch. This works best longwise, from the bottom to the top of the cone.

3. You now have a cone to hold seeds and to gather treasures such as acorns. The leaf cone can also be useful for holding popcorn as you sit by the fire.

You will need:

- A large sycamore leaf

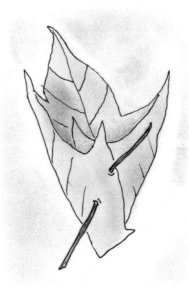

Besom Brooms

Celtic New Year is celebrated at this time, honouring the dead and welcoming in the new souls. Birch is recognised as the tree of new beginnings and is traditionally made into brooms to sweep away the old and cleanse the space for the new to arrive. The leaves have fallen, the seeds have flown and the tree's energy has moved into the roots for winter's sleep. It is a good time to re-spectfully harvest some of the silver birch's dark purple twigs... Halloween is here – you can use your broom to fly to other worlds!

To make:

1. First make the brush of the broom. This is easi-est with two people. Gather the materials and lay the birch twigs thin end to thin end, and fat to fat, in a bunch that looks ample. One person holds this in the middle as the other cuts the fat ends (handle end) flush with secateurs.

2. One person holds the brush in the middle and the other takes a decent length of string to tightly bind it about 2.5cm (1in) from the han-dle end. Tie a strong knot.

3. Bind another length of string about 5cm (2in) along, and knot. Create a third binding another 5cm (2in) towards the brush end. The brush is complete.

4. To make the handle, cut a suitable stick and whittle one end into a point. Insert this, with some force, into the handle end of the brush, at least a few inches in. It needs to be a tight fit in order to be strong.

5. The broom is complete. Children can make smaller versions of this and have fun having broomstick races and flying through the woods...

You will need:
- Freshly cut birch twigs
- A good stout stick for a handle
- Secateurs
- Pruning saw
- Knife
- Strong string

Faery Pine Needle Brooms

1. Make miniature brooms by gathering little bunches of pine needles, binding them with coloured thread or wool at one end.

2. Find a small twig for a handle. If need be, whittle it to a point and insert to the bound end of the broom as with the besom brooms.

These faery brooms are easier to take on magical journeys...

Acorn Ink

Oak galls were used to make manuscript ink for many hundreds of years, right the way into the 20th century. Because of its long-lasting quality, oak gall ink was used for important documents, such as royal decrees, as well as for musical scores, drawings, letters and maps. It was popular with artists for its strong deep tones. Acorns were used to make ink even before gall ink. Galls are rarer than acorns, which grow in abundance. Acorn ink is a rich brown-black colour.

TO MAKE:

1. To make four small pots of ink, you will need three adult handfuls of peeled acorns. (If the acorns are fresh, first dip them for 10–20 seconds in boiling water, then, on a chopping board, slice longwise in half with a knife. Children can then easily peel them.)

2. Place the acorns in a pan, cover with water, put on a lid and simmer on a low heat for approximately two hours. It is an advantage to use a cast iron pan, for it is the chemical reaction between the iron and acorn which makes the ink.

3. Remove from the heat. Add three tablespoons of vinegar and a handful of iron. Stir well.

4. Allow to sit overnight, and next day simmer again with the lid on. Add water if necessary to keep the water covering the acorns and iron.

YOU WILL NEED:
- Acorns
- Rusty nails / wire wool
- Vinegar
- Honey
- Alcohol (optional)
- Jars

5. On the third day, simmer again for about an hour, with the lid on. Then strain through a sieve lined with a cloth. Return the liquid to the heat, adding a tablespoon of honey. This replaces a substance called gum arabic, which helps the mixture stick together better. Simmer gently, with the lid off, until the dark liquid reduces by at least half. Test out the ink with a paintbrush and return to the heat if you want a darker colour.

6. Pour into a jug, allow to cool and add a splash of alcohol (e.g. vodka) to help preserve the ink. Pour into jars, label and store. Use in fountain pens or with feather quills.

Feather Quill Pen

You could make a feather quill to use with your acorn ink. Goose, swan and turkey feathers have all been used to make quill pens. (The word 'pen' comes from the Latin word *penna,* which means 'feather'.)

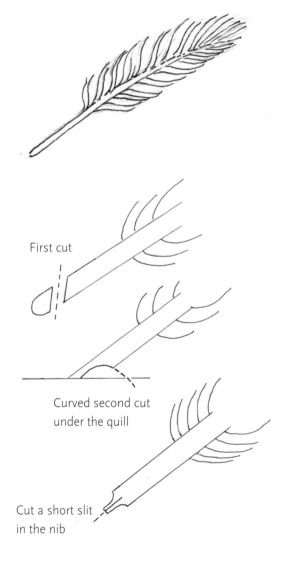

YOU WILL NEED:
- Feathers – flight feathers of large birds work best
- Scissors or small knives (please see Appendix p 317 for safe tool use)
- Cleaning tool, e.g. a straightened-out paper clip or thin stick
- Ink

First cut

Curved second cut under the quill

Cut a short slit in the nib

TO MAKE:

1. Use your fingernail to scrape away the scale on the shaft of the feather, to leave it smooth and even.

2. Using scissors, or a small knife, slice the end of the feather off at about a 45° angle.

3. Make a curved second cut on the other side of the quill from the first one.

4. Clear out the dry husk inside the quill, so that the feather-shaft near the nib becomes a hollow tube (which can hold ink). You may need to use a tool to do this.

5. Make a short slit in the nib for the ink to flow down. Dip your pen in ink and try it. Re-trim the writing point if necessary, until it is satisfactory.

Birch Bark Faery Letters

As birch bark is full of oils, it can often be found intact long after the wood has rotted down. This bark provides tinder for lighting fires and also 'paper' for writing on, as you can write directly onto birch bark with a pen. You could use your acorn ink.

YOU WILL NEED:
- Pieces of birch bark
- Sharp scissors
- Pens

TO MAKE:
1. Cut the birch bark up into tiny faery-sized pieces.

2. You can write letters to the faeries and leave them in holes at the bottom of the trees, or anywhere you think the unseen creatures of the forest may live.

If they are lucky, perhaps the children will find that the faeries have written back!

Mushrooms

Mushrooms are vital to all life in the forest and beyond. Fungi are the web of connection below the surface of the earth, within the soil. They link the trees together like a huge underground web, helping the trees and plants to speak with each other. They also add their mycelium (their threadlike bodies) to the roots of the plants, helping them to receive more water and food from the earth. They are helpers in many ways, also breaking down the dead bodies of plants and animals, making food in the soil so new life may grow. The mushrooms that we see above the soil are the fruiting bodies of the whole being, which lives mostly underground. Some are deadly – beware! Others are good food and some are wonderful medicine. Have a mushroom hunt, exploring the woods in autumn. Be respectful and careful by not touching or harvesting, unless with an expert. Instead, marvel and find out who they are, using field guides to help you.

Making spore-prints is a useful and fascinating way to get to know the mushrooms. Take the cap of the mushroom, remove the stalk, and place, gills down, onto a piece of paper or card. Some mushrooms have white spores (the guide books will help you identify which ones); for these mushrooms, use a dark coloured paper. The mushroom needs to be left overnight to create a spore-print.

Carve a Wooden Mushroom

This activity is good for practising tool use with older children. For younger children, make mushrooms out of clay and leave to dry before painting.

To MAKE:

1. Using a knife, carve the end of the stick into a smooth rounded mushroom cap shape. (See Tool Safety p 317 for tool use.)

You WILL NEED:
- Green wood, e.g. hazel. A section approx. 30cm (12in) long and 4cm (2in) wide per child
- Pruning saw
- Carving knife
- Field guide and paints (optional)
- Sandpaper

2. Use a pruning saw to make a stop cut, a straight ring around the base of the mushroom cap, to prevent the carving knife from going too far.

3. Carve the stem of the mushroom by cutting in towards the stop cut.

4. When the basic shape has been completed, use the saw to cut the mushroom off the rest of the stick. Use sandpaper to smooth the surface.

5. The mushroom can then be painted using the field guide as a reference.

Fly agaric mushrooms are bright red with white spots; they look lovely as Christmas tree decorations. To do this, paint the mushroom and when the paint is dry screw a small metal hoop into the top. Add thread to hang.

Bones of the Earth

Samhain is the time of the ancestors, a time to remember the many lives lived before ours. Buried beneath our feet, the earth's secrets and treasures are hidden. Here lie layer upon layer of soil, fossils, bones and rock, formed from the bodies of all the millions of plants, trees and animals who lived in this place before us.

It may take hundreds of years of fallen autumn leaves to create one fine layer of good soil. Like the rings of a tree which show each year of its life, the earth beneath us shows layers of time. Within these layers lie stories of all those who lived here. Beneath us lie the bones, tools and ancient fireplaces of our ancestors. Here are the stories of how the great waters moved across the land, of ice, snow and wild fire. If we imagine the earth as a tree of life, these layers of the past are like the heartwood, supporting the green growth of our present lives, whilst we are like the living outer layer of the tree, living and breathing in the sunlight. In time, we too will become the heartwood, supporting the generations to come and our stories will be written in the hidden world beneath the ground. Nature is a perfect circle, in which death supports birth, so that life continues.

Soil is a magical substance. The topmost layer is full of living beings. There are more creatures below the surface of the earth than there are above. In a healthy forest, in an handful of soil the size of an acorn, there may be several billion minuscule beings. Together with worms and fungi, they turn the fallen leaves and dead bodies of plants and animals into soil. Without them our beautiful, rich world would not exist. They mix the minerals and air into the soil so that the earth can birth life, sprout seeds and feed them as they grow. Soil is immeasurably precious.

We rely so much on our sight that we are hardly ever aware of the hidden world beneath us, a world of roots and fungi that connect and are communicating with each other. Animals live in holes, burrows and sets, their tunnels and bedrooms held in the roots of trees. Underground streams flow. Rocks, minerals, metals and crystals lie buried. Seeds lie sleeping.

Blindfold Earth Walk

The surface of the earth is like the skin of a huge drum. In summer there is a lot of busy activity above the skin. At this time of year, the energy of the trees and plants has moved down below. To gain a sense of the life below, we can take a blindfold walk through the forest, walking as silently as possible. Children can hold a rope with a leader who has eyes open and a protector at the rear who can also see. It works best to all hold the rope on the same side, have ample space between the children and keep the rope fairly taut. In the forest, it works best with maximum of eight per rope. Ask the children to imagine they have eyes in the soles of their feet and can see or sense the world beneath them. Can they sense animal burrows or underground streams?

Bone Hunt

Sometimes we come across bones in the forest or an animal that has died. Children are naturally curious and often want to take a close look and ask a lot of questions. It is a fascinating quest to try and discover whose bones they might be and, if there are several, to piece them together. You may find owl pellets or those from other birds of prey. Be careful not to disturb roosting birds. These pellets are not like poo. They are made of fur and bones that the birds cough up. They reveal the bones of the creatures the owl has eaten. You can soak the pellets in water to make them easier to examine. Can you find tiny skulls and bones of mice or voles?

We once found a dead fox curled up in a hollow tree. The children were in awe and showed huge respect. Over the following weeks and months, we watched how its body became food and earth, till only the bones and leathery skin remained. Over the weeks and months these were scattered in the woods by other animals. The children would gather them up and bring them back to the hollow with interest, care and reverence.

Deep in the Earth

Steiner Collection song

Blow north wind, blow, Au-tumn leaves are fall-ing, Cold, frost and snow,

Wint-er is a-call-ing, Mo-ther Na-ture's sleep-ing. All the land is ba-re,

Deep in the earth, she hides her trea-sures rare.

A Samhain Treasure for your Magic Pouch – Acorn Cup Whistle

Carry an acorn cup whistle to call for help.

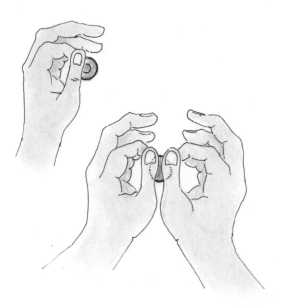

YOU WILL NEED:
- An uncracked acorn cup

TO MAKE:

1. Choose an uncracked acorn cup, and place it upon the first and second fingers of both hands, with the acorn bowl facing you.

2. Place the top part of both thumbs on the cup, leaving a small space between your thumbs – shaped like a narrow slice of pie.

3. Place your lips so they cover the cup, and blow into the gap. This whistle takes practice but is surprisingly loud. The acorn cup can also be used to gather tree drops for medicine. (See Acorn Cup Dew Medicine, p 210)

Sense Awareness Activity – Intuition Game

As well as the five physical senses we have a deep inner knowing. Here's a simple activity designed to help awaken trust in our intuition.

It's helpful and fun to use blindfolds to take away our main physical sense, sight.

TO PLAY:

1. In secret, send one person off to hide in a designated place.

2. Ask everyone to close their eyes or put on blindfolds and follow a sound such as a tinkling bell. Younger children can just close their eyes and hold onto a long rope, guided by the leader. Ask them to relax and to trust their feet.

3. Lead them to somewhere near to the hidden person and ask them to sit down, still blindfolded or with eyes closed and listen to the sounds around them. Ask them to listen with their inner senses.

4. Allow some time for this then tell them there is a person hidden nearby and ask them to point to where they feel that person is, using their intuition.

5. The children remove their blindfolds and open their eyes, and we ask the hider to reveal themselves.

This is best played several times to increase confidence.

Samhain Game – Hibernating Hedgehogs

At this time of year hedgehogs are foraging for worms, berries, beetles, roots and nuts, eating well before settling in for their winter sleep. They must be careful of badgers and foxes as they root around. It is important they create a warm snug place to sleep before the cold fingers of Jack Frost come creeping through the land.

There are two versions of this game, one for younger children and one for older children.

Version for younger children

TO PLAY:

1. Ask the children to be baby hedgehogs, snuffling around in the forest. As they are busy doing this call, 'Winter is coming! Hibernate hedgehogs!' The children snuggle up with the person nearest to them to hibernate, hiding their eyes as they crouch down.

2. You quickly place a large cloth over one pair, and then ask the others to come over and guess who the hibernating pair are.

3. When they have guessed, reveal the hibernators and carry on snuffling.

Related activities

- Talk about ways of keeping warm through the winter months to come.
- Make piles of leaves and sticks in undisturbed places for hedgehogs to hibernate in.
- Make pinecone or pompom hedgehogs.

Version for older children

TO PLAY:

1. All the children go into pairs and become hedgehogs foraging and snuffling about, eating and gathering big piles of leaves. They must keep aware because a fox or badger may come a-hunting. The predators are played by an adult. When the hedgehogs see the predator, they must curl up in a ball to escape being caught.

2. First the children are given time to play hedgehogs foraging. After a while, the adult calls 'Winter is coming... Hibernate hedgehogs!' One hedgehog from each pair curls up by their pile of leaves and the other quickly covers them. The adult gives them a little time to do this, then calls, 'Here comes Jack Frost!'

3. The children have to stop and wait as the adult comes to each hibernation pile and seeks any uncovered part of the child with frosty fingers. If any part of them is left uncovered, they may not survive the winter. (If, for example, a child's feet are peeping out, the adult playing Jack Frost can give their toes a gentle tickle. This hedgehog may not survive the winter.) Then the children swap and play again...

Pine Cone Hedgehog

The fallen leaves of autumn make warm beds for sleepy hedgehogs. Amidst the leaves, pine cones can be found on the forest floor, and transformed into hedgehogs.

TO MAKE:

1. Gather some pine cones.

2. Each child has a pine cone and a small ball of clay (or soft beeswax).

3. Mould the clay (or wax) into a cone shape – for the hedgehog's nose – and smooth this onto the end of the pine cone.

4. Add eyes and a nose.

YOU WILL NEED:
- Pine cones
- Clay or beeswax
- Beads or tiny balls of darker beeswax – for eyes

Acorns – Gathering and Processing

The oak provides shelter and nourishment for many forest creatures. Acorns are a very special wild food for people too, full of goodness to sustain us with the strength and perseverance of the oak. They require a vital washing process to make them edible and taste good. The washing process is called 'leaching', and removes tannins. The tannins can be used to preserve leather ('tanning') and the acorn water can be used to heal wounds and sore gums. All around the world, where oaks grow, the indigenous people have eaten acorns and had traditions to gather and process them. Acorns provide a staple food, rather like wheat, corn or rice, and, once prepared, can be eaten in many ways, sweet or savoury.

Gather the acorns from the second drop in late October. The first drop, usually in September, is when the tree shakes off the acorns that are unhealthy. Only pick the unblemished acorns from the ground. Peel away the shells. This is made easier by dipping the acorns in boiling water for 10–20 seconds. Then an adult can cut them in half long wise and the children can peel them. Here are two methods of washing (leeching) the acorns. Prepare in advance for this activity; just as the oak is slow to grow, the acorn process also takes time.

Stream washing

This process is ancient and energy conserving, but does require an unpolluted running stream. It takes at least a week, so plan ahead! Peel the nuts and crush into tiny pieces in a cotton bag using a small log or rolling pin. Tie the bag tightly shut with strong string or rope, leaving a long line to lower the bag into a deep, fast-flowing part of the steam. Once it is submerged, secure the other end of the rope to a nearby tree. After a week the flowing water should have washed all bitterness away. Taste to check and submerge until the taste is mild and free of bitterness.

Boil washing

This method takes at least a couple of hours, depending on how many acorns you are processing. Place peeled acorns into a large pan. Fill the pan with water and bring to the boil. This needs to boil for at least 45 minutes before you remove it from the heat. Carefully tip away the water, using a cloth-lined sieve, as the acorn meal becomes powdery and can be lost through a sieve. The acorn water will be dark brown from all the tannins. Add fresh water and re-boil. The acorns can vary in bitterness but English oak will usually need at least three long boils to clean them for eating. The only way to know when they are ready is to taste them. If any bitterness remains, boil again. Importantly, for the final pour, use a cloth-lined sieve, as the acorn meal becomes powdery and can be lost through a sieve. After the final pour, squeeze the cloth when cool enough, to remove all water. Spread out the acorn meal so that it can dry out to make a flour, or use damp for immediate use. You may dry the acorn meal in a low oven to make a flour that can be stored.

Samhain Wild Plant Recipes
Acorn Bread

TO MAKE:

1. Mix together all the dry ingredients in a large bowl.

2. Dissolve the molasses in the warm water in a jug and add to the dry mixture. The dough may be quite wet, especially if the acorn meal is still damp. This is preferable for acorn bread. You may be able to knead the dough but if it is too wet mix well with a wooden spoon for 5–10 minutes.

3. Leave to rise for at least an hour. Stir or knead again for 5–10 minutes.

4. Grease a loaf tin and then dust it with flour. Pour the dough into the tin and allow to rise for half an hour or so. You can plan this so that you can take the dough into the woods and bake it in a Dutch oven over the fire.

YOU WILL NEED:
- 200g (2 cups) acorn meal
- 300g (2 cups) flour (light spelt is good)
- 1 teaspoon yeast
- 1 teaspoon salt
- 300ml (2 cups) warm water
- 1 tablespoon molasses

5. Bear in mind that all these timings are estimates. The principle is to allow sufficient time for the dough to rise twice before baking. It helps to have a damp cloth over the dough bowl. Bake for approximately 40 minutes. Best served warm with butter in the forest by the fire.

Dutch Oven

The Dutch oven is a cast iron pan with a close-fitting lid, which is designed for cooking on a fire. It is a wonderful way of cooking in the forest and can be used for a myriad of recipes from breads and cakes to casseroles and soups. Here is a simple and effective way of using the oven, which requires a trivet.

TO USE:

1. Light the fire at least half an hour before you plan to bake, as the oven needs a good bed of hot embers to warm it through.

2. Once the fire has a good core temperature, place the trivet over the fire and carefully bang the legs into the ground a little way to ensure it is stable.

YOU WILL NEED:
- Dutch oven
- Fire gloves
- Trivet
- Spade or trowel

It also helps if the distance between the oven and ember bed is not too wide.

3. Place the oven on top of the trivet, above the fire, and preheat for 5–10 minutes.

4. Use the gloves to open the oven, put the cake tin filled with mixture inside and close the lid.

5. Now use the trowel to carefully move the logs to the edges of the fire and cover the top of the oven with embers. At this stage there should be hot embers below the oven and on top. The oven works best when there are no direct flames below it, as these will burn the food.

6. Now wait approximately 20 minutes depending on the heat of the fire and size of the cake. It is an intuitive magic that is needed. Ask the children to help feel when it is ready.

7. When it feels like time, use the fire gloves and remove the ash from the top with the trowel and carefully blow the last bits away before opening the pan... a wonderful surprise awaits.

Samhain Plant Lore

Wild Rose

GAELIC NAME: *Dris* (meaning 'briar') or *Coin ròs* (meaning 'dogs' rose' – *coin* is plural of *cù* – 'dog'

LATIN NAME: *Rosa canina*

Character

I am Wild Rose, summer heart of the hedgerow, jewel of the autumn.

My thorns are sharp to protect my flower and fruit, and hooked to help me climb towards the sun, my king.

I am flower of love, Rose of Britain. Five delicate pink hearts joined at the centre full of gold.

My leaves and petals stem the blood from a wound.

In autumn my berries, rosehips red, shine in the hedges and where they climb through the trees, bright against a blue sky, I call to the birds who will eat my young and take them to new homes.

I bear the secret sign of five, star of protection of the rose tribe I belong to.

Locked inside my fruits are golden seeds with fine hairs. Take care, for they itch!

My hips are treasure for you, full of goodness to keep you strong through the colds these months bring, and good to ease the aching of joints in these damp lands.

I am noble and pure of heart and offer you my strength.

Samhain Wild Plant Recipes
Rosehip Pulp

One of nature's most delicious treats is the pulp of rosehips. As the autumn nights grow longer and colder, the berries begin to soften. Here is a simple way to squeeze out the pulp without the seeds and the irritating hairs coming out too.

TO MAKE:

1. Pick the soft berry and you will see a hole in the skin where the stalk joined. Place your index fingers on the berry, either side of the opening.

2. With thumbs and middle fingers, carefully squeeze. The pulp will ooze out between your index fingers. Stop squeezing before the seeds come out.

3. Eat the delicious red puree and put the rest of the rosehip somewhere where birds or mice can finish eating the fruit and disperse the seeds.

Rosehip Tea

TO MAKE:

1. Gather rosehips when they are deep red.

2. Bring water to a simmering boil and add a handful of fresh hips for a teapot's worth. Simmer until the fruits are soft.

3. Mash to a tomatoey-looking pulp (a potato masher is ideal). Strain through a cloth placed in a sieve over a jug. The cloth removes the seeds and their irritating hairs.

4. Squeeze the cloth and serve the delicious syrupy tea, which is full of vitamins and goodness.

Samhain Tree Lore

Ash

GAELIC NAME: *Craobh uinnseann*
LATIN NAME: *Fraxinus excelsior*

OGHAM: *Nuin* (the letter N)

Essence
Ancestors ~ Connection ~ Key

Character

I am the Ash, Tree of Connection.

Tall and graceful, with deep strong roots and wide, embracing branches.

High in the canopy, my leaves are delicate and spacious, letting the light of the sky shine, dappled, on those below.

I am wind pollinated and my trees are either male (pollen bearing) or female (seed forming), opening their clusters of tiny purple-black flowers in spring before the leaves unfurl. Come close and see my intricate beauty.

I have the special gift of being able to change sex from year to year as nature requires. My seeds, hanging in bunches, are known as 'ash keys'. Autumn winds catch them and they fly, spinning far, to find their home, where they will grow fast and strong in spring.

When I sleep in winter, my bud tips are like charcoal sceptres.

In dreamtime I am the Tree of the Worlds, known as *Yggdrasil* by those of the North. My great trunk is the axis of the world. My deep roots touch the underworld.

My branches reach into the heavens. I am connected to the worlds within and without, above and below, and to the past and future generations. All life is connected.

Lie beneath me and relax into the earth. Close your eyes and feel my deep, deep roots beneath you... You are connected to the centre of the earth... Branches reach up high, touching the sky, the stars. You are connected to the universe. Open your eyes and look around you. Notice the beauty of the forest. Close your eyes, see a forest within you... Imagine a key falling gently from my branches into your open hands.

Place it in your heart. It is a gift from your ancestors to unlock a talent within you that has been sleeping... One day you will pass this gift on, to others yet to come.

Gifts

My wood is strong and flexible. Able to take strain and shock, I am perfect for a bow, and handles on tools. I am loved by the carpenter for the quality and many uses of my wood; I am good to carve for bowls and spoons.

Upon the trunks of my old and dying trees, a small, black mushroom grows – the same colour as my winter buds. It looks like the buns King Alfred burnt, hence the name 'King Alfred's cakes'. These can be dried and used to catch the fire's spark. My wood is favoured firewood by many – burning hot, bright and slow.

My keys are good food when they are small, soft and tender in late spring. Gather them and simmer in several changes of water, till all bitterness is gone. Serve hot and seasoned, or pickle them in vinegar to store.

Drink my young leaves in tea, as people once did to take down a fever. I bring long life and health.

Ash Song

Anon.

Steady

1. Ash, ash, fea - thered one,
Branch - es like lan - ces of old,
Gre - en leav - ed and smo - oth skinned, Your
roots hold - ing deep our land's soul

2. Black budded, deep in sleep,
Soft-barked dream of Winter,
Your leaves in Spring show us
    shadow and light,
Make ready for gifts of Summer.

3. Star branched, Spring sapped,
Full of the song of the clouds,
Teach us to dream with you,
So those who have gone
    would be proud.

4. World tree, bridge the realms,
As in the stories of old.
From the skies to the depths of
    the earth and between,
The keys to all kingdoms you hold.

Yew

GAELIC NAMES: *Iuthar* (yew wood was used to make bows and arrows, which were poisoned with its juice, hence in Old Gaelic it was called *iogh* – 'severe pain'. Another form of the name is *eo* – 'grave'.)

LATIN NAME: *Taxus Baccata*
OGHAM: *Ioho/Idad/Iodhadh* (the letter I)

Character

I am Yew, Tree of the Ancestors.

I am the oldest tree in this land and one of the most ancient beings on this Earth.

Essence
Ancestors ~ Death and Rebirth ~ Span of Ages

For several thousand years I may stand, clothed in green through every season. Many lives come and go. I witness the procession of your generations. All of you are like leaves that grow from your Family Tree and fall in autumn to nourish the soil for those to come in spring. The ages pass. The celestial worlds turn. Life changes but always continues.

No other grows as I do. Within my living tree, I die and am reborn throughout my life. It is not easy to tell my age, for I grow new trunks from my roots, which merge with my whole form. Where I grow freely, my branches may root where they touch the earth. My central tree eventually dies. In this way, over the course of thousands of years, too slow for your human eyes to see, I walk. I can walk up hills and down valleys, through the ages.

I have much to teach about embracing death as a vital part of the sacred journey of life. By accepting death within my ever-changing form, I am able to span the ages.

My tree is deadly poisonous to people. Take care! I am a gateway keeper, but do not wish you to leave this world before your time. My wood makes the huntsman's bow, to carry death, so others may live.

In spring you may see my golden pollen rise like smoke from my male trees. In autumn, my mother trees ripen with sweet red berries and feed the birds. I was planted in sacred places long before churches were built. Nowadays, churches with aged yews in their graveyards mark the places considered sacred in ancient times. I watch over those who have died and hold the presence of continuing life for those

who remain. Come beneath my boughs and feel my otherworldly spirit, the connection my long life holds to the many generations that went before you. Their lives brought you the gift of life you have today.

Gifts

My wood is of a radiant reddish-orange hue. I am durable like the long-lived Oak and shock absorbent like the Ash. I am traditionally used for hunting bows, wheels and cogs, boxes and furniture. My wood, when used for wand or staff, offers connection to the ancestors.

I am deadly poisonous to people and must be known and respected as such. The red sticky fruit of my berry is the only part of me that is not toxic, but, beware, the seed inside could take your life! Please do not tempt children by telling them my berries are edible. One crunch could be the end. Keep your distance. Let the birds eat and disperse my seed. Your lives are short and precious. Live them well.

Song of the Yew Tree

Lyrics by Anna Richardson
Traditional melody*

Slow and sombre

1. Down to the for-est I shall go. Down a down hey
down a down. Cloaked in da-rk green th-e Yew the-re grows, Der-ry
down. Oh ring your lit-tle bells of red, You hold a key so
it's been said, With a down der-ry der-ry der-ry down do-wn.

2. Oh will you give a huntsman a bow?
Down a down hey down a down.
For life to take of stag or doe?
Derry down.
Oh sing your song of light and dark;
Watch over those we love who part,
With a down, derry derry derry down down.

3. Oldest tree in this green land,
Down a down hey down a down.
For many thousand years may stand,
Derry down.
Respect we give to those who hold
Life and death since times untold,
With a down derry derry derry down down.

* The melody of this song is from an old English folk ballad called *The Three Ravens*. It was printed in a songbook called *Melismata* compiled by Thomas Ravenscroft in 1611. However, it is most likely much much older.

Samhain Animals

Tawny Owl

I am the Brown Owl, the Owl of the Woods. I roost in old trees or high among the creeping ivy.

I fly by night. My flight feathers have fringed edges, so I glide in silence. At moon-time, I hunt insects, mice, voles and birds, catching them in my powerful talons. My hearing is sharp as my talons. The ring of dark feathers which surrounds my face channels sounds to my ears; I can pinpoint the movement of my prey. I can hear a mouse in its hidden tunnels beneath the snow. My large eyes are keen too – I am far-sighted.

The parts of my food that I cannot digest, I cough up. Look below my roosting places and find my pellets; full of the fur and the bones of the animals I have eaten.

By the light of the moon, listen for my voice. The familiar call, 'too-whit, too-whoo', is the sound of two owls – I call my mate – 'ke-wick' ('too-whit') – and he replies: 'hoo-hoo-oooo' ('too-whoo'). Cup your hands with slightly parted thumbs, and blow; you too can whistle like us, and, if you are patient, we may respond to your call.

Hedgehog

I am Hedgehog; my ancestors have been here for many ages. I love to root through hedges and undergrowth to hunt out insects and earthworms, snails and mice. As I snuffle, I grunt little pig-like grunts, hence my name. I live and move all my life close to the earth – come close to the ground and smell the sweet fragrance of the earth beneath us.

I am well protected; to keep me safe my coat is made of thousands of spines. My nose can sense trouble as well as food and I curl up in a ball when I am frightened. Sometimes I am hunted by badgers and foxes, so I must stay aware.

I am nocturnal, so in the dark I do my rounds, using my nose, ears and intuition to guide me. When it is dark, trust and be guided by your inner knowing.

I have four or five babies. When my baby hoglets are born, their spines are soft. I feed them with my milk for one moon, until they can root out food for themselves.

When the leaves begin to fall and the fruits and nuts are ripe I must root and munch all I can, for the cold is coming and when Jack Frost touches the land with his icy fingers I must build a nest of leaves and grass to snuggle up for the winter.

Now to deep sleep and to dream I go. Listen to your dreams. See you in the spring.

Remember, Remember

By Anna Richardson
*Traditional melody** *

Slow and sombre

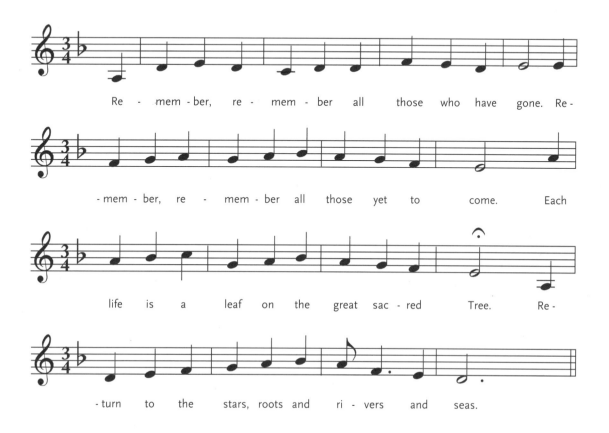

Re - mem - ber, re - mem - ber all those who have gone. Re -

- mem - ber, re - mem - ber all those yet to come. Each

life is a leaf on the great sac - red Tree. Re -

- turn to the stars, roots and ri - vers and seas.

* The first line is the melody from 'The Copus Christi Carol', a traditional English song.

Samhain Celebration

Fire Shrines

Samhain is a potent time of year; death and rebirth are powerful and profound. Samhain is the time of the ancestors, when many cultures honour their dead. The other side of death is birth. Dead leaves nourish new life. At Samhain, trees release their old leaves and their new seeds. Recognising that Samhain is a time not just of death, but of rebirth, Celtic peoples celebrated Samhain as the Celtic New Year. Create two shrines with a fire in the middle.

To MAKE:

1. One shrine is for the ancestors, those who have passed. You could make the base from mole mud, which is considered by some cultures to be sacred, since it comes from deep inside Mother Earth.

2. Place a lit candle in the middle and ask the children to find woodland treasures such as stones, bones and brown autumn leaves to put on the shrine.

3. The other is for the future generations, those yet to be born. You could make the base from a golden or green cloth and place on it forest finds that suggest new life – small treasures such as acorns, sycamore seeds and rosehips.

4. Make the fire in the middle. Ask the children to choose a special stick to place on the fire for someone they know who has died, perhaps a pet or family member.

5. As they carefully place the stick on the fire they can say, for example, 'This is for Patch' or 'This is for my Grandpa'. Ask them to do this in turn.

6. You could touch on the circle of life – how everything that is alive dies, and life begins again.

It is the end of the old year and the beginning of the new in the cycle of the earth. Everything has been harvested or has fruited and now it is time to wait for the new seed to grow. Tell the children that one day they may be an ancestor – they could be their grandchildren's ancestor. Ask them how they would like to be remembered?

7. Sing the Samhain song, 'Remember, Remember' (see p 271).

8. Make some food on the fire and before you eat prepare two bowls to leave on the shrines. You can all come together in a circle around the fire, with the people bearing the bowls leading a figure-of-eight procession. Circle around the ancestors' shrine, leaving a bowl of food on the shrine, past the fire, and around the future generations' shrine, leaving a bowl on the shrine and circling back around the fire.

9. As you process you may sing, 'Remember, Remember'.

10. After the procession, sit and share food, stories and song together.

Winter

In the cycle of day and night, midwinter is akin to midnight, the time when most creatures are asleep and dreaming. It is the darkest time of the year.

The earth journeys around the sun – one cycle is one year. As the earth circles the sun, it also spins on its own axis. Because the earth's axis is at an angle, as the planet revolves, sometimes the northern half (the Northern Hemisphere) of the earth tilts towards the sun, and sometimes it tilts away from the sun. On the day of the winter solstice, the northern half of our planet is as far away from the sun as it can possibly be. When this happens, we experience the longest night and the shortest day of the year, and at this same moment the Southern Hemisphere experiences the longest day and the shortest night; summer solstice.

At Winter Solstice, known in olden times as yule, we celebrate the return of the light, because from now onwards the hours of light lengthen every day. It is also the time to celebrate the inner light, which keeps us going through dark times. Our ancestors understood, and the animals know now, that winter is the hardest time of the year. Though the cold is pure and cleansing, it can also be cruel and harsh. So, we gather around the warmth of the fire and strengthen our hearts with generosity and goodwill, celebrating and giving gifts to loved ones.

The Forest in Winter

In winter some things are revealed and others are hidden. Beneath our feet, hibernating animals sleep in their burrows. Trees and plants are storing their energy in their roots, deep in the earth. Above our heads, last year's birds' nests and squirrels' drays are revealed, and on the ground, tracks are seen more clearly in the bare earth.

Jack Frost visits the land and everything magically transforms, sparkling in the winter sunshine. When snow covers the earth with its breathtaking beauty, there is a deep silence.

Notice the different colours, shapes and textures of the trees in winter. Feel the sticky buds of the horse chestnuts, find the velvet-black sceptres of the ash and count how many oak buds are on each twig.

See the shapes of the trees silhouetted against the sky and look up in wonder at the clear stars at night. Beneath your feet, under the earth, seeds lie dreaming, the spark of life sleeping within.

A Story for Winter, to Share Around the Fire

The Gift of Fire

A folktale from the island of Islay, in the Hebrides

This is the story of a little bird, the redstart. The female redstart is small and brown, with a long flickering tail. Her tail feathers are red as fire. Now, the redstart is a summer visitor to the islands of Britain, but once, long, long ago, one little redstart came in the heart of winter. Back then, she did not have a tail of red; her feathers were dull brown all over, the colour of winter mud.

Back then, the redstart lived over the western sea on the island of the blessed – the land of the ever-living, Tír na nÓg – with the Gods and the Goddesses.

There was the Good God Dagda, with his beard and his belly, and his magical Cauldron of Plenty, which, no matter how many warriors or champions brought their wooden bowls, was always brimming with warm rich stew. His fort rang with loud laughter, and the clinking of cups, and the music of the Dagda's harp, which played the songs of the four seasons, so the notes drifted like spring blossom, or sparkled like winter snow.

And outside there were fair lands, enchanted forests. On the top of a hill grew a grove of oaks. In the heart of the grove was a clearing. And in the centre of the clearing was a fire. The flames flickered, yellow as sun-sparks, red-gold.

The fire was tended by the Goddess Brigit. Brigit with her cloak of green, her gown of white, and her hair, red-gold. For Brigit is the Goddess of the Sacred Flame – the hearth fire of the home, the smith's fire of the forge, and the inner fire of the poet. She tended the fire and kept it always alight.

The little bird, the redstart, loved to perch in the high branches of the oak, and gaze into the heart of the fire, and sing. But the bird looked further, and she saw over the treetops, over the seas, to the lands of earth.

And she saw the people there suffering. For, in those long ago days, the people on earth had no fire. And in the deep winter they were bitter cold. They were damp to the bone in the wind and the rain, and they were miserable. The little bird felt for the people. What could she do?

She hopped down to the hem of Brigit's cloak. 'I will take a spark of fire to the people of earth.'

Brigit looked down at the tiny bird, and she smiled, her eyes dancing like flames. 'Yes, little one, share the gift of fire, but give it to someone like you, someone who wants to share their gift.'

The bird flew to the fire. And Brigit took a spark from the blaze, and placed it on the tail of the little bird. It glowed red.

And the bird flew, up and away, over the treetops, over the crashing waves, through the shining mists. Through the storms, the redstart carefully carried the spark of fire, all the way to the island of Islay.

And there on the shore, right away, was someone to receive her gift! A fisherman, kneeling on the sharp rocks, fingers numb in the freezing waters of a rock-pool, fishing for a skinny crab or a slimy ribbon of weed; anything to stop the growl of his hunger.

The redstart landed on the rock beside him. 'I bring a gift for the people of earth. At the tip of my tail is a spark of fire. It is tiny. Tend it...' But the fisherman wasn't listening. All he could hear was his own stomach. When he looked up at the bird, all he could see was meat. He seized a rock, and drew back his arm...

The bird flew up, away, her heart beating, into the forest. And here was someone to receive her gift: a hunter – someone who had learned to listen to the voices of the birds. Perched in the treetop, the redstart sang, 'I bring a gift for the people of earth. At the tip of my tail is a spark of fire. It is tiny. Tend it and it will grow.'

But the hunter sneered. 'A tiny gift? I'll take the whole bird!' And he swung his sling, spitting grit. The bird flew, her heart hammering. But she was determined.

This time she did not fly to a person; she flew to a bird. The great white owl, wisest of all the birds, who lived in a tumbledown croft on the far side of the forest. The owl listened as the bird shared her story. 'This task is too big for one alone,' said the owl. 'Fly out over the island – ask all the birds to help you.'

So the redstart flew out over the island – over heather and stone, moss and moor, loch and burn and shore. And she returned to the croft leading birds of every feather: guillemots and gulls, kittiwakes and kites, wild geese, white swans, a honking line of ducks. Even the golden eagle was there. They all settled together into the croft. The owl told them what to do: 'Fly out over the seas to all the islands; tell every man you meet to come to this croft, to receive the gift of fire.'

There was a great flapping and fluttering as all the birds rose into the air and flew out of the open roof in every direction. And, after a time, the croft was heaving with men.

The owl told of the precious gift of fire; its light, its heat, its power. How, on winter evenings, the warm purr of the flames and the golden glow of the firelight cheer the heart.

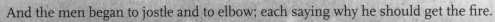

And the men began to jostle and to elbow; each saying why he should get the fire.

'I was here first...'

'I came the furthest...'

And because everyone was talking at once, and not one of them was listening, they had to raise their voices to be heard.

And as their voices rose, so did their tempers. And one man shoved. And another man pushed back. Before long, the croft was loud with the fury of fighting.

The owl hooted. 'This is no place for us. Fly away home, little bird! Go back to Tír na nÓg. There is no one here to receive your gift.' And the owl flew up out of the broken thatch, and away into the forest. And the little redstart followed. But she had already flown far and wide, back and forth, over the whole island, and she was exhausted. Before she had even reached the sea, she dropped from the sky, and fell with a thud.

She lay on the damp sand, in the needling rain, the stinging wind lifting her feathers. Her eyes closed. The spark of fire on her tail, that tender ember, dimmed and shrank. The bird and the fire were all but dead.

Then, along the shore came a boy. A little boy pocketing pebbles – treasures from the sea. The boy had lived on the island his whole life – he didn't mind a bit of rain. He was picking up smooth stones and shiny ones, round ones and... 'Oh!'

And the boy lifted the bird in his hands and carried it home to show his mother.

'Ah, poor wee thing. Warm it in your hands for a while.'

So the boy warmed the bird in his hands. He gave it water to drink and seed to eat. The bird sat up; it opened its eyes. Saw the boy and his mother, with the babe at her breast and the little children all around her skirt. The little bird sang out, 'I bring a gift for the people of earth...'

'A gift?' said the woman. 'Oh, thank you!'

And the spark of fire on the bird's tail glowed.

'Are you one who shares their gifts?' asked the bird.

But the woman just laughed. 'Me? Get away with you! I'm that busy digging or darning or sweeping or spinning. Gathering nuts and berries with the barins. No, I'm not gadding about sharing gifts! Not me!'

But the bird's eyes shone.

'Can you fetch me some twigs of pine?' she asked the boy. 'Twigs and sticks and branches.'

'Yes, of course I can.' And out he ran to the forest, with all his brothers and sisters, and back they came, their chubby little hands full of twigs.

'Can you find me something soft and dry?'

'Yes, of course I can.' And out they all ran, and back they came with dry grass and brown bracken and fluffy white down.

'Now, can you make me a nest?'

The little boy shaped a nest, and lined it, soft and snug.

And the bird fluttered down and sat upon the nest. She flicked her tail. And, like a falling star, the spark of fire blazed. The bird spread her wings and fanned her feathers, breathing the fire to life.

The Fire Bird flew.

From the rafters, the redstart looked down; at the flames, sun-yellow and red-gold, and at the children, stretching out their hands to the warmth, their eyes a-sparkle with fire-light. Over their heads flew the bird, flicking her tail feathers – tail feathers as red as fire.

Home she flew to Tír na nÓg, singing all the way.

As for the woman, she tended the fire well and kept it always alight. And she called friends and family, neighbours and strangers, and bid them all, 'Bring a branch, take a flame...'

And so, thanks to Brigit and the bird, the mother and the child, now we all share the gift of fire.

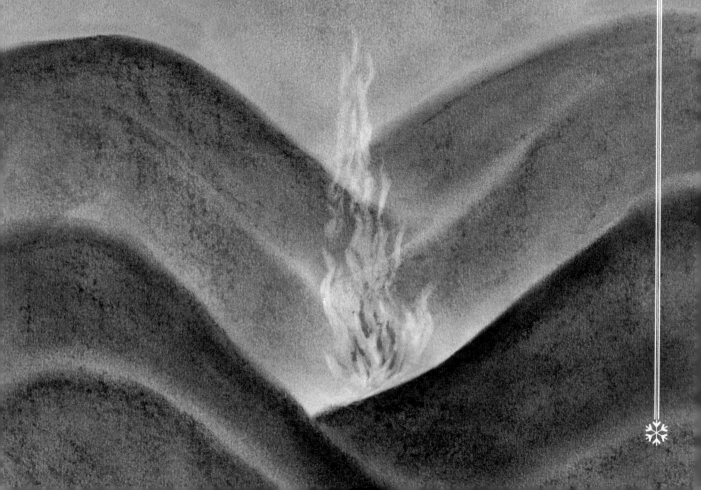

Winter Imaginary Journey

An imaginary journey can give children an inner experience of the energy of the season. In the cycle of day and night, midwinter is akin to midnight, when we enter deep sleep and dreamtime. When children are settled comfortably and wrapped up warm, guide them through a midwinter dreamtime journey:

- Wear or imagine a woollen cloak wrapped around you. Close your eyes and breathe deeply.

- Feel the warm weight of the blanket around you and let yourself sink into the comfort of the dark earth, as if you were in your own bed in the deep of night. Enjoy being completely still. Rest. Feel how peaceful the quiet is. Only your breath moves within.

- Imagine the night sky above you, and through the silhouette of the bare branches see the stars sparkle. Below, in the dark earth, through the web of bare roots, see the seeds sparkle with new life. The seeds are dreaming; the acorn is dreaming of becoming an oak. What are you dreaming of becoming? What would you like to do? How would you like to be?

- Give a little dreaming time.

- Now it is time to return from the land of dreaming; gently wiggle your fingers and toes, stretch your body and slowly open your eyes.

- Invite the children to share their dreams, if they would like to.

Winter Activities, Crafts and Games

Stillness Bird Feeding

This activity gives children a focus for sitting quietly in the forest. Explain to the children that if you are completely still, it is possible to feed wild birds from your hand. If you truly want to experience this for yourself, you will need time, patience and a quiet mind, visiting the same place again and again, to gain the trust of the birds.

Give each child a handful of seeds. Ask them to find a place away from distraction and to sit silently, with the bird feed in their hand or sprinkled on the ground nearby.

A child we knew did this in her garden, standing quietly with bird seed in her hand every day. Her patience and stillness were rewarded; the robin began to trust her and finally fed from her hand.

Silent Movement

The surface of the earth is like the skin of a great drum. When we move upon its surface, the vibration travels to the beat of our footsteps. Animals are experts at moving silently across the surface. Watch and listen to a cat moving in the garden; they walk, run and leap on silent feet. It is said in the stories of old that the Fianna, the Irish warriors, trained so well that they could run through the forest barefoot and never snap a single twig.

Practise moving without creating a sound on the drum skin of the earth. Can you walk, run and jump silently? Play games to test each other's skill. A simple game can be played where one person sits beside the path wearing a blindfold. In their lap they could have a small collection of pine cones. Everyone practises their silent movement as they walk by in single file. If the blindfolded person hears someone's footfall, they can gently cast a pine cone towards their legs.

In the winter, the energy of the forest is underground. The trees are sleeping in their roots. The seeds are nestled in the dark beneath us. Badgers sleep in their setts below. Take a silent walk through the woods – be aware of the life underground. Usually, deer and other animals hide when they hear us coming. If you can move silently, and with a quiet mind, you may be lucky enough to see the creatures of the forest.

Staff Making

To carry a staff is practical and offers the companionship and support of one's favourite tree. Staffs are useful for jumping over streams, climbing hills, opening up pathways, driving back wild beasts! The trees all have different energies and characters and we may find that we have particular love for certain ones. Perhaps they also have a particular feeling of kinship with us?

YOU WILL NEED:

- A straight stick, cut to measure to shoulder height. It needs to be at least 2cm (¾in) in diameter
- Knife to cut sticks (see p. 318)
- Peeler
- Sandstone or sandpaper
- Hazelnuts for oiling
- Clay, feathers, chalk or charcoal for decorating the staff

CUTTING:

1. The winter is the best time to cut sticks, as the energy of the tree is in the roots. Hazel has been used for coppicing for generations because its straight wood is good for staffs and it regenerates quickly after it is cut. It can be recognised by its bushy shape and the many trunks and thin sticks coming from the main body. Also look for the yellow catkins that appear during the winter. Always cut hazel at a slight angle away from the trunks. This ensures the rain runs away from the main body of the tree, preventing rot and infection.

2. You may also find a suitable stick from other trees; try to recognise the tree that you have cut your stick from by its buds. Some easily recognisable ones are: sticky horse chestnut buds, black ash buds, the cluster of tiny oak buds, the delicate spears of the beech and the green opposing sycamore buds.

PEELING:

1. Younger children can use a peeler to remove bark from their staffs.

2. Always peel away from fingers and work an arm's length away from other people. It is much easier to peel when the wood is fresh and green.

CARVING:

1. Older children can carve their staff with a knife, making notches and patterns.

SANDING AND OILING:

1. Staffs can be sanded and oiled. After peeling, leave the staff inside to dry for at least a week.

2. Then use sandstone or sandpaper to sand the staff.

3. One shelled hazelnut is said to have enough oil for one walking stick. Simply rub the nut along the length of the stick. Other nuts can also be used.

DECORATING:

1. Clay figures can be made to adorn the top of the staff – temporary, but lots of fun. Or bind feathers or wool to the top.

2. Chalk, clay and charcoal can also be used to paint the staff. To make paint, simply crush the dry materials to a fine powder and add a little water.

The Coppicing Song

By Hannah James

Cut this young maid - en right down to the ground. As I
sleep in a blan - ket of Win - ter, So
I may re - turn with a prim - ros - ey crown, And bring
life to the wood - land for - ev - er.

Bury me underground, starve me of air.
Sit up with me all through the nighttime,
And as dawn follows night, if you've tended me right,
You'll have charcoal to warm you in dark times.

Cut my long fingers to baskets and bowls,
Strong hurdles to keep out the weather,
Or a broom for to sweep out the old or for you
And your love to fly over together.

And when you are old and your branches are frail,
And your hair has turned snowy and silver,
Remember to leave what you've learnt to your children,
And I'll see them through to next Winter.

Pine Cone Gnomes

Gnomes embody the spirit of the element of earth; guardians of earth's treasures and caretakers of roots and seeds, rocks and minerals.

YOU WILL NEED:
- Pine cones
- Clay
- Sheep's wool or lichen
- Small black beads (optional)
- Cocktail stick or toothpick (optional)
- Leaves or felting wool for hats

TO MAKE:

1. First mould a ball of clay to resemble two chunky gnome's feet joined at the heels.

2. Onto this base, firmly place the pine cone and smooth the clay onto the cone to hold it in place. Make a worm-shape by rolling the clay in between your hands. Wrap this around the pine cone and join at the front for arms and hands.

3. Roll a ball for the head and firmly attach the clay head onto the top of the cone, smoothing it on with your fingers.

4. Press gently into the clay with your index fingers to create eye sockets and into these push two small black beads for eyes. Add a tiny ball of clay and mould a nose, and add clay ears.

5. Use a cocktail stick or small twig to carefully attach a beard of sheep wool or lichen under the nose and around the chin. You can make eyebrows in the same way.

6. Create a hat by rolling a leaf into a cone and pinning it together with a tiny stick.

7. Or you can make a wool hat by rolling and teasing coloured felting wool and using the cocktail stick to push it into the clay.

MAKE A HOME FOR YOUR GNOME:

1. Children can work on their own or in pairs to create a beautiful gnome home in the roots of a tree.

2. Give each child a ball of clay to make furniture or accessories for their home. Children become completely absorbed in this activity, creating clay stairs, mossy beds and leafy blankets.

Winter Gnome Grotto Celebration

While the children are busy making their gnomes and homes, create a beautiful gnome grotto for all the gnomes. Light it with candles and hang a special gift (such as a star biscuit, a walnut treasure or a little bell) for each child on the lower branches surrounding the grotto. To gather the children back to the grotto you could sing a song, play a tune or ring a bell. Invite the children to bring their gnomes and place them into the grotto. Give the children a moment to sit before the grotto and enjoy the sight of their candlelit gnomes. Honour each child by speaking aloud a gift or quality that they bring to the group (such as kindness or enthusiasm) as one by one they come to collect their woodland treasure.

Close the celebration by singing a winter song together.

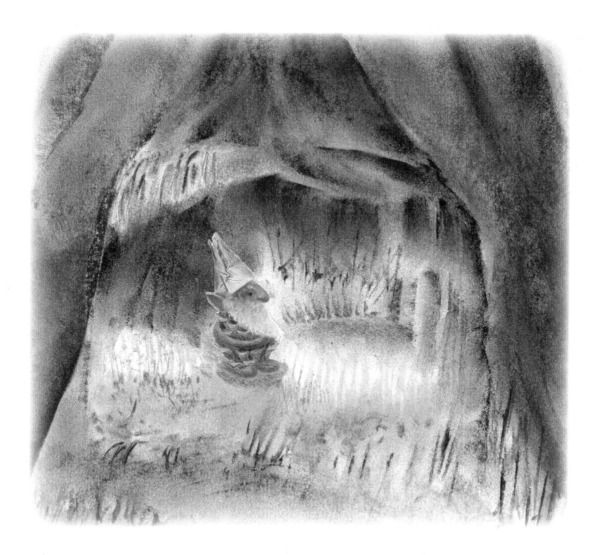

Pattern for a Woollen Cloak

Woollen cloaks inspire the imagination, bringing alive the feeling of fairy-tale adventures of long ago. People of the past wore cloaks to keep them warm, as well as using them for bedding and to carry possessions. Old wool blankets are easy to come by. The following is a simple design for making two children's cloaks from one large woollen blanket.

To make:

1. Mark out the blanket with chalk to the design shown. Carefully cut the cloth as shown.

2. Place the hood pieces together, matching top to top and back to back. With right sides together, pin and sew the top and back of the hood.

3. Tack one of the long sides of the main cloak about 1cm (½in) from the edge, then gather the cloth to the same measurement as the bottom of the whole hood.

4. Turn the hood so the sewing is on the inside. Now pin and sew the gathered main cloak to the bottom of the hood so that the overlap will be on the inside when the cloak is finished.

5. Sew on ribbons or a clasp around the neck, or perhaps a wooden button or toggle (see p 290). Repeat this process with the other pieces so you have two cloaks. Dye or embroider patterns on your cloak as you wish.

You will need:
- One large blanket
- Scissors
- Chalk or pencil
- Strong thread and needle
- Pins
- Toggle, ribbon or clasp
- Tape measure

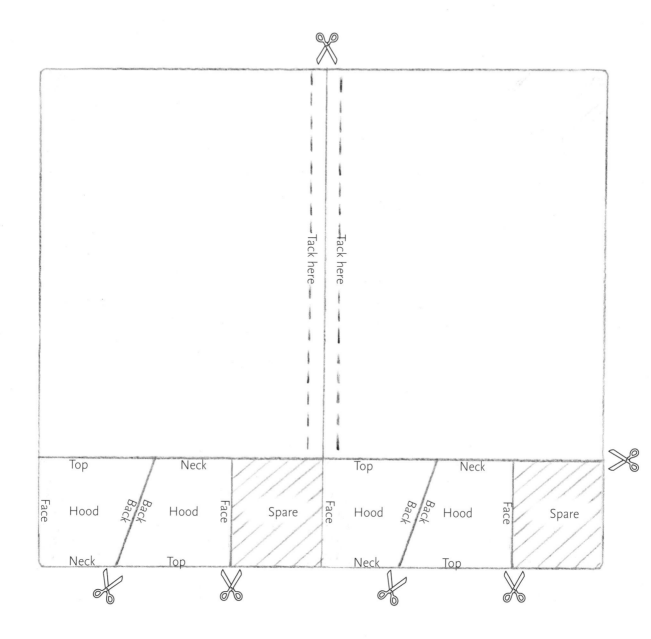

A Tree Toggle or Button

Use your button to transform an old wool blanket into a cloak. Woollen cloaks inspire the imagination, bringing alive the feeling of fairy-tale adventures of long ago.

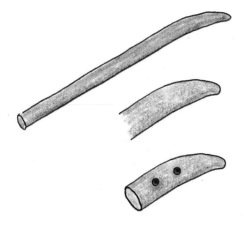

YOU WILL NEED:
- Knife
- Wood of choice
- Pruning saw
- Palm drill
- Sandpaper
- Hazelnut or walnut
- Leather thong
- Needle and thread

TO MAKE A TOGGLE:

1. Cut a twig approx. 1.5cm (¾in) diameter and 15cm (6in) long from the wood of your favourite kind of tree. (See the Appendix p 320 for how to harvest from trees respectfully.)

2. It is important to keep the full length of the stick while carving the toggle, to provide something to hold onto while you carve.

3. Carve the end of the stick into a toggle shape and, when complete, cut from the rest of the stick.

4. Sand and oil. You can oil the toggle by rubbing the surface with a walnut or hazelnut. Use a palm drill to make two holes for threading leather.

TO MAKE BUTTONS:

1. Find a branch from your favourite kind of tree which has a diameter the same size you would like your button to be, for example 2.5cm (1in).

2. Use a pruning saw to cut a length of wood from the end of the branch. The length should be long enough that you can hold one end steady while sawing the other end.

3. Cut a disc of wood from the end of the length of branch. (See Appendix p 317 for safe tool use.)

4. Sand and oil your button. Use a palm drill to make two holes for threading.

Willow Star Wands

Winter it is a good time to cut willow, when the energy is in the roots. Its flexible branches can be used in many craft activities, and can be planted into the earth, where they will grow again.

Stars, which are invisible in the light evenings of summer, shine bright on clear winter afternoons. Willow stars are simple to make and can be used for Christmas decorations in the home and in the garden. Star wands can be used to create a little winter magic.

YOU WILL NEED:
- Lengths of willow
- Ties – you can use garden wire or raffia
- Small bell (optional)

TO MAKE:

1. Take a length of willow and firmly fold it in half to create a stem and a tail.

2. A finger's length away from the fold on the tail end, make another fold to create a triangle.

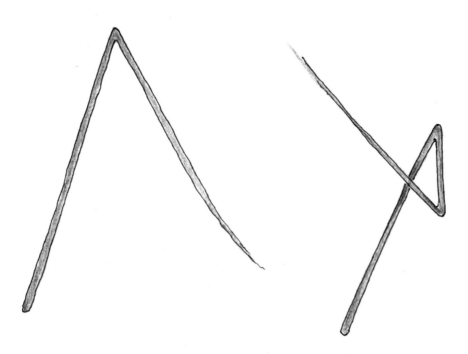

3. The tail of the triangle makes the shape of a number 4.

4. Make another fold in the tail of the 4, a finger's length from the stem, back over the horizontal piece and over the triangle.

5. Make the last fold a finger's length from the edge of the triangle, and tuck this length of willow behind one stalk and over the next to secure it into the star shape.

6. You may need to secure the tail to the stem with a tie. It can also be secured by wrapping the tail a few times around the stem.

7. You can tie the little bell to the place where the stem meets the star.

Star Wand Magic

Walk through the woods with your Willow Star Wand, on your own or in procession. Children can blow a wish through the star, or send out good wishes with the tinkling of the bell.

   If someone you know is going away, or moving on, you could use the Willow Star Wands to wish them well – stand in a circle and ask the person who going on a journey to stand in the centre. Children surround the child with wands outstretched. Starting with wands held low and gradually moving them upwards, the children sprinkle their friend with good wishes.

Inner Light Walnut Candles

In the spirit of winter, this craft encapsulates the magic of hidden inner treasure and the return of the light. Walnuts can be gathered in the autumn months and stored in preparation for Yule. These walnut candles can be prepared in advance as gifts for the children or made with them as Christmas gifts for others, and are ideal to hang on the Christmas tree. These candles are floating candles and look beautiful in a water-filled bowl or in natural waters. (They must be floated in water, as this prevents the shells from catching fire.) A simple and beautiful ceremony can be created by lighting the candles with a wish and setting them afloat on a pond, lake or slow-moving stream.

To make:

1. Put wax on a gentle heat to melt.

2. Carefully open the walnut without breaking the shells, by inserting the tip of a knife into the blunt end of the nut and twisting.

You will need:
- Walnuts
- Beeswax
- Wick
- Scissors
- Knife
- Vessel to melt and pour wax
- Ribbon or thread for hanging

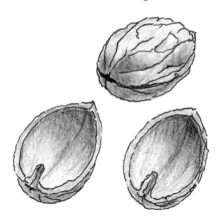

5. Once dry, cut the wick into pieces around 1.5cm (¾in) long.

6. Pour wax carefully into the walnut shells.

3. Enjoy eating the nuts and keep the shells in their pairs, positioned upright ready to pour wax into. Sand, loose soil or moss can help keep them steady.

4. Dip a length of wick into the melted wax and dry straight. This makes the wick more solid and easier to insert into the candles later.

7. Allow to dry until the top just begins to solidify and then pierce the centre of the wax with the small wick, being sure that the wick reaches the bottom of the shell. When the wax is set the candles are ready.

To make hidden walnut lights:

1. Cut a ribbon or thread about 15cm (6ins) long and tie a knot to create a loop from which to hang the walnut.

2. Place the knotted end of the loop in the middle of one walnut (completed candle) half.

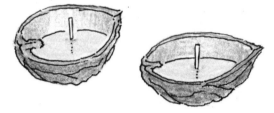

3. Using a small stick, smear melted wax over the rim of the shell and quickly rejoin the two halves of the walnut.

4. The nuts can be opened by inserting a knife into the blunt end of the nut and twisting. They are lovely gifts to open on a special occasion such as solstice or Christmas.

A Winter Treasure for your Magic Pouch –
Lucky Stone

Once in a while as we are walking along a path, or on a beach, or digging in the mud, we may find a special stone that shines out and asks us to pick it up and look more closely. Perhaps we are drawn to its colour and patterns, its shape and weight? As we hold it in our hand and weigh it, it feels just right. It gives us a good feeling. This could be a lucky stone, a treasure of the earth who would like to befriend you for a while. Stones and crystals are ancient and mysterious. Who knows what stories they could tell if only we could slow down enough to hear them? They can bring healing and strength. If you find one in this way, you could add it to your Magic Pouch. When they have finished their work with us, lucky stones often disappear as curiously as they arrive. Or feel the moment when it is time to return your stone to the wild once again.

Sense Awareness Activity –
Bark and Twigs

As we become more familiar with the trees in the forest, it is easier and easier to recognise them during the growing months by their leaves, flowers and seeds (which may be berries and nuts). Learning to know our tree friends more deeply, we notice them in every season. In the winter, it is the time to seek to know them by their bark and the shapes of their twigs and branches.

Take a walk and meet the trees in their winter sleep. Feel the bark, notice the form of the bare branches, the twigs and closed buds. Buds are sensitive to sunlight sensing the length of the days and when it will be time to open. Respectfully prune a few twigs from different trees and ask the children to close their eyes and try to recognise the tree from the feel and shape of the twig. The buds of each tree species have their own unique shape, size and colour. In pairs, ask the children to take turns closing their eyes and leading each other to different trees. Can you recognise the tree from the feel of its bark? When everyone has had a turn, place the twigs in a vase of water for the children to sketch. Sketching encourages us to look with fresh eyes and really see. In the winter months, it is lovely to have a vase of winter twigs on the table.

Winter Game – Fly, Robin, Fly

This is a fast run-around game to warm the inner fire on cold wet days in the woods.

Set the scene

Tell the children that Jack Frost and his Frost Sprites come in winter to cover the land with icy stars and crystals. Everything they touch freezes. Many moons ago, they even stole the people's winter fire, so that they were cold and shivering. At this time, a little brown bird, a friend of the people, listened to their stories and sang them songs. Now, she wants to help them to recover their fire. Her Robin clan can help find the warmth hidden by the Frost Sprites and return it to the people. But can they find it before the Frost Sprites freeze them too?

The robin is our most familiar winter bird. You can play this game with the birds as robins. Or, to highlight the connection with the Winter Story, 'The Gift of Fire', you can play that the birds are redstarts. In this case, at the end of the game, tell the children that the Fire Spirits gave the redstarts their red tail-feathers.

> **YOU WILL NEED:**
> - Three red cloths to represent the warmth of the fire

TO PLAY:

1. Make a circle of sticks (or use the fire circle before you light the fire).

2. Split the group into two teams; Robins and Frost Sprites.

3. Set the boundary area appropriate to the children's ages and abilities.

4. Robins stay inside the stick circle and hide their eyes, counting to 30.

5. Frost Sprites hide the red cloths in the playing area, making sure they are hidden in such a way that when the Robins fly around the cloths will be visible, e.g. hanging in a tree.

6. After 30 seconds the adult shouts, 'Fly, Robins, fly!' and the Robins run off to find the cloths and bring them back to the circle. The game is complete when the Robins have all three cloths in their circle.

7. The Frost Sprites try to catch the Robins. When caught, Robins must freeze and can only be unfrozen by another Robin. A Frost Sprite can take the red cloth from the frozen Robin and hide it again. The Frost Sprites cannot guard the Robin but must swirl away to chase another.

8. If all the Robins have been frozen you can end the game there. Another option is to have the adult call out that a thaw has come over the land; in this case all the Robins are unfrozen and the Frost Sprites must lie still for 5 seconds. You could also play the game with a time limit.

9. At the end the game you can tell the children that the Robins were given red breasts by the Fire Spirits for their love and bravery, which they still carry to this day.

Winter Wild Plant Recipes – Winter Tree Tea

In the winter months, drinking hot tea in the forest is an important way to stay warm. Children delight in finding and harvesting nature's medicinal plants, and can sit and hold the warm brew while listening to a story. Keep a flask of tea to hand in case small children get cold – holding a warm cup in cold fingers, as well as drinking the steaming tea, helps bring back the joy of being in the forest in winter. Of course, you can boil a kettle on the fire to make the tea too.

TO MAKE:

1. Chop one whole apple and put into the flask with a cinnamon stick (or a spoonful of powdered cinnamon) and a tablespoon of honey.

2. Fill with boiling water, fasten tightly and take a cup for each person in the group.

3. Take a journey into a wood where you know pine trees grow. Add a good handful of pine needles to the flask and allow to steep for at least 15 minutes before serving.

4. There are many evergreen trees, so take care to identify the right one by using a field guide. Here is a helpful rule:

> *Pines have pointy sewing needles,*
> *And Firs are furry.*
> *Spruces are spikey,*
> *And Cypresses are scaly.*
> *But Yews could be the end of you!*

5. Gather a selection of evergreens and explore their differences with the children. As the poem suggests, pine needles are the same length as an average sewing needle and have a pointy tip. Fir needles are round at the ends, so when you stroke them they

YOU WILL NEED:
- Pine needles
- Apple
- Cinnamon
- Honey

are soft and furry. Spruces on the other hand have sharp needles and are spikey when stroked. The cypresses include the western cedar and leylandii, commonly found in gardens – look at their beautiful leaves like waxy, scaled feathers. Yew is very dark green and, like the firs, is soft. Yew is deadly poisonous, so take the time to learn its form, leaves, bell-like red berries and dark reddish bark, which is characteristically yielding when pressed.

6. Look. Feel. Smell....only taste when you have given the time to be sure of who the plants are. The evergreen trees are wonderful to learn about in the winter when they really shine out. Many of them have medicinal qualities; some are poisonous. Pine is our native conifer, which can be made into healing tea.

7. Pine needles have a delightfully zingy flavour and are good on their own as well as blended with other ingredients. Pine helps open the chest to clear the airways. It is full of vitamins C and A, strengthening the immune system and helping us resist infection.

HARVESTING TIPS

It is easier to find pine needles in the winter, as the wind brings small boughs of the tall pine to the forest floor. If you're harvesting directly from the tree, the pine needles come away more easily when you pull the needles backwards by the tips. If you gather from a small pine tree make sure you collect only a few from each tree.

CAUTION: Avoid pine tea during pregnancy.

Winter Vegetable Soup, Cooked on the Fire

TO MAKE:

1. Ask everyone in the group to bring a few vegetables. In this way the right amount is always made for the size of the group. Peel and chop the vegetables into small pieces. Always supervise when children are using sharp tools (see Appendix Tool Safety p 317).

2. Some wild edible greens can be found over-wintering, and make a lovely addition to a soup. Even on a frosty morning, you may be able to find cleavers, sorrel, plantain and ground ivy (catsfoot, not climbing ivy) leaves. Chop finely and add to the pot.

3. Add water to cover and put on a trivet over the fire. If time is limited, you can add hot water from a flask to reduce cooking time.

YOU WILL NEED:
- A few vegetables
- Peeler
- Small knife
- Wild edible greens
- Trivet
- Vegetable stock or miso

4. Boil up the soup on the fire, until the vegetables are tender, stirring occasionally.

5. Add vegetable stock or miso near the end of cooking to taste.

6. Serve and eat around the fire.

Winter Tree Lore

Scots Pine

GAELIC NAME: *Giùbhas* (which means 'juicy
tree' – from the abundance of pitch or resin
the wood contains)
LATIN NAME: *Pinus sylvestris*

OGHAM: *Ailm* (the letter A)

Essence
Divine Light ~ Sky ~ Cleansing

Character

I am Pine, the Tree of the Heavens.

I am tall and strong, growing straight towards the sky, my trunk glowing orange-purple in the sunlight.

I have watched over these lands since long before people came. I grow in the vast forests in the North, stretching from Scandinavia across Russia and Siberia. I love to grow in the high places with my crown in the heavens.

My high branches bear needle-like leaves, evergreen and hardy in snow. Like brushes, they sweep the wind clean, keeping the air of this world fresh and pure.

Lean your back against my trunk, close your eyes and hear the wind sigh and sing in my boughs. Breathe deep of the pure air I share.

In late spring come and see my upright golden candles of pollen-rich catkins. My pollen brings fertility to my flowers and blows in great abundance across the land.

Where it falls, it nourishes the earth, bringing life and vigour to many beings. Look closely, and above my pollen candles see that some of my shoots are tipped with a small, pink-red cone-shaped flower. These will grow into the cones that house my seeds.

Come on a warm spring day and you may hear these woody cones pop and crack, opening in the sun, finally releasing my golden seeds to fly away on their translucent wings.

Find an open cone upon the ground. Can you find my golden treasure inside? My seeds and pollen are a rich food that people have long gathered. I offer great nourishment to many.

I am known by many as Tree of the Light.

People light bonfires of my wood on the winter solstice to celebrate the return of the sun.

In Eastern Europe my glades were decorated with candles, and shining treasures representing the Divine Light and everlasting life. From these older celebrations comes the tradition of the Christmas tree, celebrating the awakening of the light within and the return of the sun here on earth.

Spend time in my presence. I have deep strength and peace, carrying your mind above its small view, up to the heavens, to the greater view of our connection with all life.

Gifts

I am second only to the oak in the gifts I share with people.

My wood is strong, durable and resinous. It burns well and is used for flaming torches. Because of its straightness, it is used for ships' masts and, in modern times, for telegraph poles; it has many building uses.

My aromatic resin can be made into glue and ointments to help draw out splinters.

My resinous wood can be used to make pitch, tar and turpentine.

My inner bark can be eaten when the sap is flowing most strongly and is a traditional food amongst traditional peoples.

My thin roots can be used as lashings and as cord.

Pine pollen is a good food and medicine.

My nuts, though small, are edible.

My needles make excellent tea, which is full of vitamin C and is especially good for clearing the chest.

Stand tall and breathe deep.

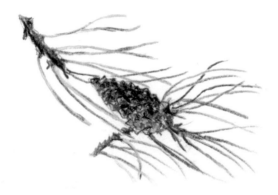

Winter Seasonal Song

By River Jones

The Pine Tree Song

O Pine tree stand-ing tall, from the hills I hear your call a-
-ris-ing clear and strong, in my heart I hear your song.

To sing as a round, begin the second group halfway through the song.

Holly

GAELIC NAMES: *Cuileann* (from the root word *cùl*, meaning 'guard defence')
LATIN NAME: *Ilex aquifolium*

OGHAM: *Tinne* (the letter T) – from the Old Irish *teine*, meaning 'fire'

Essence
Everlasting Life ~ Sanctuary ~ Protection

Character

I am Holly, the Holy Tree.

I share the kingship of the forest with the Oak, watching over the land with protection and care from midsummer to midwinter, for during the time of the waning light I am always green, a sanctuary for life in the forest.

My spiky, shiny leaves are tough and leathery, resilient in summer sun and winter snow alike. Through the seasons I am constant. I am protected from the weather and am known by country people for offering safe haven in storms and from lightning. Deer like to sleep beneath my trees. Look for their beds under my boughs and find the white hairs they leave behind.

When the storms of life feel harsh, and you feel troubled, seek my sanctuary. Sit beneath me and feel my protection – feel held, feel safe.

In the summer months I bloom. My sweet-smelling white flowers have four petals, shaped like a cross – a sacred symbol in many cultures; the holy crossing-place between the earth and the heavens.

As the sun wheel turns, my flowers ripen into shiny berries as red as blood – food for my friends the birds and a favourite of blackbird and thrush.

Find me growing under old oak or beech, where they like to roost high in the branches, spreading my seeds in their droppings. Here I grow, evergreen. Many people through time have gathered my boughs in at Yuletide. Some took my sprigs into special dwellings for the tree spirits during the great sleep of winter.

Still today people bring my boughs into their homes at Christmas, harking back to the old ways. I bring protection and blessings and the presence of the holy ever-lasting life.

Gifts

My wood is white and strong and burns bright and hot, making a tinkling sound like tiny bells. My trunk is hard and has a green hue. I am the original greenwood tree.

I have been known over the ages, in my kingly role, as a tree of justice and of the warrior, my wood often chosen for weapons such as spears and arrows to protect the lands.

I am good for carving and make excellent staffs that can help bring protection from wild animals and lightning.

Though birds enjoy eating my berries, be aware – holly berries are poisonous to humans.

My leaves can be used – holly leaf tea is medicine for coughs and fever.

My flower essence is for healing strong, spiky feelings of jealousy, revenge or hatred.

I remind you that love is the greatest protection of all.

Holly Song

Slow and sedate

By River Jones
and Anna Richardson

CHORUS

O Ho-lly _____ O Ho-lly tre - e, How

green you grow, green in sun and green in snow _____ .

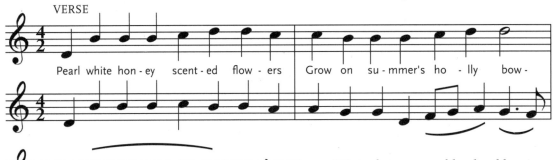

VERSE

Pearl white hon-ey scent-ed flow-ers Grow on su-mmer's ho-lly bow-

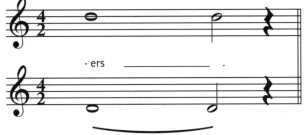

- ers _____ .

Winter brings your blood-red berries,
Blackbirds' and the thrushes' cherries.

Safely rest the deer below,
When the winds bring ice and snow.

Holly fires warmth and light,
Heart in deep midwinter night.

Bright protector, constant friend,
Your shining thorns our land defend.

Sylvan spirit sanctuary,
Everlasting greenwood tree.

Ivy

GAELIC NAMES: *Eidhion / Eidheann-mu-chrann*
(which means 'clothes of a tree')
LATIN NAME: *Hedera helix*

OGHAM: *Gort* (the letter G)

Character

I am Ivy, I cling and bind, evergreen vine of the forest.

My leaves gleam with a leathery sheen and have delicate tendrils that grow and cover earth or tree.

I can grow old and strong, weaving my way up trees to the sky. Sometimes I smother but rarely so; my way is to weave and climbing grow.

In autumn months my flowers bloom, rare beauty, globes of green-gold flowers, honey-scented. See the wasps and bees come for sweet nectar, the last in the wild for this year.

Later, berries dark, and poisonous for people, ripen to feed the birds and seed my young.

In winter I shelter the birds that bravely stay in this land. I am food for deer and sheep who have few greens to keep them strong through snowy times. I am said to be woman, as Holly is man.

At Yuletide, when you bring us both together into your homes, we bring harmony to man and wife and the presence of everlasting love and life.

Weave a hoop with my tendrils, together with Holly, to make a wreath for your table or your door.

My dead twigs and those of Holly are some of the finest forest kindling for your winter fire.

Sphagnum Moss

GAELIC NAMES: *Còinneach boglaich*
(which means 'bog moss')
Còinneach dhearg ('red moss')
Mointeach liath (moin – 'peat' –
and *liath* – 'grey')
LATIN NAME: *Sphagnum spp.*

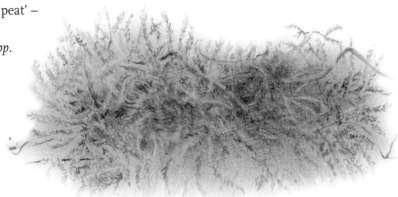

Character

I am Sphagnum Moss, healing moss of the bogs. Soft as cushions, I grow in wet boggy places and like a sponge I soak up the waters.

I like the soil where heather grows. Find me in damp hollows in pine-birch forest, on moor or heath; tiny stars of vivid yellow-green or glowing pink-red.

I grow in big families throughout the Northern Lands, from America, through Europe, to Russia. I am a kind friend to people, and was the first plant your ancestors met when they were born; my soft mosses were used to gently clean newborn babes. I was also used for nappies!

When dried, I can absorb twenty times my own weight in liquid – more than any cotton. I heal too and clean wounds from infection. As a wound herb, I have saved many human lives. Gather me and dry me out. Store me in a little cotton bag to use for healing a bleeding wound. For the worst wounds, soak my dry moss in a strong brew of healing herbs, such as St. John's wort.

NB: In World War I millions of wound dressings were made from sphagnum moss, saving thousands of lives. Sphagnum is the primary peat-forming moss and is used extensively today as a soil conditioner in composts, because of its miraculous water-absorbing qualities. Extensive commercial use of this plant is leading to destruction of natural moss bogs, which are delicate environments and take hundreds of years to restore.

If you have the right kind of soil, you could propagate sphagnum moss, as it grows easily. To give sphagnum moss a new home in your garden or local forest simply break a piece of sphagnum moss into pieces and sprinkle the pieces in a swampy, boggy spot.

Winter Animals

European Robin

I am Robin. My song is clear and melodic.

I sing all year round to tell other robins where my territory is. My song tells hen robins that I have a safe place where we can rest and find plenty of food for our young.

In summer, I like eating insects. Long ago, when wild boar dug the ground, nosing for food, robins followed, enjoying the earthworms. Now instead of wild boar, gardeners enjoy my company, as I look for worms in their freshly turned earth. Late in the year, when the ground is hard, I eat fruit and berries too. I love elderberries, rowan-berries and blackberries.

When I have found a mate, I bring her gifts of good things to eat, like wiggly caterpillars. She makes a nest of leaves, moss and grass, lined with soft feathers, in a sheltered hollow or leafy hedge. Sometimes we even nest in an old watering can or the shelf of a garden shed. Whilst the hen sits on our eggs, I bring her lots of food to eat.

When our babies hatch, my mate and I both feed our chicks; we look after them together.

In the winter, when the cold winds blow, I'll puff out my feathers to keep myself warm. When the ground is hard, I'm happy to find food on a bird table. I am bold and I can be fierce. I am curious of people and will come to listen to your stories. See me in the branches as you sit around the fire.

Badger

I am Badger, the Keeper of the Roots.

I live with my family in an underground maze of tunnels called a 'sett'. We have rooms for sleeping and rooms for rearing babies, and we clean them out regularly. We like to dig our homes in banks of sandy soil, in the roots of trees. Some of our setts have been here since before the great ice covered the world. We still follow the ancient pathways that were started by our ancestors.

We have five toes and strong digging claws to find worms, our favourite food. We can eat more than 100 every night. Look for our large paw prints; you can see the outline of our five toes and the deep gouges made by our long claws.

We can smell grubs and bluebell bulbs under the earth, and dig them up to eat. We like eating insects and berries too.

We live most of the time underground and come out at night to eat and play. When the moon shines, our black and white faces seem to disappear amidst the stripes of shadow and light.

Winter Solstice Celebration

Midwinter is the darkest time of year, the shortest day and longest night. From now on the days will get longer, although not yet warmer. We are now in winter's grip; it is time to turn inwards – to honour the wise and ancient dark from which all life springs, to rest and to find the light within.

YOU WILL NEED:
- Fire kit
- Frankincense or pine resin
- Cloaks and blankets
- A large bowl of water
- 1 walnut candle per child (see p 293)
- Winter Tree Tea (see p 297) or Winter Vegetable Soup (see p 298).

Light the fire, using holly and pine if possible. Create a double spiral in a forest clearing, using greenery, leaf litter or sticks:

TO MAKE A DOUBLE SPIRAL:
Start in the middle by leaving an S-shaped path on the ground and making two spiral arms that finish opposite to each other:

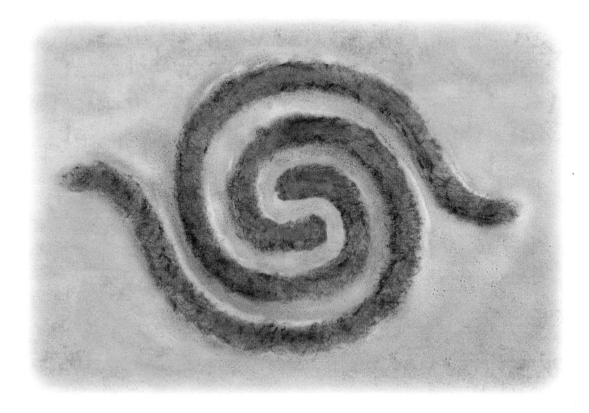

THE CELEBRATION:

1. Place the bowl of water in the middle of the spiral with a large candle to light the walnut candles from. (It can be helpful to have an adult in the middle, especially for younger children, who may need help to light their candles and place them in the bowl of water.)

2. Opposite the large candle, in the second centre of the double spiral, place a mound of mole mud, decorated with crystals, to give the children a picture of the dark of the earth and the treasures of winter.

3. Gather around the fire.

4. Children find a place, somewhere near the fire and near to each other, to make a little 'deer bed'. They can be covered with their cloaks or blankets.

5. When the children are settled comfortably, snuggling under their winter cloaks, sing them the winter lullaby 'Sleep, Children, Sleep' (p 311). Give them time to enjoy the feeling of resting in the arms of Mother Earth.

6. After a little resting lullaby time, each child may line up with a walnut shell candle and walk the spiral in silence. At the centre of the spiral, each child lights their candle and sets their light afloat on the dish of water. This simple gesture creates a vivid picture of the birth and growth of the light.

7. Back at the fire, each child can put a small piece of pine resin or frankincense into the flames, with their silent thanks for whatever their heart feels grateful for.

8. Share a drink of Winter Tree Tea or a bowl of warming Winter Vegetable Soup to complete your celebration.

 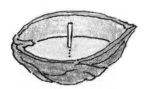

Sleep, Children, Sleep

Lyrics by Anna Richardson, Dawn Casey and Helen d'Ascoli

Slow

Sleep, ch-ild-ren, sleep, In earth that's warm and deep. And

lay your head do-wn safe and sound, so sleep, ch-ild-ren, sleep.

Sleep, children, sleep.
Stars shine down on you.
On earth your dreams are starlight too,
So sleep, children, sleep.

Sleep, children, sleep.
The snow lies thick and deep.
Winter lays her blanket down,
So sleep, children, sleep.

Appendices

The Central Fire

Just as the sun is at the centre of our solar system, the fire is at the centre of our time in the forest. We gather around the fire to celebrate, craft, cook and share stories and songs. The fire gives us warmth and light and brings us together in a circle. We create a spark as the ancestors once did. Like a falling star it is caught in a soft dry nest of tinder. We gently blow life into it and flames are born. With care, the sticks are fed to the fire, and we sing:

Fire Song

By Anna Richardson and Helen d'Ascoli

Fi - re, fi - re burn - ing bight, danc - ing flames of

shin - ing light, we cir - cle round since times of old, to

share your warmth and heart of go - ld.

Fire Making

The ancestors' spark

Our ancestors carried the sacred knowledge of how to birth the spark of fire and this was carefully handed down to each generation. Perhaps the oldest form of fire making was discovered when certain stones were hit together, such as flint and iron pyrites, a method known as 'fire by percussion'. Later, with the discovery of how to extract metal from particular rocks, iron strikers were developed.

Fire by friction has been used throughout the world and there is evidence of this method from ancient Egypt, the Americas and Aboriginal Australians and throughout Europe. This technique requires certain woods or plant stems to be rubbed together at speed to create a source of heat which then ignites the dust formed by the friction. Two main styles still practised to this day are hand drill and bow drill. These skills take diligence, dedication and years of practice to master and are well worth the effort and time for all the personal development provided along the way – fire is a great teacher.

Today we have many easy ways to light fires including matches and lighters. There is also the modern fire striker, which provides a strong spark, even when wet, and plays an important role in outdoor education.

Materials for catching the spark

The spark must land upon suitable material that can nurture and grow the coal before it is big enough to ignite the tinder. Our ancestors used certain dried fungi to catch a spark or extend a coal in order to carry fire from one place to another. Some examples are King Alfred's cake (*Daldinea concentrica*), a black knobbly fungus that commonly grows on ash; this must be totally dry and works well when cut open. Another common fungus that works well is artist's fungus (*Ganodernam applanatum*) often found on dead or dying beech. It needs to be dried and the velvety top part shredded.

Charcloth

The easiest way to catch a spark for the tinder bundle is to use charcloth. To make your own use an old piece of natural cotton cloth and place in a tin with a tight-fitting lid – a small golden syrup or sweet tin is ideal. Make a small hole in the tin and place the whole thing in the embers of a fire. Allow to burn until it stops smoking. Once cool, you can open the tin – the charred fabric will now light easily.

Tinder nest

The spark must have a nest in order to be born into a fire; this nest is made of tinder. Understanding the natural tinders available from the local environment is wonderful knowledge and children enjoy gathering and creating a tinder bundle. Tinder is any dry, fibrous material that easily ignites.

Into this nest we direct the fire's spark and, with the help of the wind, breathe the flames of the fire into life. Each environment and season provides different plant sources of tinder. Here are some good examples of plant tinders in the forest that work well in their dried form:

- Silver birch bark
- Cleavers (sticky weed)

- Bracken
- Honeysuckle bark
- Inner bark of some trees, e.g. sweet chestnut and lime

Lighting the fire

This method describes using a modern striker for the spark, though the following process is the same once the coal is created.

- Strike the sparks into the middle of the tinder bundle. Watch for a glowing ember to form.
- Hold the nest up and away from the face, at an angle that allows you to blow onto the coal. Have your back to the wind so the smoke blows away from you.
- After a while, the tinder will combust. Carefully lay it on the raft and add the thinnest kindling twigs gently on top.
- Now feed the fire the next size sticks and keep a good flow of air by blowing from the side into its heart.
- Welcome the fire with songs, jokes and stories. Fire is a gift to treasure and respect.

Gathering wood

Gathering suitable wood for a bright fire is a skill in itself and an activity which develops wood lore.

- The driest sticks are found hanging in trees – dead wood that has been blown down by the wind and air dried.
- Gather piles of different sizes from the thinnest matchstick width upwards.
- Sort sticks into size piles in the hearth area. This is a good activity for children.
- A raft of dry sticks in the centre on which to build the fire helps to preserve the dampness of the ground.

Woods to burn

All the trees have particular special qualities and these affect the nature of the wood and the way they burn.

- Ash, oak, holly, beech and hornbeam all burn hot, bright and slow, as they are hard woods. They are good for making beds of embers for cooking as well as warm fires in cold times.
- Hazel, willow, poplar, sycamore and birch burn well but faster than the harder woods and are good for fire by friction.
- Pine burns well but spits. As does sweet chestnut.
- Blackthorn and hawthorn burn hot but care is needed as the thorns can cause nasty infection.
- Elder and yew should be avoided, as they release mildly toxic fumes.
- Horse chestnut and elm are poor burning woods.

Choosing a hearth in the woods

- Choose a site that will have the least impact on the ecology of the land. Consider the plants and animals who live in that place.
- Avoid positioning a fire too close to trees and shallow root systems and avoid overhanging branches.
- Avoid peat-rich soils, which can ignite and send the fire travelling under the ground, whence it can rise up again in other places many hours later. Leaf litter under conifers is also extremely flammable.
- Clear the area of debris being extra careful in dry conditions.
- Keep the fire small and appropriate to the place and its intended use. This also limits damage to the seed bank in the soil.

- A designated fire circle is good in woodland for long-term use.
- Seek permission to light a fire from the landowner. Many woodlands are nature reserves and will not permit fires.

Fire safety

Go through these safety points with children before making a fire:
- Make sure all long hair is tied up and no loose clothing or scarves are worn.
- Take heed of where the wind is coming from and sit with your back to the wind (otherwise you may get fire blowing towards you).
- The fire circle should be a safe space where people never run and only enter when interacting with the fire.
- Have a bucket of water near the fire in case of burns.
- Sticks should be placed rather than thrown onto the fire, as throwing them in can cause dangerous sparks to fly.
- Once a stick goes on the fire, it stays in the fire; sticks with glowing ends can be hazardous.
- Fire is sacred and should only have wood as fuel (no rubbish, as the fumes are toxic).

Forest School Good Practice

The activities in the book encourage you to take children out in the woods, regardless of your experience or qualifications. All great educators of the past, including Froebel and Steiner, have advocated the importance of spending time in nature.

When taking groups out to the woods, responsibility must be taken for:
- Safety of the group
- First aid
- Ratio of adults to children
- Safe use of tools
- Safety around the fire
- Risk assessment
- Emergency plan
- Care for the environment

We have included tool safety tips but this book is not an alternative to Forest School or outdoor learning training. When taking groups into the woods in a professional capacity, there are legal requirements that must be met in order to ensure safe practice.

We recommend that if you are taking groups out to use tools and make fires, you have some practical training. The Forest Education Network has information on courses with the Council for Learning Outside the Classroom, the Institute of Outdoor Learning and Forest School training. The Forest School Association is the professional body for Forest School practitioners and provides resources and guidance on Forest School.

Toolkit

- Bow saw
- Pruning saw
- Secateurs
- Loppers
- Palm drills
- Peelers
- Fixed-blade knives
- Fire strikers
- Water container
- First aid kit
- Emergency whistle – to be worn at all times, but used only in an emergency

Tool Safety

A high ratio of adults to children is needed for working with metal tools, ideally 1:1 with really young children, moving to 1:5 with eight years and above, until a good level of competence is reached. Only teach tool use with tools you are personally confident with using. You must understand the techniques and hazards for each tool. Keep tools sharpened and check them regularly.

The hazards are obviously bodily harm in the form of cuts. The protection is common sense, clear instruction and absolute focus upon the task. The adult must sensibly assess the risks, the character of the child, the situation and the task and make sound decisions.

Bow saw

This tool is good for cutting wood thicker than 10cm (4in) diameter, such as logs for the fire. The bow saw is ideal for using with young children because the adult and child can hold one side each with two hands pulling and pushing together. The child must hold the saw with two hands at all times. Keep the blade guard on when the saw is not in use.

Younger children can sing a rhyme as they saw, to help get into a rhythm. We sing this simple song to the tune of 'Frère Jacques':

Forwards backwards,
Forwards backwards,
Sawing wood,
Sawing wood.
Put it on the fire.
Put it on the fire.
Saw saw saw,
Saw some more.

Pruning saw

This tool is designed primarily for green wood. It is good for thinner branches and coppicing for staffs, or cutting slices of wood such as pendants. This tool cuts on the pull rather than the push. It is safest for the dominant hand to use the saw and the other hand to cross over and brace the wood on the other side, so that if the saw jumps out of the groove the other hand is not cut.

Secateurs

Use these to cut wood no bigger than the thickness of a finger. They are good for cutting thin willow, e.g. for star wands (p 291). Make sure the catch is closed after use and return to a safe place.

Loppers

These are for cutting wood about thumb thickness and a little bigger. Do not let one person hold it while another cuts and always return to an adult after use.

Palm drills

Useful for making holes in wood, such as for buttons or toggles. It is important to use palm drills by pushing down while twisting on a flat, stable surface, such as the top of a log (never onto your body).

Peelers

Use peelers on green wood, which peels more easily than seasoned wood, for example on a wand or staff. They are good for peeling veg for soup too, though they can be just as sharp as a good knife and inflict deep cuts when used unsafely. Always ensure the peeling movement is away from the body.

Knife safety protocol

- Have a high adult to child ratio and supervise all knife work.
- Keep the tools sharp and well maintained, and secure in a box or bag when not in use.
- Always use knives while in sitting or kneeling position (not while standing or walking).
- It is good to have logs to sit on and a designated area for tool use. It is safest to use fixed blade knives rather than foldable ones because the latter can fold while in use and cause accidents.

Safe whittling practice

- Find a safe place to sit.
- Ask the children to create their 'safety bubble' by sitting in position and reaching their arm out in a sphere around their body, checking no one is within arm's reach.
- Take care when taking the knife from the sheath as cuts can happen if the holding hand is near the blade.
- Always whittle away from the body.
- Put elbows on knees and whittle in a forward position to avoid cutting the legs,

especially the femoral artery. Another safe position is to whittle to the side of the body.
- Use common sense and encourage children to be careful and wise with tools.

Working in the woods

The woodland is an ecosystem, all parts relying on each other for survival and a balanced healthy existence. If you are working in a wood on a regular basis remember that you are part of the ecosystem of the wood. Treat the woodland with respect, only take what you need for your activities and aim to leave it as you found it. Some projects need to be left for a few weeks but always return the wood to its natural state when these have finished.

When you are harvesting wood, aim to take branches that are rubbing against each other or that are overshadowed by larger trees or not in a good place to grow healthily. Help the woodland by leaving spaces for nature to be undisturbed and by leaving some dead wood, which is an important habitat for many insects and invertebrates, birds, lichens, mosses and fungi.

Boundaries

Always set clear boundaries, so the children know how far they can roam, explore or run during games. Agree on a signal for returning to the group, such as a wolf's howl or crow call or a whistle. Only the adult uses this call to regroup. Practise this regularly. Safe and clear boundaries enable the safety, success and enjoyment of the whole group

The importance of mud

Playing in the mud maintains physical and mental health. Mud is an integral part of

Forest School and is actually good for you! Recent research has found that being in contact with beneficial microbes, *Mycobacterium vaccae*, which we inhale and ingest when we dig in the earth, increases levels of serotonin in the brain. Serotonin is a natural anti-depressant and strengthens the immune system. Mud is also a wonderful open-ended medium for exploration and play, there is no end of opportunities for learning through mud and it is freely available in abundance.

The importance of games

Nature awareness games are a great way to teach children about nature and to embody learning, as well as being lots of fun.

Joseph Cornell, President and Founder of Sharing Nature Worldwide, asks, 'How can we help others experience nature deeply when their minds and bodies are so restless? The secret I've discovered is to focus their attention with nature activities that engage their senses in a fun and captivating way.'

Games bring people together and can create unity and give an opportunity to work as a team. Playing is important at any age.

The importance of free play

Encouraging free play fosters children's healthy development; it is the natural process by which children learn about the world around them.

In free play, children can direct their own learning and go as far or in-depth as they need to. They will be able to test their edges and challenge themselves.

Non-competitive forms of social play are essential for developing a sense of belonging, equality, connectedness and concern for others. Playing games is an ancient form of bonding which helped hunter-gatherer children develop into co-operative adults.

In self-organized play, children learn to get along with diverse others, to compromise and to anticipate and meet others' needs.

The importance of risk-taking

Children love to explore and have adventurous play outdoors. They need adventure and challenge in their play in order to learn essential life skills such as risk management, problem solving, perseverance and working as a team. In striving to achieve something that is challenging, we overcome our own boundaries, increasing feelings of self-esteem and achievement.

Children who spend more time playing outdoors grow fitter and healthier, and learn to value and protect their environment.

'No one will protect what they don't care about;
and no one will care about what they have never experienced.'
David Attenborough

Useful Resources

- Field Studies Council ID charts
- Magnifying lenses
- Tarpaulin (we use a clear, reinforced plastic tarp or a lightweight nylon one)
- Paracord for tying up tarps and knotwork
- Natural twine
- Small gathering baskets
- Cooking equipment without plastic on the handles or lid
- Tins with lids for making charcloth and charcoal on the fire
- Horseshoe trivet (for putting cooking equipment on over the fire)
- Tool box or safe storage for tools

Cooking in the Forest

- Use fire-gloves to remove hot pans from the trivet over the fire.
- Do not use aluminium or non-stick pans.
- Do not use pans with plastic handles.
- Use wooden rather than plastic spoons for stirring.

Foraging considerations

Wild plants are nutrient rich and are strong health-giving foods. Less of them is needed by the body than of shop-bought food. It is good to try small amounts at first, especially as some sensitive people may have reactions to new foods.

Considerations for safety

- Be careful of poisonous lookalikes. Always doublecheck you are certain before sharing wild plants as food with children.
- Ask children to always check with an adult before eating wild plants.

- Avoid plants growing on roadsides, as they pick up heavy metals from fumes.
- Avoid plants growing in or near water you suspect may be contaminated.
- Avoid all plants that may have been sprayed with chemical weedkillers.
- Enjoy the special gift of foraged wild food and always use common sense.

Respectful Harvest

- Approach the plants with respect.
- Only harvest from areas where the plants are abundant. Leave plenty for others so that the plant community will continue to flourish.
- Leave the grandparent plants – the biggest and strongest – to make strong seeds for the future.
- Ask permission of the plants, wait for a feeling response and respect the answer.
- Ask if there is anything you can do in return (perhaps sow their seeds or clear around them). It is an old tradition in the British Isles to give a small offering of oats or barley for the gift of medicine from a plant.
- Harvest with care and the least harm possible.
- Only take what you need.
- Share the food or medicine with others as the plants have shared with you.
- Give them thanks for their gifts.

Thanksgiving

Thanksgiving helps us to develop a healthy, respectful relationship with the natural world. It is a lovely way to come together as a group to begin or end a session. For example, at the beginning of a ceremony, thank the directions and elements, and, at the end of a day in the forest, children can share with everyone in the circle one thing that they are thankful for.

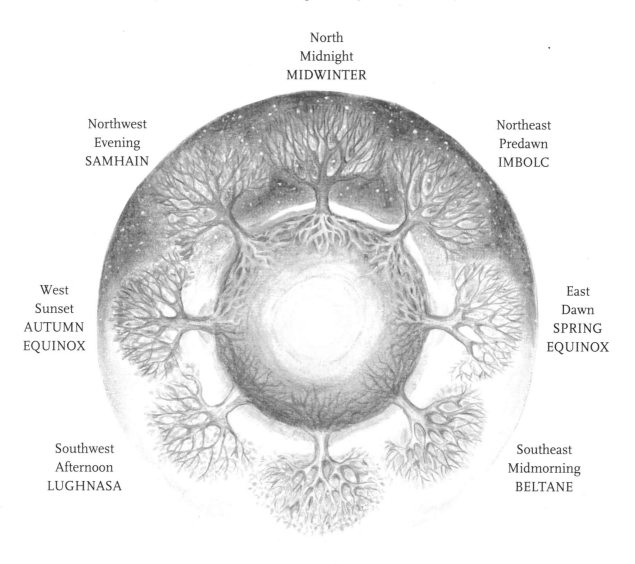

North
Midnight
MIDWINTER

Northwest
Evening
SAMHAIN

Northeast
Predawn
IMBOLC

West
Sunset
AUTUMN
EQUINOX

East
Dawn
SPRING
EQUINOX

Southwest
Afternoon
LUGHNASA

Southeast
Midmorning
BELTANE

South
Midday
SUMMER SOLSTICE

Imbolc – Northeast – Stars

Thank you stars for watching over us and guiding our way.

Spring – East – Air

We thank you air for your breath of life.

Beltane – Southeast – Plants

We thank you plants for your generosity, beauty and all your precious gifts.

Summer – South – Fire

Thank you fire for your warmth and light and thank you sun for bringing life to the earth.

Lughnasa – Southwest – Animals

Thank you to all the wonderful creatures, great and small.

Autumn – West – Water

Thank you sacred life-giving water.

Samhain – Northwest – Rocks

Thank you rocks, bones of the earth, holding ancient memories of the land

Winter – North – Earth

Thank you Mother Earth for giving life to all the beings of the world.

Centre – Mystery

Thank you for the mystery and magic of life and the sacred power of love.

The Ogham and Oghma

The 14th-century *Book of Ballymote* (*Leabhar Bhaile an Mhóta*) states that Ogham was invented by the legendary champion Ogma: 'The father of Ogham is Ogma, the mother of Ogham is the hand or knife of Ogma.' It is possible the word *Ogham* comes from the Irish *og-úaim* (point-seam) – the seam made by the point of a sharp weapon.

All surviving Ogham inscriptions (such as those in Kerry, Cork and Waterford in Ireland and those in Pembrokeshire in Wales) are on stone, and many are personal names, suggesting that they are monuments marking territory or graves. Early Irish legends also tell that Ogham was used on wood for records, messages, magic and divination.

Ogham is also known as the 'Celtic tree alphabet', since, according to the Old Irish manuscript *In Lebor Ogaim* (*The Book of Oghams*), many of the letters of the Ogham alphabet are also the names of trees. For example, the letter B is called *Beithe*, or 'birch', and the letter C is *Coll*, meaning 'hazel'. A text thought to date from the seventh century, *Auraicept na n-Éces* (*The Scholars' Primer*), assigned a tree to every letter of the Ogham alphabet. The *Auraicept* is the source of the tree names given here.

Ogham – The Celtic Tree Alphabet

Ogham is an ancient form of writing – used from at least the fourth century, and perhaps even from the first century – found carved on monuments throughout Celtic Britain.

The original forms of Ogham represented approximately 80 sounds from Gaelic, with 20 symbols arranged in four groups of five. Each group was made up of single strokes, easily carved into wood or stone, with each letter represented by one, two, three, four or five strokes, to the right, to the left, diagonally or through the 'stem':

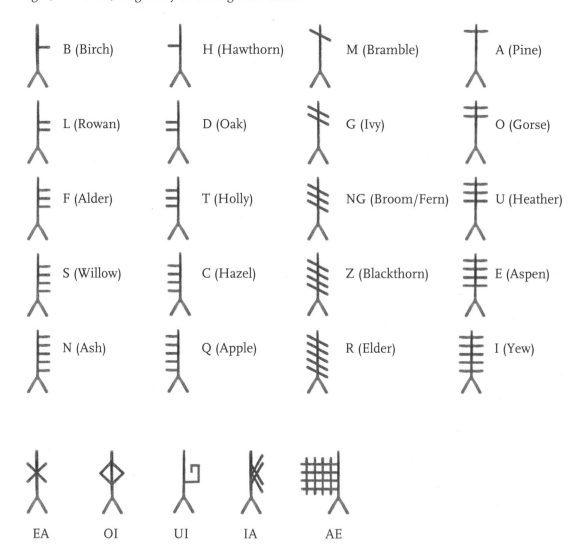

EA   OI   UI   IA   AE

The last set of letters were invented later than the first 20 letters, in the Old Irish period, and are known as *forfeda* – or supplementary letters.

Gaelic Plant Names

We chose to use the Gaelic names for plants, as these were the names given to the plants by the indigenous peoples of the lands where they grow. As John Cameron notes in his book *The Gaelic Names of Plants*, the names for the plants often come from their appearance, uses, habitats and associations, and help us learn more about our ancestors' understanding of, and relationships with, these plants.

Story Sources

Our ancestors lived close to the earth and to each other. Stories were known by heart and told by mouth. The tales that have come down to us are the ones that have been consciously passed on through generations.

Stories speak direct to the soul in the language of dreams, resonant with universal images. They are open, offering many meanings. We each receive what we need from a story, to heal or learn or grow, in the journeys, challenges and transformations of our lives.

Imbolc: *Brigit and the Cailleach*

'This is Brigit the female sage or woman of wisdom – Brigit the goddess whom poets adored, because very great and very famous was her protecting care.' *Cormac's Glossary*

The powerful figure of Brigit lights both the pagan festival of Imbolc and the Christian celebration of Candlemas. The tenth-century *Cormac's Glossary* tells us Brigit was daughter of the Dagda, the Good God of the Tuatha Dé Danann, and that she had two sisters – Brigit the Physician and Brigit the Smith. It is thought all three were aspects of the one goddess of poetry, healing and smithcraft.

Some historians identify the Irish goddess Brigit with the British goddess Brigantia. The Brigantii, the largest Celtic tribe in Britain, were named after their goddess Brigantia, Sovereign of the Land, whose image still appears on British coins. Many places still echo her name: Breconshire in Wales, Brent in London and Brechin in Scotland.

With the coming of Christianity, the powerful energy of the pagan goddess Brigit was transmuted into Ireland's beloved St Brigit. In evolving from goddess to saint, Brigit gracefully bridged Celtic and Christian traditions. The coming of Bride was celebrated in the Highlands and Islands of Scotland, and in Ireland, with heartfelt prayers, songs and rituals. In pre-Christian times, priestesses gathered on the hill of Kildare (Cille Dara – the Church of the Oak) in Ireland to tend a fire sacred to the goddess Brigid. When St Brigit built her church in Kildare, she continued the custom of keeping the flame alight. The flame burned until the 16th century, when it was extinguished during Henry VIII's Dissolution of the Monasteries. In 1993 the sacred flame was rekindled, and it is still alight.

The Cailleach, in folktales from Scotland and Ireland, is a divine ancestor, a creator goddess and a weather deity. She is ruler of the winter months. In Scotland, the last months of winter, the 'wolf-months', are named *A' Chailleach* – the time when the Storm Hags, the Cailleachan (old women), raise their storms. Craggy mountains and prehistoric cairns in Ireland and Scotland still bear her name.

Carmina Gadelica: Hymns and Incantations, Alexander Carmichael, T. A. Constable, Edinburgh, 1900

Scottish Folk-lore and Folk Life, Donald A. Mackenzie, Blackie and Son Ltd, 1935

Mackenzie states that at the end of winter the Cailleach transforms into a boulder, or is changed from an old woman to a young maiden. He records how she threw her magic rod beneath a holly tree. Mackenzie also refers to an Argyll tale in which the Cailleach is guardian of a well at the summit of Ben Cruachan. When the spring overflowed as she slept, Loch Awe was formed.

These strands of folk-story, as well as snippets of folklore drawn from the following books, inspired the weaving of my own tale, a story written to honour the goddesses of our lands and to express the spirit of the season.

Myths and Legends of the Celtic Race, T.W. Rolleston, Harrap, 1911

Gods and Heroes of the Celts, Marie-Louise Sjoestedt, Methuen, 1949

The Silver Bough: Scottish Folklore and Folk-Belief, F. Marian McNeill, William Maclellam, 1957

Celtic Heritage, Alwyn Rees and Brinley Rees, Thames & Hudson, 1961

My gratitude goes to William Thompson, my mother-in-law's father, a lover of Celtic myth, to whom many of the above reference books belonged.

Spring: *The Golden Egg*

The *Kalevala* is the national epic of Finland; a nineteenth-century work of poetry compiled by Elias Lönnrot from Karelian and Finnish oral folklore and myth. The *Kalevala* is sung using the same precise metre as the folk poetry it was drawn from. I drew on two English translations, by John Martin Crawford and William Forsell Kirby, which follow the rhythm of the original Finnish. I have also heard the story told by British storyteller Nick Hennessey.

Beltane: *Tamlin*

Tamlin is a character in a legendary ballad from the Scottish Borders. Fourteen variants of the ballad are collected in: *The English and Scottish Popular Ballads*, F.J. Child, 1882 (Ballads 39A – N). The story is also included in: *More English Fairy Tales*, J. Jacobs (G.P. Putnam's Sons, 1894). I have also heard the story told by British storyteller Hugh Lupton.

Another Scottish ballad collected by Child, 'Thomas the Rhymer', comes from the same

Borders landscape as 'Tamlin', and also tells of a young man falling into the power of the Elf Queen. In the ballad, the 'Eildon tree' under which Thomas the Rhymer sees the Faery Queen is thought to be a thorn tree. I have woven this story-strand into my re-telling of 'Tamlin', since the magical blossoming hawthorn feels to me fitting in this Beltane tale of true love.

Summer: *The Children and the Sun*

My interest in San culture began when travelling in the Kalahari Desert. I read this story in: *Specimens of Bushman Folklore,* W. Bleek and L.C. Lloyd, Daimon, 1968. I also referred to *The Girl Who Made Stars and Other Bushmen Stories,* Wilhelm Bleek and L.C. Lloyd, Daimon, 2001, as well as the work of anthropologist Marjorie Shostak. The names of the children, their ball game with the melon, and the use of the buchu herb are strands I wove into the story myself, drawn from my reading and research.

The San are one of the oldest indigenous populations in the world. Their hunter-gatherer culture continued unchanged for more than 20,000 years. At the time of writing, the San face many challenges.

My deepest gratitude goes to Emily Fawcett, who carried my re-telling with her to the Ju|'Hoansi, and received their permission to share this story. My humblest thanks to the Ju|'Hoansi. It is my hope that sharing this tale will raise awareness of the challenges facing the San people, and inspire readers to take action to help. A living history museum of the Ju|'Hoansi San in Namibia (www.lcfn. info/hunters), initiated by the San hunter !Amache, fosters pride in San heritage and aims to conserve and pass on traditional San culture. A portion of the money earned from the publication of this book will be donated to Survival International, and to the living history museum of the Ju|'Hoansi San. www.survivalinternational.org

Lughnasa: *The Coming of Lugh*

Lebor Gabála Érenn (*The Book of Invasions*) is the earliest known history written by the Irish, an 11th-century manuscript preserving the pagan myths of Gaelic Ireland.

Lebor Gabála Érenn tells us of Tailtiu that 'Cian, gave her [Tailtiu] his son in fosterage, namely Lugh, whose mother was Eithne daughter of Balar,' and that 'the wood was cut down by her, so it was a plain under clover-flower before the end of a year... Tailtiu died in Tailtiu, and her name clave thereto and her grave is from the Seat of Tailtiu north-eastward. Her games were performed every year and her song of lamentation, by Lugh. With gessa and feats of arms were they performed, a fortnight before Lughnasadh and a fortnight after: under dicitur Lughnasadh, that is, the festival of Lugh.'

Tailtiu (now known as Teltown) is at the curve of the River Blackwater in Co. Meath. As long ago as AD539, August would see the area lively with the celebrations and athletic games of the traditional harvest-time fair; Lughnasadh – 'Lugh's Fair'. The fair at Tailteann continued for over 1,000 years. For ease of pronunciation, I use the modern spelling of Lughnasa throughout this book.

There are many versions of the story of Lugh, with significant differences. (For example, in the Manx tale, after being thrown into the sea as a baby, Lugh is found and raised by Manannán, God of the Sea.) In weaving together my own version, I drew strands from the following sources:

Aonach Tailteann, Caun O Lothchain, 1006

Gods and Fighting Men, Lady Augusta Gregory, J. Murray, 1904

Celtic Myth and Legend: *Poetry and Romance*, Charles Squire, Gresham, 1905

Celtic Wonder Tales, Ella Young Dublin, Maunsel, 1910

Myths and Legends of the Celtic Race, T.W. Rolleston, Harrap, 1911

Gods and Heroes of the Celts, Marie-Louise Sjoestedt, Methuen, 1949

The Silver Bough: *Scottish Folklore and Folk Belief*, F. Marian McNeill, William Maclellam, 1957

The Celts, T.G.E. Powell, Thames & Hudson, 1958

Celtic Heritage, Alwyn Rees and Brinley Rees, Thames & Hudson, 1961

Invoking Ireland, Ailiu Iath N'herend, John Moriarty, Lilliput Press, 2005

I also created a few strands of my own to embroider threadbare patches, and weave together different story motifs. I added the knotted wind charm, inspired by charms traditionally used by sailors, and wove together story motifs from different sources to create a patchwork picture of Lugh's childhood. Thank you to Anna for adding the rowan tree.

Autumn: *The Apple Tree Man*

In Somerset, the oldest apple tree in the orchard was called 'the Apple Tree Man', and the spirit of the orchard lived within it. The story was heard by Ruth Tongue from an old man in Pitminster, Somerset, around 1920. She recorded the story in her book *The Folktales of England*, University of Chicago Press, 1968. She notes, 'Pitminster was the place where, in my childhood, I was gravely and proudly conducted by a farm-child to a very old apple-tree in their orchard and told mysteriously that it was "the Apple-Tree Man".'

This story is well preserved by Katherine Briggs in her books *Abbey Lubbers, Banshees and Boggarts: A Who's Who of Fairies*, Kestrel Books, 1979, and *The Dictionary of British Folk Tales*, Routledge & Kegan Paul, 1971.

Samhain: *Vasilisa*

Russian Fairy Tales, Aleksandr Afanasev, Pantheon Books, 1945

The story of Vasilisa is well known. Some say Vasilisa's doll represents the internalised voice of her mother, or the power of a mother's love. Some feel the doll represents Vasilisa's intuition. To me, at this moment, the story speaks of drawing on the wisdom of our elders, our ancestors. I find its theme of the 'sifting and sorting' that follows the harvest particularly fitting for the time of Samhain.

Winter: *The Gift of Fire*

I was delighted to unearth a tale on the origin of fire which comes from the islands of Britain, in the book: *Tattercoats and Other Folk Tales*, Winifred Finlay, Kaye Ward, 1976.

In Finlay's re-telling, the redstart receives the gift of fire from 'the God of... Tir-nan-Og'. Celtic legends tell that the inhabitants of Tír na nÓg are the Tuatha Dé Danann ('the people of the Goddess Dana') – the gods and goddesses of pre-Christian Ireland. Much Irish mythology was first written down by Christian monks. My sense is that the idea of a singular, male God of Tír na nÓg is a later, Christian belief. So, in my re-imagining of the tale, I people Tír na nÓg with the deities of the Tuatha Dé Danann, and specify 'the God of... Tir-nan-Og' from whom the redstart receives the spark of fire as the Goddess Brigit.

Dawn Casey

Trees give us air.
Trees give us rain.
Trees give us fire.
Trees give us food and medicine.
Trees give us shelter and homes.
Trees give us buildings and tools.
Trees create and protect soil.

Forests give us a solution to climate change.
Forests show us how to live in community.
Forests provide an infinite world of play, exploration and relationships.

Let us remember to give back.
Let us plant, tend, restore and protect forests throughout the land.
For the benefit of all life, let us create
The Children's Forest.

Index

Acknowledgements

Thanks to Lisa Stevens for teaching us mystery animal tracking. The Woollen Apples craft (p 204) was featured in the Autumn 2016 Edition of *Kindling: The Journal for Steiner Waldorf Early Childhood Care and Education*. The Felted Wood Mice craft (p 176) was also featured in the Autumn 2016 edition of *Kindling*.

Thanks from Anna Richardson

To my son Oran Ash and all the children we have spent time with in the forests. You have inspired this book. To the plants and animals who teach us so much by the way they live.

To all my teachers along the way.

To Tree Choir for singing to the trees and all those who have shared their beautiful songs in this book, especially River Jones.

To all my friends and family who have offered time, support and help to make this book a rich treasure trove. To all those dear friends and colleagues who are out in nature helping tend the children's fire, fortunately too many to name.

To Helen and Dawn for our shared vision and heart.

To this deeply magical land.

Thanks from Helen d'Ascoli

To my parents who gave me the freedom to explore nature and be free. To Mark, Isis, Finn and Eden for being there for me. To the dedication and inspiration of Dawn and Anna. To Kevin Fossey and the Dharma School for allowing me to follow my passion. To Mark and Debby Hunter and the Annan School for seeing the spiritual heart of Forest School.

To Rachel Bennington and all the people who have helped me find my woodland path.

To the magic of the forest.

Thanks from Dawn Casey

To Brigit, for her bright flame of inspiration. To Alastair, Heather and Megan, and Mum and Dad, for your constant support and love. To Emily Fawcett, for carrying the San story back to its homeland, and to the Ju|'hoansi, who listened to my re-telling and said 'yes'. Deepest gratitude.

To my agent, James Catchpole, for unwavering guidance and support. To Nicky Singer, and Alan Durant, Guy Parker-Rees, Miriam Moss, Will Mabbitt, Leigh Hodgkinson, Ronda Armitage and Amy Rogers, for giving your time, insight and expertise so generously.

To Kevin Crossley-Holland. In the forest of old stories, your work lights my way. I feel privileged, and so grateful, to have received your warm encouragement and gracious support.

To Cliff Wright, for sharing the journey with integrity, wherever it led.

To River Jones, for the music.

To all the forest mentors who cared for my children in the woods while I worked: Anna, Helen, Carrie, Alice, Phil, Vicky, Ed, Cathy, Daniel, Jill and Feathers.

To all the storytellers before me who carried the tales and shared them. To the Sussex downs and the wild Isles of Britain, my homelands.

To Anna and Helen, with love.

Other books from Hawthorn Press

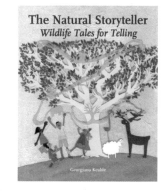

The Natural Storyteller
Wildlife Tales for Telling
Georgiana Keable
ISBN: 9781907359804

Making Woodland Crafts
Using green sticks, rods, beads and string
Patrick Harrison
ISBN: 9781907359842

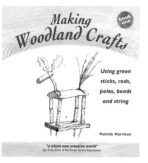

Making the Children's Year
Seasonal Waldorf Crafts with Children
Marije Rowling
ISBN: 9781907359699

All Year Round
A calendar of celebrations
Ann Druitt, Christine Fynes-Clinton, Marije Rowling
ISBN: 9781869890476

Findus, Food and Fun
Seasonal crafts and nature activities
Eva-Lena Larsson, Kennert Danielsson
and Sven Nordqvist
ISBN: 9781907359347

Hawthorn Press

Stockists
Order direct from our website **www.hawthornpress.com**
or BookSource: Tel (0845) 370 0067 orders@booksource.net